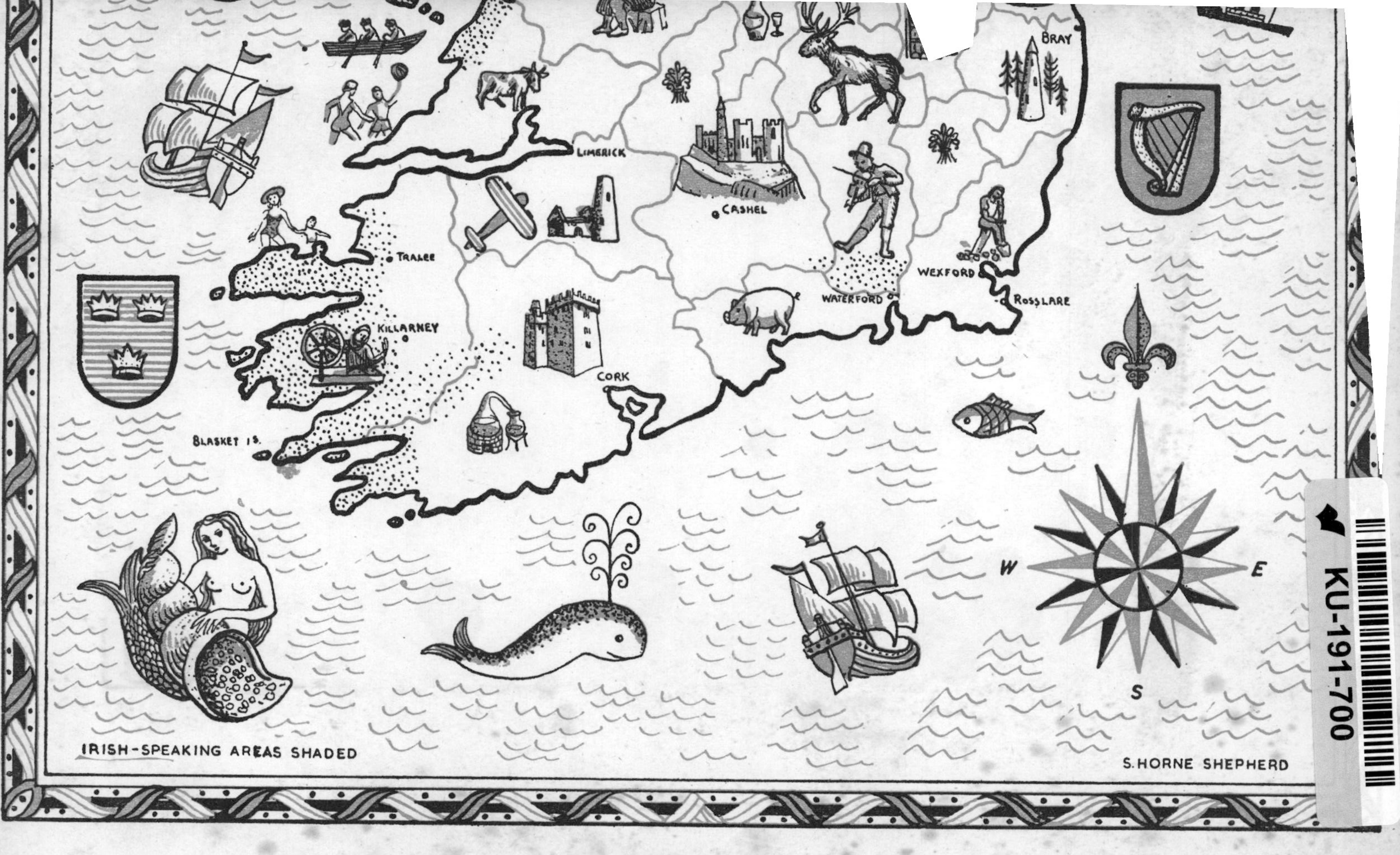
BRAY
LIMERICK
CASHEL
TRALEE
WEXFORD
WATERFORD
ROSSLARE
KILLARNEY
CORK
BLASKET IS.
W
E
S
IRISH-SPEAKING AREAS SHADED
S. HORNE SHEPHERD

IRELAND AND THE IRISH

Other Works by Charles Duff

A HANDBOOK ON HANGING
THIS HUMAN NATURE
THE TRUTH ABOUT COLUMBUS
NO ANGEL'S WING (Autobiography)

Plays:

IRISH IDYLL
MIND PRODUCTS LIMITED
OILFIELD (with Leo Lania)

IRELAND AND THE IRISH

Charles Duff

LONDON * NEW YORK
T. V. BOARDMAN & COMPANY LIMITED
14 Cockspur Street, London, S.W.1

To the Memory of
TSUI CHI
Poet—Philosopher—Friend

PRINTED AND BOUND IN ENGLAND BY
HAZELL WATSON AND VINEY LTD
AYLESBURY AND LONDON

CONTENTS

PART II

SEEING IRELAND

ILLUSTRATIONS

Each photograph is marked with the letters ITA or UTDA, which indicate Irish Tourist Association and Ulster Tourist and Development Association.

End papers and maps designed by S. Horne-Shepherd.

PREFACE

THIS book was written in response to a request for a work in one volume which would give the person who knows little or nothing of Ireland and its people a general account of their historical background, literature, folklore and way of life, in order that a visit might be more intelligently rewarding. It is, nevertheless, hoped that many who may not be able to visit the country will also find it of interest, especially as no other single book deals with this many-sided subject as it is dealt with here.

I wish to acknowledge my indebtedness to the Irish Tourist Association (Dublin) and the Ulster Tourist and Development Association (Belfast) for having helped me in various ways, and especially for the photographs reproduced in this book. I also wish to thank friends who desire to remain anonymous for suggestions of which I have taken advantage, and for criticisms of the book in typescript which I found helpful and encouraging in dealing with a subject as ambitious as the title indicates. Without this help I should often have run the risk of drowning in these deep Irish waters, even though I have tried to avoid the deepest.

C. D.

London, 1952.

PART I

BACKGROUND

What is the cause of thy journey or thy story?
The cause of my journey and my story?——
The men of Erin, yonder, as we see them,
Coming towards you on the plains . . .

From *Ultonian Hero Ballads,* by H. MacLean.

CHAPTER I

INTRODUCTION

I found in Innisfail the fair,
In Ireland, while in exile there,
Women of worth, both grave and gay men,
Many clerics and many laymen.

I travelled its fruitful provinces round,
And in every one of the five I found,
Alike in church and in palace hall,
Abundant apparel, and food for all.

I found strict morals in age and youth,
I found historians recording truth;
The things I sing, in verse unsmooth,
I found them all—I have written sooth.

From the Irish, translated by James Clarence Mangan.

1

The Homeland

If the prospective visitor to Ireland could be changed, for preference on a summer's day, into one of those happy birds that are able to poise themselves in the air and enjoy the view below, he would be enchanted by what he saw on looking down from a point above the geographical centre of the country.

Here, on the fringe of the European continent, is an oval-shaped island pointing from south-west to north-east. The colours which dominate its surface are green and brown, but they are often intermixed with others, in which there is a great variety of blues. For the greater part of the way around the coast of this island inroads have been made by a pitiless ocean which, in an incalculably remote age, was aided by furies of volcanic upheaval. On the eastern side, and only in a few stretches, are there semblances of a straight coastline. The rest of Ireland's seaboard is irregular beyond description: fjords, inlets and bays cut into it everywhere, some on a scale to provide accommodation for the combined fleets of the world, others as if specially made to give shelter to the small craft of humble fishing communities.

The greater part of the central area of the country is flat. Here the colour brown is almost unchallenged. To the north, south, west and all but a part to the east of the Central Plain are uplands. They rise from gentle hills to impressively grim mountains, and both hills and mountains vary from isolated peaks to ranges some of which stretch as far as the eye can see. Hills and mountains provide a variety of colours to satisfy the most exacting artist in search of exciting landscape. Perhaps the most striking feature of the Irish panorama will not be found in the multiform reliefs and colours of its hills and mountains, but in the peculiar, unique quality imparted to them by its abundant waters. Ireland is a country of waters. There are those waters of the ocean which break the coastline everywhere; and the fresh waters inland. Wherever you set foot in Ireland, you are never far from water: water in every shape, every form and in every sort of movement or in every sort of peace. The abundance of the fresh waters is due to the configuration of the surface as well as to the rainfall, for Ireland has been so designed by Nature that the rainfall is slowly collected and usually makes its way in relatively slow measure and often by roundabout routes until the excess finds its outlet to the sea in its own time and in its own way. Thus it is that there are so many spring wells, so many brooks, streams and rivers, slow or fast-flowing, twisting and turning among the hills and mountains, often enlivened by rapids and waterfalls; and there are also some partly man-made canals which still carry a useful traffic. And then there are the many very beautiful lakes or loughs; and even chains of loughs, as on the great River Shannon. The Shannon is the longest river, not only in Ireland, but in the British Isles; Lough Neagh is the largest lake, and the Erne comes next.

There is no country in the whole world which, for its size, has so much variety in its geography as Ireland. The visitor soon discovers that it must also be one of the best recorded in the geographical sense; for almost every field, every hillock, every little path and every rivulet, however small, has its name—and often its story going back beyond the memory of man. The countryside, the towns and the cities are saturated with story. You can hardly move far outside the towns with-

Lough Bofin—Co. Leitrim
ITA

Desolate Mount Errigal—Co. Donegal ITA

Killarney Lower Lake, Evening ITA

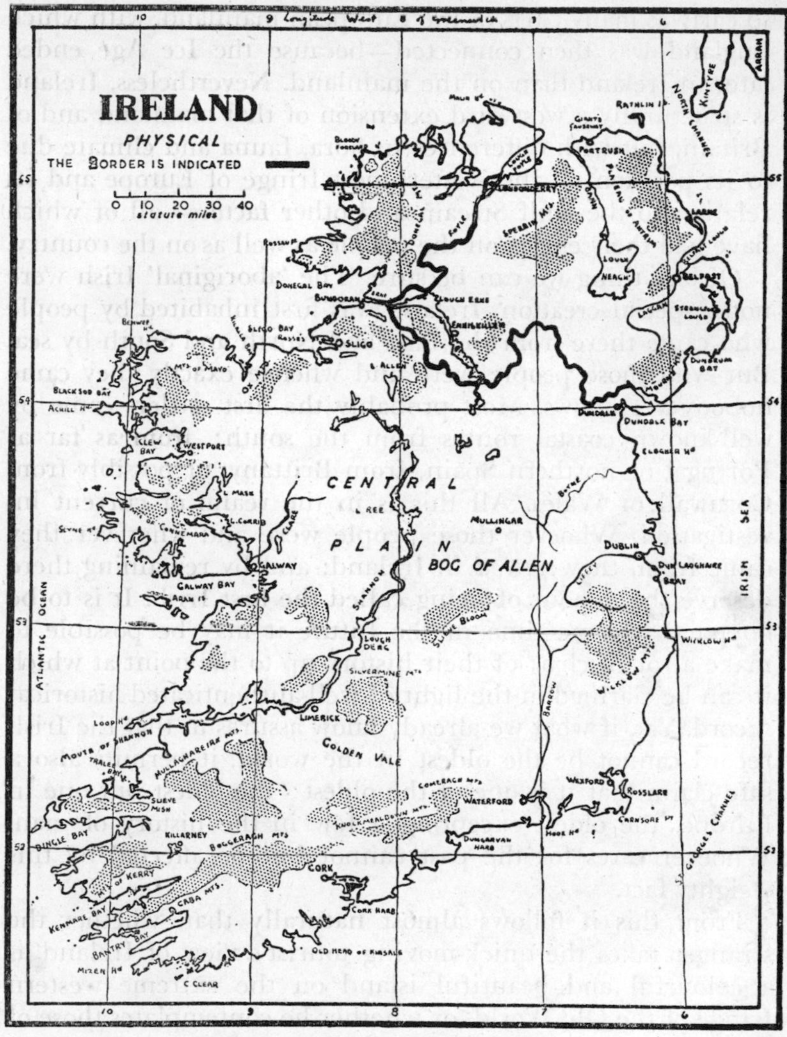

out experiencing the feeling that you are surrounded by strange and curiously remote traditions.

The latest estimates indicate that Ireland has been inhabited perhaps since the later Palæolithic period and certainly since the Mesolithic period; which means anything up to 10,000 years. It seems now to be fairly well established that this western island was not inhabited by human beings so early as many parts of the European mainland, with which England was then connected—because the Ice Age ended later in Ireland than on the mainland. Nevertheless, Ireland is structurally a westward extension of that mainland and of Britain, but with differences in flora, fauna and climate due to its position on the westernmost fringe of Europe and its relation to the Gulf Stream and other factors—all of which have had their effects on the people as well as on the country.

Of one thing we can be sure. The 'aboriginal' Irish were not a special creation. Ireland was first inhabited by people who came there from the East and North and South by sea. But who those people were and whence exactly they came nobody yet knows. Most probably the first settlers came by well-known coastal routes from the south: from as far as Portugal or northern Spain, from Brittany, or possibly from Cornwall or Wales. All this is in the realm of current investigation. Whoever those people were and wherever they came from, they *settled* in Ireland; and by remaining there deserve the honour of being called the first Irish. It is to be hoped that some time in the future it may be possible to make a rough chart of their history up to the point at which it can be clarified in the light of well-authenticated historical record. Yet, if what we already know assures us that the Irish record cannot be the oldest in the world, it permits also a safe claim that it is one of the oldest: the oldest but one in Europe, the oldest excepting a few in the history of man. Whoever cares for the past cannot but be affected by this weighty fact.

From this it follows almost naturally that, whether the stranger takes the quick-moving tourist's view of Ireland as a colourful and beautiful island on the extreme western fringe of the Old World, or whether he contemplates those of its present inhabitants with whom he comes into contact, he will find more than enough to interest him on all sides. He will surely find many things to puzzle him in both the country and its people. It is to help the sympathetic and interested visitor that this book has been conceived and written. Here a brief personal statement seems to be necessary.

The reader of these pages is entitled to know by what

right or authority a work with so comprehensive a title is written. I can only reply that I have neither right nor authority; but that at least I have what I hope will be justification or, at the lowest estimate, an excuse. By a throw of Nature's dice I was born north of the line which now divides Ireland politically, but of *Irish* parents who came, the one from south of that line in the old Ulster county of Monaghan, the other from Connacht, to the west of it. To be born in a 'border' county, of parents from the other side of it, has its advantages in helping to keep the mind receptive to what people think and what is happening on both sides of that Border. What may count for more is that I have enjoyed the additional advantages of schooling in both Northern Ireland and in the South: a bi-partisan education which was rounded off in England and in the university of life, the latter, by good fortune, including a period on the Continent of Europe as well as extensive travels in the Americas. One result of all this is that I am not only conscious of our Irish shortcomings as well as of our good qualities—"inferior and superior to the rest of humanity"—but the circumstances of birth, education and of life generally have made me tolerant and, I do not deny it, more inclined to look for the good than for the bad in humanity generally, and particularly among my fellow-countrymen. That great Englishman Dr. Johnson regaled some of his admirers with a famous witticism about the Irish in these words: "The Irish are an honest people—they seldom speak well of one another." The Irish can afford to allow the witticism to pass, especially as there is more than a grain of truth in it. I shall leave, in Johnsonian terms, to more 'honest' Irishmen than myself the rôle of denigration.

The starting-point of a book dealing with so ambitious, so impossible a subject as is indicated by the title *Ireland and the Irish* presents few problems to the bold writer who is prepared to seize the pig by ear and tail. It resolves itself at the outset into whether to begin with Ireland or the Irish. Here we strike the first spark. For centuries there has been a rumour so widespread and persistent (one for which Irish and English are jointly responsible) to the effect that the Irish are not only difficult people, but even difficult to understand. History has given some support to the content of the rumour; for Ireland, having been conquered, showed that she was not conquered; having been, as most men thought, killed, she refused to die; having been exploited down to her shamrocks and, it seemed, all but skinned alive, she survives to become relatively prosperous in a semi-prostrate Europe; and, as the British Empire loses the claws of imperialism and much of its old strength, the 'sister island' seems capable of rising from her ashes and ready to take a new lease of life. All this is very mystifying, and one need not be surprised to learn that some years ago a nonplussed and crabbed author gave the world his views on the whole Hibernian roundabout in a work with the pejorative title *The Impossible Irish*.[1] It was a rereading of that angry book which tipped the balance for me and made me decide to begin with the most difficult and most delicate aspect of the frightening Janus. The people must come first; their demesne will take shape as we progress.

At the risk of forestalling what should become clear later, a great secret may now be disclosed: one which may well take the breath from many upon whom it is abruptly thrust. It is this. All things considered, the Irish seem to be human beings more or less like other western Europeans, with certain characteristics and idiosyncrasies of their own, but not fundamentally different from those others. It is the characteristics and idiosyncrasies which make the Irish an interesting people, but one must try to avoid falling into the error of believing that the peculiarities of their temperament are the most important part of it, for the truth seems to be that those very peculiarities are as often as not a mixture of curse and blessing. Having said that, the rest of the story will tell itself later; and story there is.

Ireland herself is another matter: Ireland, the collectivity, people, climate, soil and landscape; Ireland at work and at play; Ireland of life and of death. There is also something called Irishness—a psychological phenomenon of which we have a more or less vague picture in our minds as the word occurs. The word 'Irishness' is not unlike the word 'elephant',

[1] By Tom Penhaligon, pen-name of a well-known English journalist. Published by Routledge in 1935.

in that it conjures up an image but, when it comes to defining it in terms of words, formidable difficulties spring up before us. But even that must be attempted.

And so we shall first take the Irish—the people now living in Ireland in the two political divisions marked on the maps of our times as Northern Ireland and the Republic of Ireland—as our starting-point.

One word of explanation of the terminology I use throughout this book. Northern Ireland, also known as The Six Counties, I call simply *The North*. The Republic of Ireland, until recently The Irish Free State, and Eire, I call simply *The South*. The terms are not geographically exact, but they are widely used in Ireland and have the advantage of simplicity.

2

The Desire to Please

Some years ago a friend whom I met in the street one evening in London informed me that he was on his way to see George Moore in his Ebury Street beehive, and asked me to go with him. As I had never met Moore in the flesh, I took advantage of the opportunity. On arrival I found about half a dozen people there, including a thin boy who had made a reputation for himself as a never-failing Irish wit, a man who for this purpose may be called Fingal. Fingal, of course, was a poet; and not a bad one. He used to make a living partly by practising a learned profession and partly by writing prose for America, where his fame is greater than on our side of the Atlantic. But his real occupation in life has always been bright Irish conversation. For this he has a great reputation, especially outside of Ireland. When I saw Fingal I approached him and said: "Tell me now, you know George Moore very well—what do you think of him?"

He looked at me narrowly and enquired: "Do you mean the man or his work?"

"The man," said I. "His work has always been available to me, but not so the man. I am about to meet him for the first time and would like to be armed."

Fingal laughed. "Between you and me," said he, "Moore

is one of the biggest bores in Christendom." I thanked him for the expert judgment, and in due course was introduced to the Great Man himself.

Moore was very pleasant to me, particularly so when he found that I liked cats. He leaned forward from the edge of an armchair. I sat respectfully at his feet on a pouf. After his disquisition on cats—a truly delightful one lasting about ten minutes—he looked at me with the cynical eye of a parrot and said: "I saw you talking to Mr. Fingal a moment ago—is he a friend of yours?"

"I can hardly claim that," I replied; "I know him very slightly. But tell me, Mr. Moore, what do you think of him?"

He sat up suddenly, showing distinct signs of interest. His voice changed and he asked: "Do you mean his work or the man himself?" Moore affected a French accent which he blended with his native mixture of excellent County Mayo and mannered Horse Show way of talking.

I said the man.

"The man . . . the man . . . *aha,* the man." Moore made a priestly gesture, the fingers of one hand pointing heavenwards and said very solemnly: "He's not a bad fellow . . . very kind and well meaning. But, God save us all, what a bore!"

A very Irish situation and I laughed to myself. I had to see George Russell (Æ) before I went home that night. The old sage was then living in Bloomsbury. I often used to call on him for a chat, on which occasions he invariably produced a cup of bad tea, the badness of which went completely unnoticed while I was with him, and only occurred to me afterwards when I was thinking things over. I told him the story of Fingal and George Moore, whereupon George Russell's eyes sparkled and he uttered a quiet little laugh. He held his teacup at arm's length, pointing it at me like a pistol and said in that messianic way of his: *"Do you know, they were both right."*

The story could end there, but it has a sequel. Thinking it amusing, I told it to a friend who was a well-known Dublin publisher until about the tail-end of the Irish Literary Renaissance—before the 1922 Treaty, that is—a wonderful little man known as 'The Leprechaun' because of his astounding ability for appearing suddenly as if from nowhere to join full-time drinkers and talkers wherever they happened to be gathered together and there was lush. I was taken aback by his reaction.

"George Russell! *George Russell!!* One of the biggest frauds and hoaxes even Ireland ever produced! How that man ever got away with it *I* don't know. But he did, he did." He finished his glass in an angry swallow as if to clinch it.

"Now, Leprechaun," said I, "he can't be such a fraud and hoax as all that! The shrewd Dubliners, of all people, would have spotted him before he got far with his fraud and hoaxing."

"Of course they spotted him. Everybody in Ireland spotted him"—the Leprechaun made a sudden gesture of impatience —"but I suppose it's easy enough when all's said to understand why he got away with it."

"How so?"

"Well now, you know as well as I do that the Irish are so easy-going and tolerant, so smooth and glib-tongued and full of blarney, so full of imagination that, whenever they want, they can create illusions like George Russell, providing they have a lead. George gave them the lead by not merely telling them that he believed in fairies, but by *painting pictures of fairies which he'd seen*! That did it. From then on he never looked back, for in Ireland lots of people really believe in fairies and the rest will tell you *no,* they don't believe in them, but that they're there all the same. Russell struck a magnificent line, and that's the secret of his reputation: *fairies!*—and his blether about the Bhagavad Gita which everybody who didn't know better thought as good fun as the fairies, especially when even Yeats fell for it."

At that point I gave it up. It struck me many times since then that this story gives some indication of what one is to expect in talking to Dubliners, among whom conversation is a game and an art, and is not intended, like the Socratic dialogue, to clarify or solve some question by means of an applied dialectic. Conversation is for conversation, and so long as a speaker can make an impression on his audience—by wit, by surprise, by any sort of verbalism—both are satisfied. There is no question most of the time of relative truth but, when truth is seriously intended, it is usually stated bluntly without frills or embroidery. The Dubliners are not alone in this, but Dublin seems to be the centre in which this art of calculated conversation is most practised and carried to its highest flights. Fingal did not really in his heart believe that George Moore was the greatest bore in Christendom; nor did Moore think of Fingal as a bore; nor did George Russell really mean what he said. As for the Leprechaun, he merely demonstrated his natural acting ability to prance and cavort the moment he had a suitable opening.

It may be said straightway that all this is perfectly understood among Irish people themselves. It is a game which they greatly enjoy. But it can be disconcerting to the visitor who is unaccustomed to it. If the stranger should happen to be an American, the chances are that he will soon give up any attempt to analyse it, and either regard the speakers as a bit crazy or, if he is wise, make the best of such amusement as it can provide and leave it at that. The same applies to most strangers to Ireland, other than those of English origin. The 'pure' Englishman—about as reasonable a conception as the 'pure' Irishman, but everybody will know what the term means—is another matter. There have been English people who understood the Irish, and no doubt there are many of them living who understand them now. It may seem paradoxical, but it is precisely because of their excellent sense of character that English people most often fail to understand the Irish. This requires explanation.

Although some of the English may be unaware of it, they may take it from an Irishman that few people of any other race or nationality are better judges of character. When the Englishman meets a stranger (almost any stranger, but especially one of another race or country) he usually withdraws into his shell and discloses little or nothing about himself, but meanwhile he closely and intensely scrutinizes the other until he satisfies himself that he has the other 'weighed up'. The Englishman's judgment is seldom far wrong. In this useful old branch of what is now called psychology, it is spotting the dominants and constants which counts: factors which usually disclose themselves in behaviour and may or may not be indicated in speech. Success in the spotting demands shrewdness in the observer, but the educated English differ from most other peoples in that they instinctively cultivate, often with assiduity, such gifts as Nature may have endowed them with in the particular art of weighing up friends, neighbours and strangers.

A good case could be made showing that the success of the English in this world has been largely due to their exceptional ability in this field; and that, wherever they have met with a major failure, it has been due as much to mistaken judgment of character as to all other factors put together. Now, it is not without significance that, although the major mistakes of the astute English ruling classes have been comparatively few, among that few the outstanding errors of judgment have been made in regard to people whom they ought to have known best; but, as events have shown only too clearly, whom they cannot have understood. These people were their own colonists in America, and the Irish. The English were so familiar with both that they thought they could take chances with them. Hence the mistakes.

3
Character of the People

The problem of the American colonists duly solved itself and the United States are the result. The centuries-old Irish problem has also almost solved itself, but not so completely. Much water must flow under O'Connell Bridge before all is neat and tidy in the 'sister isle'. Even the Americans seem to be more settled and fixed than the Irish, and this notwithstanding the continued functioning of their racial melting-pot. Ireland is a small place, but its size merely scales down the dimensions, and does not alter the nature of her problems, or her nature. If the English made grave psychological mistakes with their American colonists and with the Irish—mistakes now generously admitted—one finds it difficult to understand the first of those errors but not the last. The Irish mistake can be explained, though some may think that in attempting to do so I over-simplify. It was due to a curious quality in Irish make-up which, in its strongest manifestation, is at any moment capable of frustrating all efforts by strangers—non-Irish people, that is—to weigh them up with anything even approaching accuracy.

The Irish have a strange and disconcerting capacity, one which they can turn on with lightning facility, for changing the picture of those constants which the observer may be spotting in behaviour or speech and building up in his mind. They can, so to speak, give a shake to the mental kaleidoscope, and what the other fellow thought was a fairly clear picture in clearly defined outlines becomes altogether another picture and often one that is startlingly different from the first. It is when dealing with strangers or when in a tight corner that the Irish are most likely to shake the kaleidoscope. Note that it is not they who change: it is merely that they succeed in baffling the stranger. They rarely try such tricks among themselves, for in addition to possessing the faculty for changing the picture in other people's minds, they see fairly easily into their own. In addition to this strange quality, there is one other of which many of them show signs: a somewhat mercurial, emotional and at times incalculable temperament. And with all these—to the stranger, unpredictable factors in the make-up of our Irishman—there is one which may come as a surprise to many. It is that, among themselves, the Irish are perhaps the most conservative, calculable and, I was almost going to write *predictable,* people in Europe, though that may be going too far. As for the capacity for disconcertingly baffling the stranger and for not being easily weighed up, it may be that nearly one thousand years of being pushed around by strangers has had something to do with it; and also with their own close conservatism, especially *vis-à-vis* the stranger. At heart, the Irish are the least revolutionary people in Europe, though they carry within them as much potential social high-explosive as any other. If the high-explosive is there, it is unlikely to be used for a long time, because the country as a whole is satisfied with a stability it has not enjoyed for centuries; and stability is everything to those who draw a living from the land. The possible exception to this is the one part of Ireland where industrialism rules: Belfast. And there the character of the people differs from that of the rest of Ireland, including even the rest of the Six Counties of the northern governmental area. The Belfastman is a type on his own. In the country districts of the Six Counties, the people do not differ very greatly from the countrymen of The South; and together they represent the bulk of the population.

All the Irish everywhere are recognized to be an independent people. This needs some qualification, and I think it can be stated in words which a French scholar has applied to the Celts of France in relation to Roman rule: "What they liked was not so much independence as to be dependent only on what they like." The Irish have a remarkably strong propensity for wishing to be dependent *only on what they like,* what they themselves choose to like; and they do not seem to care whether other people approve or even understand their choice. In this respect they can be touchy. I remember once having pointed out in quite a friendly way to a countryman in my own Fermanagh that the hub of the axle of his ass-cart could do with some grease, as the wheel was stiff on it and this gave the ass more work than was necessary, thereby tired it and made its efforts slower. He didn't say anything. I thought my advice had registered and that he would do something about it. He did nothing. When I returned a year later I chipped him good-humouredly about it. The old man straightened himself, looked me straight in the eye and said: "Hell to me soul, anybody would think that the cart was yours! I'll grease it when I like. And if I don't like I won't grease it: and I won't, for it has worked well enough for me these many years!" I got what I had asked for. It took some time and apologetic explanation on my part before the old man and myself were on as good terms as before.

The stranger who resents this sort of attitude is foolish. All he has to do is to remember that when it comes to any sort of interference with what—reasonably or unreasonably—they have chosen to like, the Irish, a courteous and polite people by natural inclination, are as likely as not to show the impertinent one the back of their hand. Irish tongues have a sharp edge to their soft side.

It is little things like this which are liable to cause friction. There are not many of them, and the taboos to be respected by the visitor are usually simple, easily learnt and easily remembered. The most dangerous of all is sex—anything even remotely related to sex. Whoever wishes to pursue an investigation into the reasons for this taboo must do so with his own compass and under his own power, for this is not the place to discuss it beyond recording the warning and giving it emphasis. It should be noted that it is not a taboo springing from the Roman Catholic Church in Ireland—though it is partly so—for the Protestant denominations are equally sensitive about it. In Ireland this manifestation of Puritanism is as common among Protestants as Catholics. One has to remember that the Irish—Protestants and Catholics, Northerners and Southerners, the people of the Gaelic-speaking parts and the anglicized Irish of the East coast—all have a strongly Puritan element in their make-up. The rigorous official literary and film censorship of The South reflects it and, as invariably happens to bureaucracy everywhere, the censors sometimes apply their powers with results that by English or American standards are little short of absurd.

The Irish as talkers! Here I have a twinge of conscience about letting the reader into some deeply concealed Irish secrets—things that are silently acknowledged among themselves but never publicized from the rooftops even in those moments of verbal malice with which the talkative Irishman or Irishwoman in full blast so often peppers the harangue. The twinge of conscience is relieved by the thought that, after all, what I propound may not be so deep a secret as I imagine; that in short it has been fairly obvious to many of the social anthropologists and observers of native habits who in recent years have visited our interesting island; and that even I may be quite wrong or at least have not fully understood.

One assumes that the visitor is not a member of that class —English or American—which is convinced beyond argument and lives in the blind faith that he or she belongs to a category of mankind that is superior to the mere Irish. The English who used to go to Ireland for hunting, shooting and fishing were representative of the type but, as their day is almost past, the less said about them the better. They were not liked by the Irish, who never regarded them as superiors, and they were tolerated because they often brought a little extra money where it was badly required. If any of them survive, they are welcome to keep away. One assumes also that the visitor is of a friendly disposition and anxious to make friends but not to influence people; for if the former approach is likely to open all doors to the stranger, the latter is liable to close most of them. Better not try to influence the Irish, even for their own good. The visitor who comes in the mind to treat those whom he meets as men and women in every way equal to himself, irrespective of differences in wealth or social distinctions, will always fare best. This is axiomatic. He is immediately accepted as a friend, and before long will find himself a respected member of almost any group he shows an inclination to join. This will give him an opportunity of taking part in the talk, but he must be warned at the outset against expecting Irish talkers in their native atmosphere to be always ready to perform for his benefit, as if all were born professional comedians and perpetually bubbling over with wit and humour which they are ready to turn on in volume for his special amusement. He may, indeed, be somewhat taken aback to find how serious Irish people generally are; or, though it is less common, how boring they sometimes are. He is certain also to meet some who never miss an opportunity of acting the playboy, especially when a stranger is present. As there is a fair sprinkling of playboys in most towns, in the cities and, above all, in Dublin, it may be useful to say something about them. The playboy type—occasional or permanent—is found in all grades of society, is a special product of the country, and is often profitably exported.

In the first place, the Irish playboy is a born actor who must have an audience and who will do or say almost anything that is likely to create an impression. He has a weakness for dramatizing himself in the centre of interesting or amusing situations and, as he has imagination and great facility and felicity in verbal expression, he will not, if the audience is receptive, stop at any fantasy or at putting it forward as reality—which it is to him—in order to evoke wonder at or appreciation of his performance, or to raise a laugh. There is not much unconscious wit or humour in his performance, though the fertility of his invention may sometimes surprise even himself. And in all this, *he can be deadly serious*! Success encourages him. Some Irishmen (or Anglo-Irishmen, for they too have these gifts) have risen to fame by developing this playboy temperament and canalizing it in directions where it has received widespread recognition for its art and entertainment value. It is only one aspect of these famous men's temperament and ability, and they do not use it to the exclusion of others less suspect or, if if it must be, less serious. To the Irish in general, Bernard Shaw and Oscar Wilde, for example, are in this sense great playboys: marvellous entertainers possessed of wit and imagination, verbal facility and the power to use exaggeration, paradox and unreason artistically. One meets the less spectacularly successful of the type in many a Dublin pub. Among the pub-*élites* and literary cliques one often finds a group of them in which each individual tries to out-do the others. It can be great fun. The visitor who is privileged to listen—and the privilege is rarely withheld—leaves the company unwillingly, even though his head may be swimming as a result of the verbal exaltation. Dublin stands alone amongst cities of the world in its ability to reduce to pulp and by mere talk the innocent and untrained listener. And in that, after he has left this world-headquarters for the wholesale manufacture of verbal fireworks, the stranger may suffer after-effects in a mental hangover, a bewilderment which, however, is cured when he gets his feet back again on, say, the more earthy soil of Old England. An English friend returning from Ireland with me on the Holyhead boat said: "My head is still reeling with all that talk—isn't yours?" I said no, and explained that, being Irish, I must be immune, as I regarded it as so much grand fun and not to be taken seriously.

What malice there often is in that talk! What powers of criticism! If it should happen to be literary discussion, no reputation is safe, especially no contemporary reputation. And most of the gods of the past are shown to have feet of clay. English literary gentlemen often dismiss all this kind of talk as either 'provincialism' or due to an inferiority complex or arrested development. There may be some of each of these elements in it, but I think the greater part of it is just Irish playboyism, or it may often be that not uncommon thing found everywhere, the envenomed envy of the artist: like that of the famous Italian prima donna who was once caught tearing a pair of silk stockings with her teeth because a rival had an outstanding success. The Irish are garrulous and emotional, and when emotion takes command of their garrulity, the stranger need not be surprised at anything which comes out. But he should judge the verbal performance as performance and not as the delivery of considered judgment. In that way he will enjoy it. If he takes it seriously, or in any other way, he will be doing something which the Irish themselves rarely do, knowing far better. If he should take it literally he will merely show himself to be as obtuse as the great English judge who, on being asked what he thought of *A Midsummer Night's Dream*, replied that it was just a tissue of lies and improbabilities from beginning to end.

What has been said refers chiefly to the sort of very amusing verbal capering for effect which one is likely to find in greater measure in Dublin than anywhere else in Ireland. One is likely to find it anywhere, even in The North. But outside of Dublin it is usually less exuberant. And it may take other forms. To me the most pleasant of all Irish talk is the simple, straightforward and clear-cut conversation of the people of the western seaboard and islands. My personal experience is that, with no less imagination and certainly far less conscious effort, they can produce as they wish a flow of verbal nectar which never either bewilders or wearies the listener, and usually has the effect of making him feel refreshed, as if on a hot summer's day somebody had handed him a glass of champagne, or a porringer of clear water from a mountain spring.

These are my own impressions, and they are given, not as distillations of wisdom on the Irish art of talking, but merely to provide the stranger with the rough equivalent of that useful antidote which helps to prevent or relieve air-sickness. For the Irish, they may seem gratuitous and possibly unfair; for those who are not strangers to Ireland they will be unnecessary. As we all know, nothing can be more boring than the attempt to analyse the unanalysable, and there is probably nothing more incapable of analysis than Irish talk, with its wonderful voice-play and, in terms of singing, voice-control; its natural artistry in dramatic effect; its fantasy, and often its imaginative range. I need not labour the point, more than to say that the familiar professional Irish comedian of vaudeville and the radio exaggerates it all; and, more often than not, travesties the real thing. The real thing is spontaneous; and what is not spontaneous is either completely phoney or at least suspect.

4
The Social Classes

Belfast is the only city or area in the whole of Ireland which is industrialized. With the industrialization goes nearly everything to be expected from it. Belfast and The North will be specially considered, but here it may be said that the moment the visitor finds himself in the northern countryside, he will not notice any great difference between the nature of the people and most of those whom he will meet in the southern countryside—always excepting speech and accent. In Belfast itself one finds the same social strata as in an English industrial city, but there is a difference between the ruling class of Northern Ireland and that of England where, for good or ill, Socialism has taken root in the mind of the masses and, as this is written, shows itself as a powerful element in the social system. Of Ireland in general, Beatrice Webb said: "They do not know the beginning of Socialism in this country. Every one of them is an individualist to the backbone." That was over a quarter of a century ago, but it holds good today, though English Socialist legislation is influencing The North, where an old and intractable Conservatism is still very strong. Only in Belfast is there any significant 'Leftism' or Socialist feeling, although the memory and works of Ireland's most progressive and imaginative humanist political thinker—James Connolly, executed for his part in the 1916 Easter Rebellion—are far from being ignored or forgotten. In the countryside of The North the old Anglo-Irish Ascendancy is still Ascendancy linked with

Westminster, with the traditional English ruling class and with big business. In The North there are this numerically small Ascendancy class and a considerable middle-class in the towns and among the well-to-do farmers; and then there are the small farmers and farm-labourers. Most of the towns are like English market towns. It is a close-knit society with a pattern of its own and, completely industrial in Belfast, outside the capital it bears many resemblances to what one will find almost anywhere in England outside the industrial areas.

Not so The South. One has to read Irish history in order to find an explanation of the marked differences in social structure and in the way of life between the Six County area and the rest of the country. In The South there are still many survivors of the old Anglo-Irish Ascendancy; they are politely respected but without power; and they are a steadily declining influence. Since the Treaty of 1922, a new ruling class has taken the place of the old; a new farming class, consisting mostly of freeholders, has already consolidated its position, and an entirely new bureaucracy has grown up, adding considerably to the number of the Irish middle-class. Furthermore, although in The South agriculture is of more importance than all the other industries put together, there has been a considerable movement into the towns and especially to Dublin, of which the population has increased from 373,178 in 1900 to half a million in 1950. The lower incomes are to be found among the large number of small freeholders, other smallholders, farm labourers and the unskilled workers in the towns and cities. A little better off are the artisans, the workers in the limited number of industries, hotels, restaurants, and in small businesses generally. Almost a class by themselves are the owners of public houses; and the spirit-groceries—establishments conveniently divided into two parts, in one of which you can buy all kinds of groceries, and all sorts of drink in the other, for consumption on or off the premises. With the ruling class and bureaucracy must be bracketed the Roman Catholic Church which, in The South, occupies a unique position in the social edifice, and has a power and influence of its own in virtually everything and with everybody from Cabinet Ministers down to the humblest peasants. Apart from the new peasantry, but almost in regard to them too, one may say that the Republic of Ireland is a bourgeois country, conservative in outlook, very Catholic in religion and, compared with the past, prosperous. The picture is very different from that of the old Ireland under English rule.

What has happened in Ireland, apart from The North, is that power has passed from an old ruling class to the Irish people, against whom one of the standing charges in pre-Treaty days was that they were "incapable of ruling themselves", to which was added the comment after the Treaty that they were "bound to make a mess of things". In the face of many difficulties they have survived, but what has happened in Ireland since the Treaty can hardly be called a social revolution, though some steps in that direction have been taken. For one thing, a new professional class arose because the sons of poor people now began to enter every profession and because new and very favourable land laws have helped, by a redistribution of property, to change a cruelly exploited tenantry into a landowning class. Some idea of how favourable this legislation is may be gathered from the fact that land can be bought by the tenant paying an annual sum of *half the rental* he would have been paying fifty years ago when, after a long agitation, the principle of a 'fair' rent was recognized! In comparison with Britain and the U.S.A., the system of land ownership in the Republic of Ireland is extremely favourable to the poor man who wishes to own and manage his own farm. And although there are large, medium and small farms, it is the medium farms of from 15–100 acres which now constitute the agricultural mainstay of the country. This has brought into being a new class, of which the numerical importance can be judged when we take into account that, of the total male population, some 50 per cent. are engaged in agriculture. Thus, the visitor must never forget that, of every two Irishmen he will meet, one of them is a man of the soil. The chances are that he is a freeholder independent of a landlord—which makes him feel very much freer than his ancestors could have felt since the seventeenth century. Men and women, their sons and daughters, have an economically independent spirit; and, even when times are not always good to them, that spirit remains.

Old Lady in Hooded Cloak—West Cork
ITA

Old Lady and Spinning Wheel—Donegal ITA

Woolworkers—Foxford Mills, Co. Mayo

This is true, although not always related to the standard of living. The standards of living have also changed. There are still bad patches and much real poverty, but, generally speaking, the standard of living is much higher than it was before the Treaty.

Democracy has grown in The South. With it there has appeared a really prosperous branch of the middle-class, one unconnected with hard work on the land. They are middlemen, distributors, traders, shopkeepers, small manufacturers and so forth, and they were making good money before the Second World War. Since then they have continued to make it, in many cases hand-over-fist. They, not the farmers, are the people who give the visitor the impression that The South is prosperous. Although some of the farmers do very well, it is rarely in straight farming that the fortunes are made. Those who make the biggest money in Ireland are not the people who do the vital work for the country. Ireland, on the whole, is a land of humble men and women who are so important that without them there would be no base for the others, but these others lap much of the cream from the poor man's milking.

I once discussed with a friend the difference between life under British rule and that of the Irish since the Treaty of 1922. His reply is worth noting, as I think it would be the reply of the intelligent Irishman anywhere in The South. "The Irish," he said, "could nearly always cod the people who ruled and administered for the British. The high-ups in the old régime were so far removed from the people that they knew little or nothing of the popular mentality or will. They could always be deceived. The lesser officials were as often as not Irish; and, because of the general feeling of the public in regard to many things, and because many sympathized with the people, they were inclined to let much slide. And so things were easy. But not so under our own régime. Now we have Irishmen, our own people, as lawgivers, tax-collectors and in every public office. They know us as we know ourselves. We can't cod these boys! We can get away with practically nothing nowadays, unless they deliberately turn a blind eye, as they often do, for instance, about trifles such as drinking in pubs during prohibited hours. Whatever Government happens to be in power in Dublin knows that there is no great crime when a publican sells drink out of permitted hours, so long as the fact is not shouted from the hill-tops. Besides, the revenue is helped by these legal peccadilloes and they encourage the tourist traffic. Sure nothing pleases anybody more—tourist or native—than to have a drink 'agin the law', behind the closed doors of a pub to which entry is obtainable only by giving the secret knock or password. The atmosphere of conspiracy is very pleasant. Such minor law-breaking is a source of delight, and there are not many of our rulers who have not enjoyed it themselves at some time or other. The Civic Guards are very broadminded and seldom bother much about it, so long as it is decently conducted and not associated with any more serious crime."

This is not the place for even a brief dissertation on the relations of the sexes, or on Irish married life and the family, but a few remarks may save the American and English visitor from errors which might easily lead to loss of face in more than the metaphorical sense. The Irish have as high a respect and regard for their womenfolk as any people in the world, and Irish women think as highly of Irishmen as of any others, and perhaps more so. We may perhaps take all that for granted, but I have stated it bluntly, because even within my own limited observation I have seen strange assumptions on the part of both Englishmen and Americans that the average Irish girl is ready to bow down and worship them merely because they are English or American. It is not so. Let it be understood that the average Irish girl, whether from The North or The South, is as sharp and intelligent as the average Frenchwoman, and if she has not the latter's sophistication, she has other qualities which make up for it. She can compete with the woman of any nation in beauty and natural charm and, for loyalty to the man she has chosen, is without superior anywhere. She is not easily taken in, and *never* by blarney or tall talk, having been well trained in those native arts from the cradle. She is by temperament chaste, is fortified by her religion, has a deep sense of respect for herself; and the stranger who assumes otherwise is making a mistake of which few Irishmen would be guilty in Ireland. This is not to say that she is unwilling to be friendly with a stranger, but the latter need not be surprised if she refuses to permit familiarities which women of his own country might not always resent. No need to labour the point that the visitor must behave to meet the fact that in Ireland he will find what he may well regard as a straitlaced population of women. He can be assured that, if he behaves well, he will find Irish women delightful. If he behaves badly, trouble is inevitable.

That is about the only warning the stranger need be given, though it is perhaps fair to add that he will find throughout the whole of Ireland a curious lack of sentimentality about such things as love-making. He may be struck by the, at all events, outward lack of affectionate display between engaged or married couples, almost amounting to a coldness that is not consistent with the emotional nature of the people. This is a complex question, one worthy of a monograph to itself, and demanding space and *expertise* that cannot be given here. In any rough evaluation a curious and interesting fact emerges: the women of Ireland have more children than those of any other country. And the marriage age is advanced, being over thirty. The advanced age is due partly to economic factors, partly to an old tradition of family responsibility which has the effect of making the men hesitate until the last moment about taking the plunge into matrimony, and partly to the accepted position in regard to divorce. There is no divorce in The South, the position being governed by the Canon Law of the Roman Catholic Church. Divorce is possible in The North; but it is not easy and there is little of it. All the Irish in Ireland have a stoical, fatalistic outlook on this subject, the general attitude being that, having made one's bed, one must lie on it, women and men being satisfied with the consolation, if it is necessary, that children provide the strongest means of family stability. This balances the mercurial temperament; and it works.

In England there is an unwritten law, not always strictly observed in recent years, that in certain places—pubs, for example—discussion of politics or religion is to be avoided. It is not a bad working rule for the visitor to Ireland, though discussion of politics in that country no longer carries with it the risks of the past. Religion is another matter. There can be no 'discussion' of religion in The South, for the Irish

Roman Catholic accepts his religion so fully that he will not argue about it any more than he will ever try to convince a non-Catholic of its values. The latest census gives the Republic of Ireland a population of 94 per cent. Roman Catholics and, on the whole, they are fully practising and often even devout Catholics. This 94 per cent. of Catholics accounts for what Englishmen and Americans regard as the 'large number of priests', with which often goes the accusation that Eire is a 'priest-ridden' country. The number of priests and religious who reside permanently in Ireland is increased by a fluctuating and often considerable number of Irish-born priests and religious who return home from time to time—they go all over the world—to visit relations and friends and to savour the old atmosphere of their birth and upbringing. Hence, it is easy for the stranger to get a wrong impression. What the stranger must learn to realize is that, by their own standards, the Irish do not regard themselves as priest-ridden.[1] What he should also recollect is that already mentioned fundamental trait of the Irish for always preferring to depend on something of their own choice—in this case their religion—rather than on something else which might or might not be better and the merits of which hardly interest them. Hence, if even they *are* priest-ridden, it is their own choice to be so. By English or American standards one might consider that they are priest-ridden, but English or American visitors should keep their opinions about this to themselves, for not only is it not their business, but they will be wasting breath talking about it. Thus, in The South the religious question ought not to cause the sensible visitor any trouble whatsoever.

The position in The North is different. Here the stranger must tread very warily, because the politics of Partition have made religion highly political. In the Six County Area about one-third of the population consists of Roman Catholics; in Belfast less than one-quarter of the population are of that religion. Taking the whole area, the remainder of the people are Protestants, with Presbyterians in a majority, closely followed by Church of Ireland (Episcopalians). Broadly

[1] "In England and Wales (1950) there is one priest for every 450 Roman Catholics; in Australia one for every 640; in Eire one for every 670."—Dr. J. T. Kiernan, at a meeting of the Statistical Social Inquiry Society of Ireland (1950).

speaking, the Catholic population favours the abolition of Partition; the Protestant is apparently content to leave The Border as it is. A strong and incessant anti-Partition propaganda is met by an equally strong and ever-repeated "No!", and we have a situation in which a person's political views are nearly always inferred from his religion. Catholics and Protestants in The North are fully aware of this; and behave accordingly. It is an unpleasant situation for both, and capable at any moment anywhere of causing private rows which may easily develop into public clashes. The stranger on a visit to The North may not wish to be involved in what he probably regards as a matter for the people there to decide among themselves. But it can happen that an English or American non-Catholic, unacquainted with local high tension on the Partition question, will freely express himself on the side of the anti-Partitionists. If this should happen, and if those who hear it are 'Loyal Orangemen', the stranger's remarks may be ignored—merely out of politeness because he is a stranger. But there is always the risk that there will be present at least one hard northman who will not, out of politeness or for any other reason, allow it to pass; and who, especially if elated or 'oiled', will give vent to his disapproval in terms of unchallengeable lack of ambiguity and, in extreme cases, backed by a passion which easily leads to violence. There is a pugnacity and toughness in The North which may pass unnoticed until it is aroused, but which, when once aroused, can astonish the stranger and dismay the visitor who is out for a quiet time. I hope that in saying this I have not conveyed the impression that the people of The North are all likely to 'blow off' at any moment, for nothing could be farther from my intention or from the truth. I have purposely stated an extreme case. Taking them as a whole, those people do not yield points to the people of The South in general friendliness and hospitality towards visitors. In stating the extreme case, I do so merely to give warning of a danger which can very easily be avoided by the visitor who exercises a little tact and intelligence.

I have dealt in this chapter with some aspects of life in Ireland which, I have found, always strike the first-time visitor as strange or puzzling. I have found them so myself after long absences from Ireland; and I do not claim to have said the last word about them. Almost everything I have said is the result of asking non-Irish friends for their impressions after a visit and especially for their queries about things which have baffled them. This accounts for the aspects of Irish life on which I have touched, but they are merely aspects specially chosen for this purpose, and nothing more. Nor are they exhaustive, for I do not think it is possible to have even an elementary appreciation of Ireland and the Irish without taking into consideration the complex history of their small island.

Irish people know more about their history than English people or Americans know about theirs, and time has a different meaning for them, so much so that the stranger is often inclined to think that they "live in the past". What it amounts to is that the Celtic mentality dominates time, and an event that happened a thousand or two thousand years ago is as real to many as one which happened last week.

CHAPTER II

THE CELTIC SETTLEMENT

Long, long ago, beyond the misty space
  Of twice a thousand years,
In Erin old there dwelt a mighty race
  Taller than Roman spears;
Like oaks and towers they had a giant grace,
  Were fleet as deers,
With wind and wave they made their biding place,
  These western shepherd seers.
    Great were their deeds. . . .

From *The Celts*, by THOMAS D'ARCY MCGEE.

1

A Land of Gods and Heroes: Prehistory

WHAT has been known as the early history of Ireland consisted until comparatively recent times of a corpus of the most bewildering tall stories which the rich Celtic imagination of poets, myth-makers, theorists and plain fakers could achieve. The application of modern scientific methods with the object of bringing some sort of order and reason into all this is still in its infancy. At least three new sciences are involved: archæology, linguistics and anthropology. The work of investigation, of sorting grain from chaff in each of these branches of science, is still in the pioneering stage so far as Ireland is concerned, and it is fairly safe to say that a decade or decades must pass before many of the difficult problems of ancient Irish history can be solved. There is as yet very little certainty about a number of elementary and at the same time fundamental things. The student finds himself trying to navigate in a dark ocean infested with not merely interesting creatures, but with fabulous monsters the nature of which evokes terror or delight.

For all that, it would be a mistake to assume that the labours of modern investigators are entirely valueless. On the contrary, theirs must be one of the most interesting of all fields of study, because ancient Ireland presents a microcosm, a condensed picture of a Celtic world which once extended across Europe. There is in this Ireland of our own times more evidence surviving of those widespread Celtic peoples and of their culture than is to be found elsewhere. In Ireland much of the evidence is available in forms with which the investigator can deal; and one must never forget that Irish traditions are the oldest in Europe to the north and west of the Alps. The survival down to our own times of traditions dating back beyond the beginnings of recorded history is due to a remarkable institution of the old Irish Celts. As this institution proved itself to be of such great importance, it is worth a brief scrutiny.

The institution consisted of a class or caste called the *filidh*—pronounced fill-ee, to rhyme with Bill-ee. They were greatly venerated men—poets, sages, 'walking encyclopædias' who carried in their great memories the history of the people, the epics of the heroes and of great events, the laws, the pedigrees of outstanding personalities, the works of the poets, the rules of conduct and the traditions of the race in general. These men owned no real estate, and they possessed nothing but their clothes and perhaps a musical instrument to accompany their song or declamation. They had no need of property or wealth: they were provided for. They were *philosophes,* philosophers in the French sense of the word, not metaphysical philosophers. The *filidh* travelled about the country and were welcomed in the herd's cottage or at the chief's court, by ordinary people and by kings, and as men of peace who usually avoided 'politics'—except perhaps as arbitrators endeavouring to solve some problem in a way to avoid violence—they were not merely popular but greatly beloved. It was in the memories of these men that the old history and traditions were carried, from the pre-Christian and pagan days when there was no writing until the arrival of St. Patrick with Christianity in the fifth century—and on to the twelfth century, by which time industrious scribes had taken down their oral traditions and given Ireland the permanent records which are so fascinating and so bewildering. These records are our starting-point in written Irish history. The Science of Archæology corrects or confirms the written record; and progress is thus made.

That the sum of this record is chaotic and in parts fantastic need not surprise us if we consider its nature. Not only were there innumerable *filidh* who from one generation to the next during a thousand years (and maybe much longer) transmitted the traditions, but one must always allow for the working of the fertile Irish imagination, the temptation of poet and artist to brighten a dull story or to add grace to the commonplace; the wild romanticism of some, the uncontrollable verbal impulses, the leanings towards the supernatural and the mystical of others. Generous allowances must be made for all such human weaknesses, if 'weakness' is the right word for these familiar workings of the mind. There is another factor which plays an important part in the ultimate record. From the establishment of Christianity (in the year A.D. 432) and onwards, the sages converted from their old paganism began to alter, subtract from and add to the pagan traditions, so that the latter might not conflict too harshly with the new authoritarian religion to the latter's disadvantage. In this we find confusion more confounded. What may have been originally a simple statement of truth becomes unrecognizable after an already stretched or distorted tradition has been edited and retouched by the conscientious Christian scribe. What has been said will give some idea of the problems which face the modern investigator from the linguistic and literary aspects alone. And before the results of such investigation can be finally acceptable, they should be confirmed by the work of the archæologists and anthropologists. Having thus warned the reader of the curious and baffling compositions of sages, poets, mythographers and well-intentioned fakers which, until recent years, were *accepted* as ancient Irish history, we can afford to look blandly at some of those old stories. In doing so we shall often find ourselves in the realm of the supernatural, for which the Irish mind seems to have had a pronounced liking from the earliest times to the present day.

The list of dates in that early 'history' of Ireland begins with the year 2242—'in the history of the world'—when a lady named Cessair landed there.[1] That was exactly forty days before the Flood. There is a reason for the establishment

[1] For this strange chronology and the story, see *Pagan Ireland,* by the respected scholar Eleanor Hull.

of the precise date. Irish writers of mediæval times showed an irrepressible anxiety to make out that their country had been inhabited at a very early period—in which they were justified—but one suspects that they may not have been too pleased with the idea of being outdone in a claim to antiquity by those Jewish people of whom they read in the Bible. Some such inspiration must have been behind the finally recorded story of Cessair and the establishment of the remarkable date. The story is a simple one. Noah had a granddaughter Cessair (whom Moses does not mention). She and her father wished to go on board the Ark, but Noah could not find room, and therefore he advised them to make for the uninhabited far western part of the earth: a safe area, Noah thought, because being uninhabited there had been no sin there, and the Flood was a punishment for man's sin. Some accounts say that Cessair was so angry that she threatened to forsake Noah's God and take an idol with her to worship. In the end, she and her husband, with her father, brother and fifty maidens, set out and reached Ireland. But the Flood followed them there and they were all duly drowned. A date had been established in Irish history.

The *Book of Invasions* is the main source of that early 'history'. Its written record dates from the twelfth century A.D., though it was probably begun centuries earlier, and the stories in it come from perhaps a millennium before that, for all have a distinctly pagan and supernatural flavour. If Ireland's scribes liked to think of their great antiquity, her sages also liked to think that their people were of mixed origin, and the *Book of Invasions* tells of no less than five great invasions. Before the first of these influxes the country was inhabited by a race of sombre sea-spirits, the Fomorians. The invasion was led by Partholan, who came from Spain and arrived in Ireland on the 1st of May in 'the year of the world' 2520. Battle was joined between Partholan and the Fomorians, but a pestilence attacked the latter and they perished on the mythical Sen Mag or Old Plain. Another account mentions Breg, the religious centre of pagan Ireland, where there are graves.

May Day, the feast of Bel or Beltane, some thirty years later, is given as the date of the next invasion, also from

Spain and led by Nemed, who with some of his followers died in a pestilence. Those who did not perish were subdued by the Fomorians, but the sons of Nemed rose in rebellion and besieged the Fomorians who had taken refuge in a glass tower on Tory Island. This revolt failed, and in fabulous circumstances the 'sons of Nemed' were wiped out.

The third was altogether an even more mysterious and certainly a very curious invasion. The story is one of the most celebrated of Irish traditions dating from pre-Christian times. Here we have an astonishing mixture of myth and history, in which the Irish imagination runs its full course. A survivor from the Spanish invasion of Nemed founded a race which grew in numbers, and one of them, Breac the son of Starn, fled the country and went to Greece, where he had many descendants, so many that they became a nuisance to the Greeks (who do not provide any record of these interlopers). In the Irish language those people were called Fir Bolg, words which were long accepted to mean 'Men of the Bags' or leather wallets; this name having been given to them because the Greeks put them to work carrying bags of soil from rich valleys to stony heights for agricultural purposes. Speculation was that the Fir Bolg were a mixture of original Irish, Spanish invaders and inferior Greeks. After a long residence in Greece (some hundreds of years) they returned to Ireland to leave a most unpleasant tradition. In an ancient Irish work, *The Book of Genealogies* (which among other things purports to prove that the Irish descended from Japhet), a writer says of the Fir Bolg: "Every one who is black-haired, a tattler, guileful, tale-telling, noisy, contemptible; every wretched, mean, strolling, unsteady, harsh and inhospitable person . . . ; every one who loves not to listen to music, the disturbers of every council and every assembly, the promoters of discord among the people; *all* these are descendants of the Fir Bolg." To this day in Ireland it is by no means uncommon to hear an unpleasant or disliked person referred to contemptuously as a Firbolg.

The next invasion followed within half a century, that of the Túatha Dé Danann—The Peoples of the Goddess Dana—a most pleasant god-like race who came to do good and bring their civilizing influence to Ireland. The reader who would wish to see the Celtic imagination working very delightfully is referred to the *Book of Invasions* for an account of this superfabulous invasion and of the struggles on the supernatural level between the Fomorians and their gods and the Túatha Dé Danann and theirs; and of the defeat of the Fomorians at the Battle of Moytura in County Galway on the day of the feast of Samhain, that is, the 1st of November in 'the year of the world' 3330.

The fifth, and for the modern scholar perhaps most interesting, invasion was that of the Milesians from Spain. They were so called from Mile, their leader. Spain was merely a stage on their journey, and it was understood that they came originally from some place much farther away. Milesians and Túatha Dé Danann traded and fought and, in the end, the Milesians triumphed and the Túatha Dé Danann retired into *sidhe* (pronounced shee-e) or great megalithic tombs, of which wonderful examples survive at New Grange and Brug na Boinne. From the sons of Mile descended the royal clans, and altogether the Milesians were regarded as superior people. So that, if a modern Irishman claims to be a Milesian—and such a claim is not rare—what he means is that he is a superior person because he springs from that fine stock. In addition to these invasions there was still another in which a people called the *Cruithne* in Irish and, doubtfully, the Picts in English spread over Scotland and a large part of Northern Ireland. In Ulster they became at one moment the dominant power.

Such are the old stories in brief. The first reaction of the modern mind is to regard them and all such folklore as just so many tall stories. It would be a profound mistake to dismiss them entirely. The best modern scholars do not brush these stories aside. Instead, they take the myths and legends as they are and endeavour to refer them to reliable historical bases, to use the findings of the archæologists to check them, and to apply cautiously and within its limits the rather vague science of anthropology. In this way they hope that one day the hard core of truth in that ancient Irish 'history' will be found. Already encouraging progress has been made. The outlines of a picture no less exciting than that of the *Book of Invasions* and other early works are beginning to appear. Let us see where we now are.

First, we have to regard all those astonishing dates, not so much as fantasy, but as the Christian attempt to relate them to the new faith which took the place of the old paganism. To state it bluntly, as so many inventions. Next, instead of thinking in terms of 'Partholan', 'Fomorians', 'Fir Bolg', 'Túatha Dé Danann', 'Milesians', with their mixture of god-like or supernatural and human attributes, one should think of them in terms of men living elsewhere in Europe in physical, social and moral units. All the evidence indicates that, at the beginning of the Christian era, the population and culture of Ireland were largely Celtic.

So here is the link with the great Celtic peoples outside of Ireland.

2

The Celts become Irish: about 350 B.C.

The French scholar Henri Hubert in two masterly works[1] reconstructs the history of the Celts from their beginnings, and gives us a picture of all the Celts, of every part of the Celtic world. He makes clear to us the meaning of the name, and that is important. The Celts, he says, are *not a race*. The name is that of *a people or a group of peoples.* And that group is *an aggregate of anthropological types.* The area covered is a wide one: from Greece in the East to Ireland in the West; from the Baltic in the North to Spain in the South. He tells us of the separation of one group called the Goidels (Gauls in France, Gaels in Spain) from another group called the Brythons (who went to Britain); and these tall people, intelligent, excellent fighters, who about 1700 B.C. were mostly to be found in Central Europe, showed a very definite inclination to move —they may have been driven—towards the west. They reached Ireland about 400–350 B.C. It was Gaelic Celts from France or North Spain who went to Ireland. Romans and Germans attacked the continental Celts; they were con-

[1] Translated as *The Rise of the Celts* and *The Greatness and Decline of the Celts* in the History of Civilization series, edited by C. K. Ogden (Kegan Paul, London, 1934).

quered by the Romans; and what had been an empire covering a considerable part of Europe ended as groups of peoples in France, North-west Spain, Britain and Ireland. The descendants of those Celtic peoples—themselves of mixed races—are with us today in the extreme west of Europe, in islands and peninsulas. Celtic languages are still spoken in the tip of Brittany in France, in Wales, in the Isle of Man, in the North of Scotland and neighbouring isles, and until late in the eighteenth century Cornish, a Celtic language, was spoken in Cornwall. In Ireland the Gaelic or Irish Celtic language not only survives but—having survived the threat of extinction—in the twentieth century the number of people who speak it increases. In Gaelic the Irish have a beautiful and richly developed language, which, to quote Douglas Hyde, "with the exception of that glorious Greek . . . has left the longest, most luminous and most consecutive literary track behind it of any of the vernacular tongues of Europe". What is equally remarkable is that the only part of the old Celtic empire left in the world to claim itself as a Nation-State is the present Republic of Ireland.

The reader who wishes to learn more about the story of the Celts in general is referred to the work of Hubert already mentioned, and, for illumination on many of the baffling problems of early Irish history in particular, to the still more modern and illuminating work of Professor O'Rahilly.[1] The latter, especially, dispels many a cherished illusion, but here we must rest content not to become involved in the highly technical controversies which this difficult subject is apt to stimulate. One thing worth noting is that, although Professor O'Rahilly adds to our knowledge of the religion of pre-Christian Ireland, we still do not know very much about the fundamentals of either that religion or the considerable mythology embedded in the surviving records. We may speculate that the Druidism brought to Ireland by the Celts became blended with an older paganism, and that the most powerful or principal god in the realm of the supernatural —a realm populated by many gods, demigods and by heroic

[1] *Early Irish History and Mythology*, by Thomas F. O'Rahilly (Institute of Advanced Studies, 64–65, Merrion Square, Dublin, 1946).

as well as by partly human creatures—was the Dagda, the sun-god source of all wisdom, natural and supernatural. And we can hardly avoid the conclusion that the pre-Christian pagan inhabitants of Ireland were sun-worshippers—though we do not know much about the forms of their worship; and, in regard to its *ethos,* we are also lacking in knowledge. The mention of sun-worship brings us to an interesting point. The old Celtic name for Ireland was *Everio* which, for the Irish Gaels, became *Eriu.* O'Rahilly says: "That *Eriu* was the sun-goddess is suggested by her traditional epithet *án* (meaning fiery, bright, glowing, i.e., 'emitting both heat and light'.)" The sun-goddess, who was also and primarily goddess of earth and its springs, often gave her name to tracts of country and to rivers. The modern Irish name for Ireland, a very Christian country, is *Eire*; and Eire is the modern form of *Eriu,* the pagan sun-goddess. In this we have one of the many reminders which confront us today of Ireland's old paganism. Other pagan survivals in contemporary Ireland, and in many forms, are not lacking.

Although little is known about the religious beliefs of the pagan Irish, of the hard core of truth awaiting discovery which lies covered by onion-like layers which must be examined and removed one by one before the central truth can be reached, nobody can read the old records without excitement and stimulation.[1] There is a grand, free wildness, a healthy and vigorous imaginativeness running through them. We find all sorts of references to the most widely dispersed forms of human beliefs. For example, animistic worship seems to have been widespread, and was frequently associated with sacred trees, weapons and pillar-stones. The elements—especially the sun and fire—were worshipped. Perhaps the commonest and certainly the best-known belief of all was in fairies, for which the Irish word is *sidhe* (pronounced shee-e); the reader will remember that this is the same word as that for the megalithic tombs or tumuli into which the Milesians drove the Túatha Dé Danann. From the earliest traditions, from the very beginnings of old Irish literature, in fact, throughout the whole history of Ireland

[1] Those who find Professor O'Rahilly's work above their heads are referred to T. W. Rolleston's *Myths and Legends of the Celtic Race.*

and down to this moment, the fairies, often called the 'little people', have been great favourites of the Irish people. In a famous epic poem, usually spoken of as *The Táin*[1] (pronounced t'aun), of which the title in English is *The Cattle Drive of Cooley,* a work of unknown authorship first written down from oral tradition in the seventh century and telling of a famous episode of the far-distant past, the representatives of this supernatural race play an other-worldly part somewhat similar to that of the Greek gods in Homer:

> Whereat that warrior from the Shee replied:
> I am long-handed Loo the son of Ethlenn,
> Who in old days—hundreds of years of days
> Before this day wherein I speak to thee—
> Led the bright, greatly skilled Dé Danann hosts
> To that dread battle of the North Moy Twirra,
> Wherein the Fomorian hosts were whelmed and slain.
> Yea, I am he who slew the one-eyed Bahlor,
> And afterwards reigned many years in Tara
> Above the Dé Danann host. And, little son,
> 'Tis I who was thy father from the Shee,
> Sooaltim not being thy father.[2]

—lines which provide proof of the supernatural origin of the hero Cuchulainn. The ancient Irish pantheon, though richly populated, was not a highly developed, well-elaborated and clearly defined one like that of the Greeks. It is to their great credit that they had their goddess of the arts, Brigid, daughter of the sun-god, the Dagda. The latter had a numerous progeny, including one Boab Derg, who lived near the present Portumna on the shore of Lough Derg, and another named Angus Mac-in-Óg, who favoured the neighbourhood of Brug na Boyne, where there is the world-famous tumulus at New Grange, an archæologist's heaven. One could continue almost indefinitely listing those other-world beings, but enough has been said to give an idea of the importance of the supernatural to the old Irish mind; and from the remotest to the present day. As for Brigid, just mentioned, she was also the goddess of fertility. The sacred fire which burned at Kildare almost uninterruptedly until the Reformation was

[1] In full *Táin Bó Cuailnge*, pronounced *T'aun Boh Cooley*.

[2] From the translation in English verse by Mary A. Hutton (Maunsel, Dublin, 1907).

Clifden, Connemara—Co. Galway. The Twelve Bens in the Background

Celtic Cross at Monasterboice—Co. Louth ITA

Gallerus Oratory—Co. Kerry ITA

associated with her, and until at least the first decade of the present century she was "commonly invoked in the Hebrides and until quite recently in Donegal to secure good crops" [1] —another example of a Celtic pagan survival.

There were happy and encouraging aspects to that old Irish paganism. It provided among other things for an equivalent to the Christian heaven which took the form of an abode of everlasting youth and peace—*Tir na nÓg* or the 'Land of Youth', also known as the 'Land of Promise', the 'Plain of Delights'—inhabited by fairies who dwelt either in the tumuli—the *sidhe*—which was the earliest idea; or in the 'Happy Isles' (which later in Christian times became 'The Islands of the Blessed'), where immortals lived an existence of unending delight. A feature of the old religion was metempsychosis—the change from human into animal or other form—in which, constantly recurrent, were changes to the salmon, the wolf, the stag, the seal and the swan. Swans are still sometimes spoken of as the 'Children of Lir', and Lir was the god of the sea, father of the much more popular sea-god Manannán Mac Lir, from whom the Isle of Man gets its name. A strange reaction was evoked by the salmon and salmon-transformation; somewhat like our own when the serpent is mentioned, and there are still many parts of Ireland where the salmon is thought of as a 'wise' fish.

These supernatural aspects of the old religion and of the myths and legends in spite of their confusion can give us glimpses of the character of the pre-Christian Irish—indications which justifiably might be discounted but for the fact that in Ireland to this day are to be found many psychological similarities and parallels. Consider this question of the fairies, for example. The Churches frown on such beliefs; modern science pooh-poohs them as nonsense. But the elimination from the Irish mind of belief in or respect for the supernatural, and of a sense of awe about invisible and intangible phenomena which have inexplicable effects on the mind, proceeds slowly. The closer we come to the untarnished Celt the more likely we are to find either belief or at least doubts.

[1] *Encyclopædia Britannica* (XI edition). Article by E. C. Quiggin on Ancient Irish History—Religion in early Ireland—to which I am indebted for this and some of the facts which follow.

The Irishman often seems to be haunted by a fairy or fairies which help him to maintain communication with a mysterious world of the spirit, and this seems to be peculiar, not only to the 'pure Irish'—and, as we know, they are a great mixture of races!—but also to everyone born and brought up in the country, whatever his origin may be. Well did Bernard Shaw realize this puzzling, often infuriating but peculiarly Irish characteristic when he wrote *John Bull's Other Island* nearly fifty years ago. The play takes account of two types of Irish: Larry Doyle, a shrewd, practical and realistic man of affairs, the other an ex-priest, Keegan, a saintly dreamer type, far less 'successful' but much more interesting, one who, with a mind attuned to some other world, nevertheless often hits the earthly nail on the head when the realistic mind has missed it. Keegan speaks of Ireland as 'an island of dreamers' and says to the Englishman Broadbent: "Ireland, sir, for good or evil, is like no other place under heaven; and no man can touch its sod or breathe its air without becoming better or worse." This dreamer has a remarkably shrewd knowledge of the ways and wiles of men, but hardly bothers to cope with this world's problems, and nearly always shows an innate preference for the kindly, the intuitional and the emotional over the calculating and the intellectual processes. In reading the old Irish stories the non-Irish person is sometimes taken aback by the almost brutal starkness, the uncompromising intransigence of the ideas and pictures that are conjured up; and still further astonished to find this realism mixed or combined with what seems to be the most far-fetched and elaborate other-worldliness. Realism and dreaming are almost commonplace Irish characteristics. The stranger finds this sort of thing very difficult to understand and is entitled to ask a question which few Irish people will or can answer: how do they reconcile the dreaming with the realism? The answer to this might help to explain why the Celts in general and the Irish Gaels in particular never succeeded in formulating a religion. We can well understand that when the Christian missionary arrived in Ireland with his clear-cut code and the easily explained definite spiritual message of the Gospel, that all-over-the-place, easy-going and, it seems, happy-go-lucky paganism gave place very quickly to the new religion. The gentle Christianity of the fifth century presented few problems to the Irish mind, and was, so to speak, accepted overnight. It did not fundamentally change the Irish mind; nor did it eliminate all the paganism. Of the latter there remained the physical and visible signs in the forms of monuments and so forth, some of which we can see to this day. There are also some very curious and probably pagan survivals, such as the Puck Fair held each year at Killorglin in County Kerry; and the wakes which are still held in parts of Ireland.

Generous space has been given here to the early period of Irish history, which need not be embellished with dates more than to say that it came before the Christian era, and that modern scholarship seems to be agreed that the Goidels or Gauls—the French-Spanish Celts—arrived in Ireland round about 350 B.C., before which point of time everything is extremely hazy. The generous space has been given with a purpose and a simple one: Ireland and the Irish of today cannot reasonably be understood unless we have in mind at least the elements of the old stories and some idea of the implications behind them. We must not forget the vigorous humanist paganism of what might be called the 'basic' inhabitants of Ireland; or that persistent element in their character which we call otherworldliness or the capacity for dreaming; or the combination of both with a sense of realism that is so often to be found. What strikes us about the pre-Christian period of Ireland's story is the importance of invasions from abroad. But as far back as we can look, Ireland has had an almost miraculous power of absorbing or affecting whoever settles there—"no man can touch its sod or breathe its air without becoming better or worse"—to the point that, in the end, aliens become "more Irish than the Irish themselves". In the Christian era there were also invasions, as we shall see, but never at any time by the Romans; although Roman ideas found their way from Britain. It was in the Christian era that the Irish, "who claimed kinship with the Iberians because they called themselves *Hiberni,* and with the Scythians because they called themselves *Scotti*", for a change invaded Wales and Scotland. Their conquest of Wales never achieved permanency, but the Irish Gaels became masters of the rude

Picts of Scotland, consolidated their conquest, gave that country their name, and made a lasting impact. The Kingdom of Argyle ('Eastern Gael') was founded by the Antrim prince Fergus Mac Erc in the year 470. These were the only major sallies ever made for conquest by the Irish, whose destiny has been to be invaded on many occasions rather than to invade foreign countries other than peaceably.

PREHISTORIC AND PAGAN IRELAND: SUMMARY

8000 B.C. — *End of the great Ice Age.* No evidence of human inhabitants in Ireland.

8000 B.C. to 2000 B.C. — *The Middle Stone Age.* Evidence found at (1) Larne raised beach of (probably) the earliest inhabitants of Ireland. Evidence also to indicate (2) influx (invasion? immigration?) of a Baltic or Turanian people (? akin to our Finns) and also of Iberians: fair and dark skins. At Island Maghee (Co. Antrim), Cushendun and thereabouts (3) evidence has been found of hunting and fishing peoples. 1, 2 and 3 may all relate to the same peoples, but the evidence requires sifting and co-ordination before it is safe to speculate.

Some of the misty traditions and stories of the *Mythological Cycle* (Partholan, the Fomorians, etc.) might be related to these peoples, which represent two immigrations: one from northern and one from southern Europe; one of a fair, the other of a dark people. Whether the hunters and fishers represent two races nobody can tell. It is not without reason that what in English we call the Giants' Causeway is in Irish *Clochán na bhFómharach*: the 'Stoneway of the Fomorians'.

2000 B.C. to 1600 B.C. — The *Later Stone Age* and the *Bronze Age.* A period of Iberian influence, and of the earliest tumuli (Dowth, Co. Meath), providing evidence of copper and goldwork—i.e. of an early culture. Megalith Cult.

1600 B.C. to 1200 B.C. — Much evidence discovered in recent years relates to this period, an important one; but much remains to be done before interpretation can be regarded as reliable. The findings include dolmens, rock scribblings (some of which might be precursors of the often obscene 'sheelanigigs' or caricatured females cut on the walls much later of old churches and castles; and

unexplained); stone circles (resembling Stonehenge—about 1500 B.C.—and similar circles on the Continent); also burial-places, pottery and raths or forts. The evidence is indicative of civilization. This also was the period of the *Cruithne* (? Picts) mostly in Ulster. Who the *Cruithne* were (? Turano-Iberians!) is still a matter of guesswork.

1200 B.C. to 200 B.C. *The coming of the Celts:* a great western movement of racially mixed continental peoples and probably originating from Central Europe (? the Danube Basin), of which either vanguard or overflow crossed the water to Britain and Ireland. The main Celtic invasion of Ireland took place, it is estimated, in the half-century from 400 B.C. to 350 B.C. Now the Celtic language, Celtic Cults and Celtic Culture were introduced into Ireland. Celts and *Cruithne* fought. In most places the Celts won by weight of numbers, though 'pockets' of the earlier inhabitants remained undefeated. In The North, Celts and *Cruithne* intermarried, producing a strong, fighting people (whom the Normans never defeated and the English found most troublesome). The intermixture may explain why the Ulster Irish differed in so many ways from the Celts of the rest of Ireland.

From this period dates the Celtic Tradition in Ireland, one that has been maintained to this day notwithstanding many invasions. Irish history begins, is recorded in the words of the poets and singers, and transmitted orally for posterity to write it down. The *Mythological Cycle* no doubt contains some of the early history, but symbolized and still obscure. From this period the original Celtic language developed into its three branches: the *Gaulish* (see Cæsar's Gallic War), the *Brythonic* (Welsh, Breton, Cornish) and the *Gœdelic* (Irish and Scottish Gaelic and Manx). The French writer Hubert emphasizes that Celts showed a strong tendency to *move westwards*; no doubt because of pressure by Goths, Romans and others.

200 B.C. to A.D. 500 *Iron Age.* The period of pagan Druidism, with its bardic poetry, law, sense of tradition and desire to transmit the tradition. Now there is a quickened growth and development of early Irish culture embracing the arts and music, and probably also Ogham writing. First there is a slow infiltration of Christianity into Ireland and then, in the fifth century, its estab-

lishment, a period of overlapping with paganism, and the beginning of Ireland's 'Golden Age'. This lasted until the depredations of the Norseman despoiled and almost disintegrated a country which at one moment promised to become a western Greece. From the fifth century onwards, the introduction of writing based on the Latin alphabet brings greater clarity and provides written material for an interpretation of Irish history.

3

The Irish become Saints and Scholars: from A.D. 432 onwards

Until St. Patrick christianized the country in the fifth century, a considerable culture flourished in an Ireland which was mainly pastoral, divided into kingdoms often warring among themselves and where the King of Connacht, "Conn of the Hundred Battles", in the year A.D. 200 established a great Middle Kingdom stretching from the Atlantic to the Irish Sea. Conn made himself famous in a long line of *Ard Ri* or High Kings, with headquarters at Tara, where his grandson Cormac in 275 built a capital on the Hill of Tara, which has associations great and noble that are held in reverence to this day. Meanwhile, we must glance briefly at the profound impact of Christianity on pagan Ireland.

Patrick was born a Roman citizen speaking a colloquial Latin. There are doubts about his ethnic origin and birthplace, which modern scholarship tends to place as somewhere in the west of Britain. The Irish warrior, King Niall of the Nine Hostages, from a raid on West Britain in about A.D. 400 brought back a host of prisoners to be sold as slaves, among them the youth Patrick. He lived as a slave of the pagan Irish for six years and, having already heard the call of Christianity, determined that some day he would bring its message to the people who had enslaved him. At the end of six years he escaped from his bondage and went to a place in France, now called Auxerre, where during a period of fourteen years he studied to prepare himself for his mission. He returned to Ireland in 432, a year which marks the beginning of a new and 'Golden Era' in Irish history.

Patrick began his teaching of the Gospel in County Down. He made considerable progress among the people of Ulster, but must have realized that, however satisfactory the progress might be, however acceptable the new faith to the pagans of Ireland, it could never be consolidated unless it won the approval of those in power: the High Kings and the other kings and their chosen aristocracy; and perhaps of almost equal importance and even more difficult to persuade, the cultured Druids and the *filidh*. The High King of Tara's office was that of a priest-king of the old religion. His aristocracy consisted mainly of warriors ready to fight when he gave the word; the same held for the minor kings and their aristocracy. The Druids were priests whose rank equalled that of the kings and aristocratic warriors. They were the magicians, the soothsayers, the law-givers; and, as such, were possessed of a quasi-mystical power over the minds of the people. Finally, there were the sages and tradition-carriers, those very important *filidh,* a caste possessing an influence which we cannot estimate, but which we are entitled to assume was great.

Patrick must have satisfied himself that the nature of the old religion, with its lack of a discipline in any way harsh or mind-enslaving, was such that his task of converting the ordinary Irish people to Christianity did not present formidable difficulties. There are no records of 'public protests' or of 'religious riots' anywhere against his mission. We may reasonably speculate that this wise and enlightened good man decided that the most difficult task with which he was confronted was to win the approval of the powerful; or at least to persuade them to be tolerant in regard to his teachings. When we think of the profoundly revolutionary nature of those teachings, especially to people who, though often referred to in serious works of history as 'barbarous', had nevertheless a remarkable culture and a psychological unity which no historians can deny, we may well feel astounded to find that Patrick was not only given *carte blanche* by the most powerful, but even assisted with gifts of land on which to build his churches. This tolerance on the part of those Irish pagans might be called weakness; it may have been wisdom. There survives a story of Patrick's momentous interview with

Laoghaire,[1] the High King, on the Hill of Tara at Easter in the year 433. King Laoghaire would not himself accept Christianity. He died a pagan and was buried in the traditional manner of a pagan Irish chief: standing upright facing the direction of his enemy. But his brother Conall accepted the new faith and so also did his principal *filè* (a man named Dubhtheagh, pronounced Duffa: from which we have Duff, Duffy and the O'Duffys). So far as one can gather from what survives of the story, Laoghaire seems to have realized that the future lay with the new faith, but he held to his paganism because of a sort of *amour-propre,* or perhaps sentiment; a feeling that it would 'do him his time'. What is really remarkable is that, while himself holding to paganism, he was so tolerant and gave such encouragement to Patrick and his mission that from then onwards the progress of Christianity in all parts of Ireland never met with any serious reverse. The new spiritual teachings appealed to the Irish mind, to the Celtic dreamers and poets whose imagination tends to be 'unpractical' and 'useless' unless or until it becomes harnessed to something: to religion, politics, a cause, or even to a dream. Patrick and his band of ardent and single-minded teachers swept the country from north to south. He established his Archbishop at Armagh, perhaps the most famous place in Ireland after Tara. When he died in 461 the new faith was well consolidated. The great teacher and organizer was buried on the spot where he had founded his first church: at Downpatrick, on land given to him by King Laoghaire's brother Connall. St. Patrick became the patron saint of Ireland.

That harnessing of the Irish mind to Christianity achieved marvels. An already rich pagan culture became richer in many new directions; another layer was spread over the historical landscape. The Irish were inspired by a collective dynamism and Ireland was soon to become 'the island of saints and scholars'. The Latin language was studied; the Bible in the Vulgate became known; great ecclesiastical foundations were established. From the *filidh's* sense of art

[1] Pronounced Leary. Dun Laoghaire—pronounced Doon or Dun Leary—the 'Fort of Leary' is the Irish name of the port which to the English is known as Kingstown.

and the Latin alphabet there was evolved a very lovely and practical Gaelic alphabet of eighteen letters with diacritical signs in which the Irish language could be written; and was very beautifully written. The lettering, the calligraphy, the illumination of some of the books produced in the monasteries of Ireland during that 'Golden Age' represent artistic achievements of a high order. One of them, *The Book of Kells* (Gospels, eighth century), has with justice been called the 'most beautiful book in the world'—a priceless treasure which may be seen in the Library of Trinity College, Dublin. It is on view protected in a glass case. Custodians keep it from sunlight and, lest the colours should suffer from such light, the same page does not long remain on view before it is turned. Words fail to give any idea of the exquisite colouring, the perfection of the tracery, the rich ornamentation and the complete artistic harmony of this great work. What astonishes the interested visitor who goes more than once so that he may see different pages, is to find that every page in it competes in beauty with every other page. But there are other books which, if not surpassing *The Book of Kells,* run it close. For the moment, we must emphasize the tremendous fact that the success of Patrick's mission meant that Ireland, a country with an artistic and imaginative people, possessing a considerable old culture and a vast oral tradition, now became a *literary* country. What had been oral tradition became reading matter for the limited number of people who learned to read. But the traditions persisted in the minds of many and for generations. So that beside each other were two branches of culture: *Tradition* and *Reading,* each with its exponents and supporters. In regard to the almost miraculous speed with which letters spread, and the range of interests covered by the written word extended, one need not be surprised at it all if we remember that the culture, the oral tradition, the laws, the sagas, the poems and the songs were all there already and clamouring to be taken down in writing. What was required was first an alphabet, then scribes, scholars, and finally suitable conditions. The imaginative temperament of the Irish set to work with an enthusiasm which in a couple of hundred years not only transformed Ireland intellectually, but made it a centre of culture to which scholars came from all over the western world, and from which Irish missionaries radiated to the great continental monasteries and centres of learning as gifted teachers who were everywhere welcomed and successful.

The word 'efficient' is used above to describe the kind of alphabet required before that great reduction to writing and stabilization as well as diffusion of culture could be possible. It is worth noting that before the Latin alphabet was adapted to the Gaelic language, long before the coming of Patrick, the Irish had an alphabet of their own. This singular old alphabet was known as the Ogam or Ogham, for which Douglas Hyde said that the best pronunciation in

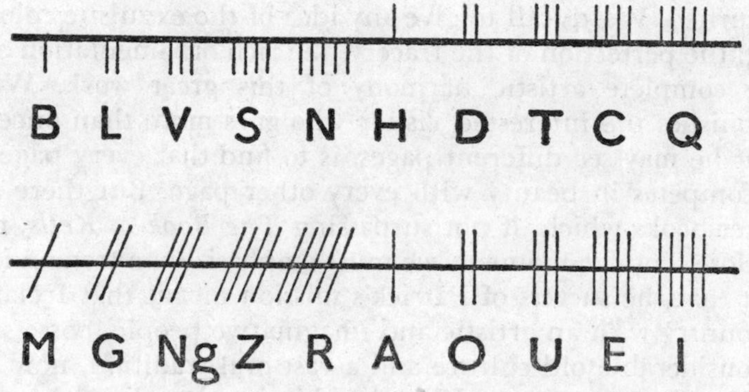

either Irish or English is as if rhyming with "rogue 'em". It is mostly found on inscribed pillars called Ogham Stones, and there are doubts in the minds of some scholars as to how far back these old monuments date, though A.D. 400–600 satisfies the majority. Douglas Hyde regarded the fixing of this date as a "very important and immensely difficult question"—one which we need not attempt to discuss technically. There are references in Irish literature to Ogham Stones in parts of Ireland where none have been found, as there are to those in Munster, where they abound. There is also a record in *The Book of Munster* of one Corc, son of the pagan King of Munster, who went to Scotland to the Court of the Scottish King Feradach, where this king's poet noticed an Ogham inscription on the Irishman's shield and read it apparently with ease. The court poet may have been Irish.

Hyde mentions 170 Ogham inscriptions of which not more than a score were found outside of Kerry, Cork and Waterford; and several specimens exist of Ogham writing cut on small articles such as gold or lead ornaments, proving that it was not confined to pillars or gravestones.

Few things could be more interesting to the archæologist and palæographer than these strange old records, of which there is a considerable collection in the National Museum in Dublin. The Ogham alphabet is one of the oddest ever devised by man. The symbols for letters consist of runes, lines or groups of up to five lines, arranged with reference to a stave line or an edge. These simple symbols could be easily and quickly carved. The inscriptions on pillars began at the *bottom* and are read upwards from left to right; the earliest examples are mostly sepulchral records consisting of a name and patronymic, thus: "Stufal the son of Ducofar". There are some delightfully interesting problems attaching to these inscriptions. The alphabet is accurate enough phonetically, but it is clumsy and uneconomical as regards the space used; and therefore unsuitable for literary records. There is no literature in Ogham writing. Instead, there are starkly simple records of persons, and it is supposed that, apart from marking burial-places, the Ogham inscriptions on stone were used to keep a record of boundaries or they were buried in tombs to indicate some man's ownership of land; in other words, as evidence of local and mundane things. The real puzzle is *why* this writing should be used for such things when the excellent adaptation of the Latin-Greek alphabets to Gaelic was already available.

For the origin of the Ogham and how it came to Ireland, Macallister [1] gives a satisfying hypothesis. It is very similar to the Chalcidic form of the Greek alphabet, current about the fifth and sixth centuries B.C. in northern Italy—"just the place where the 'Celts' or their druids were likely to come in contact with the Greek alphabet at the time when they were developing the literary traditions still current in the druidic schools of Cæsar's time". From northern Italy it came with those druids to France (where none of it has been found) to Britain (where in Wales inscriptions with Latin legends,

[1] *The Archæology of Ireland* (1949).

possibly fifth century, have been found) and so on to Ireland. An older and less convincing explanation is that it sprang from a cryptographic runic system of which a Swedish example dating about A.D. 600 has been found, which points to a Teutonic origin. The key to Ogham was clearly set out in the Irish *Book of Ballymote* in the sixteenth century, and in other ancient manuscripts. Two other features of this strange story remain to be noted. Ogham continued to be used by Irish storytellers for scribbles down to the beginning of the nineteenth century. And it can be used as a sign language or 'deaf and dumb alphabet'! The five strokes become the four fingers and thumb, and the right or left placing of the letters in reference to a stave line can be indicated by pointing the fingers right or left or, as was more common, up and down. Here, if you wish, is a fine old piece of Celtic hocus-pocus—or something with a history of sufficient interest to justify further and deeper research.

Christianity, and with it the new system by means of which the traditions could be committed to writing, gave Ireland many things in addition to the first national literature in Europe outside Greece and Rome. Artists other than calligraphers were at work encouraged by the attractive metal which was to be found at hand in fair quantities. There was alluvial gold in Ireland; and Ireland's goldwork became famous. Very beautiful ornaments were made. Great—and rich—monastic establishments sprang up, some of them in remote parts of the country, many of them not far from the sea, others accessible from sea by the inlets and the rivers running into the sea. The new faith turned Ireland from a turbulent country of many wars and much border-raiding into one of comparative peace. The former warriors devoted more and more of their lives to a simple agriculture, and still more attention to the great herds of cattle which were their chief form of wealth.

An abundance of rivers and lakes made good waterways. There were no roads in the Ireland of those days in the Roman sense. The nature of the country—mountainous, thickly wooded, boggy—meant that communities usually were small and scattered. In the turbulent times when wars great and small recurred with regularity, there had been population-grouping for mobilization and similar purposes. The groups were called *tuatha,* and each was capable in an emergency of providing from 700 soldiers upwards and, by extension, the resources of the land occupied by these men. The military side of the *tuatha* now grew steadily weaker until the word came to be applied more to tracts of land variable in extent than to fighting men. In fact, the old military organizations, even the nuclei, tended to disappear altogether. Such a country and social system provided a tempting invitation to potential marauders. And they were not lacking.

4

The Norsemen come and go: A.D. 800–1014

Three and a half centuries after the establishment of Christianity in Ireland the Norsemen—Swedes, Norwegians and Danes—began a series of marauding and plundering expeditions which were so successful that in some places they became serious invasions ending in settlements. At first the Norsemen were content to raid coastal places, or, in their long, shallow-draught boats, to sail up rivers, rob what they could find in home or monastery and make off with the booty. Politically, Ireland was in a state of disunity and, among the seven kings, a shared high-kingship and a peacefully inclined people, there was no leader with the will, military knowledge and ability to organise effective resistance to the Norsemen. They came, they robbed, they murdered and they conquered. At last, in 852, some of them settled on a hill-top not far from the mouth of the River Liffey. Their fortified place grew into a town near the 'dark pool', *dubh linn* in Gaelic, hence the name Dublin. Other important Danish settlements were on the coast at Wicklow, Wexford, Waterford, Cork and Limerick. These Danish settlements were the first real towns in Ireland, all of them built at the mouth of a river for a good reason in marauding strategy. The settlements or 'towns' were ports to which the long boats came from their homeland and from which those boats could penetrate into the heart of Ireland on the excellent waterways. And so, little by little, Norse rule extended until it covered considerable areas of the country, but not the outer islands. Dublin, perhaps a fortuitous or, if not, a brilliant choice of site, became a sort of general headquarters in Ireland for the Norsemen. Norse rule had no other objects than pillage and exploitation. A harsh Teutonic rule it was which brought little with it in the way of culture—in which the Gaels were superior—and on the whole it seems to have contributed few valuable ideas excepting that of the larger community, the walled town from which the Irish developed the general idea of the town. The Norse invasions and settlements, in spite of their military and material success, contributed little or nothing to an Ireland indifferent to either military or political considerations or unity. Yet they did have the effect of bringing home to the materially easy-going Irish that, if they would only make use of their strong psychological sense of innate unity, the story might be a different one. From the unhappy state of affairs and this growing feeling there arose one of the greatest leaders in Irish history, Brian Boru, who not only defeated the Norsemen in battle after battle—decisively at Clontarf on Palm Sunday 1014—but in the process of building up the necessary strength to this end largely remade a country that had suffered from two hundred years of pillage and exploitation. Brian almost restored that 'Golden Age' which had fulfilled so many dreams and seemed capable of fulfilling very many more. Under Brian the arts again flourished; scholarship throve in the monasteries; Irish craftsmen led the world in ornamental gold and other metalwork; very lovely churches in a new style of architecture were built. The invaders produced this healthy reaction, and in Brian Boru the Irish had a man of strong will and great enlightenment to harness and guide it. Historians seem to be agreed that, if Brian had been followed by two men of similar intellectual calibre in the high kingship, the subsequent history of Ireland would have been less sad. We need not dwell on that. Let us note that the Norse invasion and the work of Brian Boru left more marks for us to see on that already well-marked landscape.

An old Irish saga dolefully lamented: "Erinn fell by the death of Brian." Alice Stopford Green writes: "The hundred and fifty years that followed the battle of Clontarf remained practically a blank in Irish history. . . . For the present, however, there is one decisive comment on the battle of Clontarf—the word of the Norsemen themselves: 'Brian fell but saved his kingdom.' That day finally ended the possibility of a foreign Scandinavian conquest and sovereignty in Ireland. It made no severance between the whole community of the dwellers in Ireland." Those words are to be found in her enthralling book, *History of the Irish State to 1014*. Mrs. Green, however, makes a fundamental mistake that is easily corrected by more modern scholarship. There never was a *State* in that old Ireland. Henri Hubert and other scholars make it clear almost beyond dispute that a Celtic *State* never came into being anywhere at any time, though Mrs. Stopford Green shows that there was what we should now call an amorphous 'Federal Commonwealth' in Ireland. The Celts everywhere, Ireland included, had a collective consciousness, a 'way of life': loosely knit communities living in enclaves based on the family and often co-operating to make life easier, but with hardly anything even remotely resembling a *political* unity or collectivity. And with this went a *culture*: one with distinctive features of its own that is easily recognizable wherever we find it surviving, from the Danube to Ireland, from Brittany to Cornwall, Wales and the north-west of Scotland.

The other fact to which we have at least learned to pay respect is that the words 'Celt' and 'Celtic' refer to a people or group of peoples speaking a common language—*an aggregate of anthropological types*. There was and is no Celtic race! In other words, we must not attribute *racial* qualities to our Celts, because far too many types are involved to justify certainty in this respect. One does not have to be a very close observer to see in Ireland a great diversity of types even in those parts where the old Celts remained unmixed with the invaders who came after the Norsemen. For all that, one must not, on the other hand, be led into another and less pardonable error; that, because the Celts were not a race, there was not any sort of unity among them. They had long proved and since then have shown themselves to be possessed of a unique psychological unity with common characteristics in their ways of thinking, their outlook, temperament, imagination, and in many other ways which are so 'catching' that the alien who lives among them for any length of time nearly always proves receptive to their influence. When John Smith and his English wife go to live in Ireland and have a family of children brought up there, those children are usually, to repeat the old saying, "more Irish than the Irish themselves". And, what may seem still more curious and no doubt unscientific, even this acquired Irishness remains, the strain can be strong and it also seems to be transmissible! To state it otherwise, 'Celticism'—in this case 'Irishness'—seems to be a psychological trait with certain peculiarly 'dominant' qualities which come out again and again and often in the least-expected circumstances. The Irish in our own times are the most numerous and prolific Celts and, wherever they go, they and their descendants are nearly always recognizable in one way or another. This can hardly be denied, for many of us have noticed that, say, Don Guillermo O'Donajú of Buenos Aires, whose forefathers have been in Argentina for a century, looks just like Liam O'Donaghue who is still cutting turf in the Bog of Allen. If the two should meet, they would soon be toasting one another, and if they became elated—which might happen—they would sing to the sun, moon and stars. As for the Irish who migrate to all parts of the world and establish families, the 'map of Ireland' not only often survives for generations on the faces, but a characteristic Irish working of the mind persists. Compare the writings of some second- or third-generation Irish Americans with those of contemporary Irish authors and one often sees the 'Celtic' affinity—in the case of some on almost every page.

5

Gaelic Society: 1,000 Years Ago

The year 1014, in which Brian Boru defeated the Norsemen, is a great landmark in Irish history and a useful one from which to glance at certain aspects of social life in Ireland. The High King was overlord of five provincial kings who in turn were overlords of at times hundreds of minor kings. This accounts for the large number of Irish people

Clonfert Cathedral—Co. Galway.
An Irish-Romanesque Architectural Gem
ITA

Evening on Lough Fee—Connemara ITA

Little Donkey Cart and Cottage—Co. Donegal ITA

who today have what is often a fair claim to be 'descendants of kings'. Around the kings was an aristocracy. Kings and aristocracy were rulers. Next in rank came the 'Worthies', a sort of 'upper middle-class' who were permitted to move up the social scale in certain circumstances and join the 'ruling class' on the latter's terms. And then there was the 'proletariat', the plebeians, who descended in rank from small peasant landowners to slaves. Parallel with the kings and aristocracy were the Churchmen. Bishops ranked 'with but after' provincial kings, and other Churchmen were graded in steps downward parallel with those in the ruling class and, in the 'Lectors', to a rank on a par with the top rank of the Worthies. Those two groups were the *power-holders* in the material and spiritual worlds. The pattern had become fairly common all over Europe.

But now we come to a characteristic feature of Celtic life in Ireland. In addition to the Rulers and the Churchmen and the Worthies, there was another parallel class of *Ollafs*,[1] clerical and lay, who were 'doctors', learned men in the several professions. These were *filidh* transformed by Christianity and now mobilized on its side in well-defined categories covering spiritual, artistic, legal, literary and other matters of culture, including all the arts and crafts. Curtis tells us: "The poets (*filidh*) had accepted the faith with their lips, but in their hearts retained the pagan lore and the pride of their caste. Numerous and great were the rewards they demanded for their compositions and encomiums, so that their exactions became a national nuisance and a proposal was made to exile and outlaw them. But Columba, who had been trained under a Christian *file* in youth, was their saviour: a prince of the ancient race, his ardent Gaelic soul was on their side. His casting vote saved the *filidh* and turned them from a race of wandering visitants into a privileged class of letters and learning. He advised that every provincial king and every lord of a *tuath* (see page 61) should have a supreme poet or Ollaf, and in the course of centuries the *filidh* became the ancestors of the professional, endowed and

[1] Ollaf or ollav is the English pronunciation for the Gaelic word *ollamh*, which means "a master (of science or art), a chief poet, a learned man, a professor, a doctor, a director, a sage."—*Dinneen*.

hereditary (!) poets, bards and chroniclers whose order survived until 1603." In the jargon of modern politics, the *filidh* were *'gleichgeschaltet'*—made to 'line up' with the ruling powers. These, then, were the men who formed that other class—one with ranks—which occupied itself with learning and literature, the arts and crafts. It was they who, through all sorts of vicissitudes and catastrophes, maintained and preserved cultural values. So we have Rulers, Worthies and Ollafs—and the rest: the majority consisting of ordinary people, among whom executant musicians and some others were in the top grade next to the lowest grade of Ollafs. Among the Ollafs there were several ranks which stood 'with but after' the Churchmen, who, as we have noticed, ranked 'with but after' the kings and aristocracy; and three grades of Ollafs paralleled grades in the Worthies. If we remember that the status of Rulers, Churchmen and Ollafs existed on a mixed basis of *heredity* and *election,* it is not difficult to appreciate that the comparatively small numerical groupings of people who really mattered in that society represented a close preserve; and that there would be many openings for men ambitious for power and privilege. Between those of the 'upper class' and the 'plebs' or ordinary people there was a strictly defined line. The system was anything but democratic; yet rude and rough as it was, we do not find much evidence of tyranny or dictatorship. Somebody has observed that the Irish 'can be led but not driven', and there is truth in the generalization. But they will submit to and even defend an amazing amount of hocus-pocus of their own devising, or which they have been persuaded to accept as their own. The political device of 'heredity' and 'election' was responsible for all sorts of abuses even before this time, but from then onwards it became what we would now call a 'racket'. We need not enlarge on it more than to say that the Irish have always attached importance to heredity, but in the reign of Brian Boru it began to be 'political'—an integral part of an elaborate social system. It is from that period onwards that we find a steadily increasing practice of adopting family names: Ó (ui) and *Mac* were put before family names, Ó meaning 'grandson' or 'descended from', and Mac meaning 'son of'. The latter is found as far back as the Ogham Stones. There are still people about who claim that the O' before a name indicates Milesian origin! This must not be confused with the comparatively modern conceit of using the word 'The' to indicate the name and style of a Gaelic chief: as in The O'Rahilly, The MacGillycuddy of the Reeks, The O'Shea of Kerry, The MacDermot of Coolavin, The O'Conor Don, and others.

In reading many books about the period of Irish history a few centuries before and including Brian's reign, the impression is received of a rather simple and quite beautifully romantic social system. From the labours of O'Rahilly, MacNeil, Mrs. Stopford Green, the interpretation of archæological remains by Macallister, and a close scrutiny of the sagas by such scholars as that great Swiss Celticist, Thurneysen, the only possible conclusion is that Irish Gaelic society was complex and that, with its multitude of laws, rules, regulations, taboos and what-nots, there was an almost Chinese subtlety about many of its aspects. Far from being the idyllic, romantic land peopled by none but saints and scholars, Ireland was a country consisting of human beings who, in their life and behaviour in general, did not differ very greatly from other European human beings. They had the vices and virtues of the others, though there was a Celtic tendency to run to extremes: the austerity of the early Christian monks, for example, went to the limits of austerity. The sincerity of their feelings touched the extremes of human sincerity. And so it was that in the manœuvrings for power among Rulers, Churchmen and Ollafs, we read of acts of political racketeering and gangsterism which curiously reappeared in the comparatively meek and mild forms of which we read in the modern annals of Tammany Hall. In the great heroic sagas there is often a realism that is stark to the point of brutality, and from it an immediate switch-over to an extreme of gentle poetry of an other-worldliness and airy-fairiness which is accepted as a matter of course by the Celt, but takes the breath from those unfamiliar with the temperament. This is perhaps best exemplified in the *Táin*, the "Cattle Drive of Cooley", perhaps the greatest of the old Irish tales, the earliest to be recorded and the most worked on by editors, copyists and interpolators, good and bad.

Christianity in Ireland developed on lines of its own consistent with the temperament of the people, but not always similar to those of continental Christianity. Monks and monasticism in Ireland were stronger than the bishops, who were without dioceses. The monastic establishments and settlements attracted thousands. Irish asceticism went to extraordinary extremes. Some of our present Irish puritanism can be traced back to that period of flourishing monasticism which, by the end of Brian Boru's reign, had reached a stage of competent internal organization with much secular intrusion and accompanied by a considerable falling off in piety and in Christian discipline. A reform of the Irish Church was necessary—to bring it into closer conformity with Rome and universal Catholicism; and the reform duly took place, though it took time. In 1152 an important Synod was held and to it the Pope sent a Legate. The Synod reached the decision that Ireland was to have thirty-six bishops and four archbishops, at Armagh and Cashel as hitherto, and also at Tuam and Dublin. This would strengthen the position of the Church in the work of putting its house in order. The country's real weakness, from the point of view of political power, now lay in the provincial kings who, for many reasons, were not an easy problem for the Church. Kings and their aristocracies, with their Worthies, their Ollafs and a happy-go-lucky population of ordinary people, were satisfied to carry on with life as they had long known it. They cannot have been pleased to see a new power rising all around them. The leader of the reform of the Church, Malachy, Bishop of Connor, who had gone to Rome in connection with his work, had not in his travels concealed the opinion that his too easy-going country would benefit from conquest by a foreign Christian ruler.

CHAPTER III

ENGLISH INVASIONS AND SETTLEMENTS

> Had Ireland been a weak and spiritless nation, had her people had no manhood, did they 'lack gall to make oppression bitter', maybe they would have knelt down and kissed their chains; but they rose up in 'wrath and warlike gear', as the *Annals* put it, and they did battle often and valiantly against the stranger. For centuries there was no day whereon someone did not lay a lance for Ireland; and Irish blood has reddened every inch of our soil.
>
> From *The Indestructible Nation,* by P. S. O'HEGARTY.

1

The Anglo-Norman Invasion: 1172 onwards

THIS brings us to one of the most debated items in Irish history: the Bull 'Laudibiliter'. Whether it ever existed cannot be proved. But that the ideas it is alleged to contain were implemented and put into practice, as far as they could be, is not in dispute. By this famous Bull, it is said, in the year 1155 the Pope Adrian IV (Nicolas Breakspeare, the only Englishman ever to be Pope) commissioned the Norman King Henry II of England to invade Ireland, reform its Church and put things in better order. We may leave the question of the disputed authenticity of this Bull and follow Curtis,[1] who says: "There is still better evidence for a grant of Ireland in 1155. In that year the famous writer and churchman, John of Salisbury, went from Henry II to the Papal Curia and obtained from the English Pope, Adrian IV, a grant of Ireland for the Angevin king. 'At my prayer', he says in his book *Metalogicus,* 'he granted Ireland to Henry as an inheritance, as his letter to this day testifies, and also sent me a golden ring adorned with an emerald for the purpose of investiture, and this is kept in the State archives.' " From this it seems clear that the principle was established. Curtis continues: "Later generations of Irishmen up to the seventeenth century fully accepted the papal donation as a fact—witness the Remonstrance of the Irish chiefs to the Pope in

[1] *A History of Ireland* (1936).

1317—but both then and later they accused the Crown of England of having violated the rights of both Church and people."

The temptation at this point is to stop and look at the doubtful and certainly complex game of internal and Church politics in Ireland, in England and in international affairs. A full and clear account of what really happened behind the scenes has yet to be written; a fascinating and valuable story it should be. We know just enough about it to persuade us to look at the results, the first of which was that Henry II, a Norman king, began to prepare for the conquest of Ireland: the ostensible reason being to bring that country more beneficially into and under the Church, with the corollary that the barbarian Irish would also receive the benefits of Anglo-Norman civilization. The Normans, it should be noted, were descendants of Norsemen who had settled along the north coast of France, founded a state called Normandy and, partly inspired by continental ideas, had evolved for that time a very wonderful military force and organization. Norse aggressiveness was fused with French intellect. As we know, the Norsemen were fine seamen. Now they were formidable soldiers—with the man-power and resources of northern France behind them. They conquered all England after winning the Battle of Hastings in 1066 and, in the person of William I, established sovereignty over that country. William the Conqueror's grandson was this Henry II who, having inherited kingship over the well-consolidated conquest of England, now turned his eyes to the western island. Henry was a shrewd man: he chose as the time for his invasion a wonderfully favourable moment. Not only was he himself strong in the military sense, but he had the moral support of the Pope, which meant that of the Irish bishops. Ireland was in the worst possible state to resist an invader. Encouragement was given to his intentions by the Irish King of Leinster, Dermot MacMurrough, who in a local feud between himself and two other Irish kings had been defeated in battle in 1166, forced to flee the country and take refuge in England. Dermot went to Henry, who gave him permission to apply for help to any of the powerful Anglo-Norman barons. The Irishman approached Richard de Clare, Earl of

Pembroke, nicknamed 'Strongbow' because of his military prowess. Dermot offered Pembroke his daughter's hand in marriage, and also what he had no right of any kind to offer, the succession to the Kingdom of Leinster. The ambitious Pembroke decided to accept the tempting offers. Meanwhile some Norman-Welsh knights, FitzGerald, FitzHenry and FitzStephen, half-brothers of mixed Welsh and Norman blood—known to the Irish as the Geraldines—decided that they also must have a share of the Irish booty. FitzStephen quickly took an expedition to Wexford, which he captured. Pembroke and FitzGerald arrived next year with a much stronger force and captured Waterford, where the invader married Dermot MacMurrough's daughter Eva. Pembroke and Dermot joined forces and next captured Dublin in a surprise attack. Soon after this Dermot MacMurrough died, whereupon Pembroke claimed the Kingdom of Leinster. But for this important fact, these expeditions might in time have been liquidated by the Irish who, though unable to face effectively the unfamiliar tactics, weapons and well-trained forces of those Anglo-Normans, were not slow about learning new methods of warfare and their whole history had proved them good fighters. Pembroke's claim to Leinster alarmed Henry, who had the vision of a new, powerful Anglo-Norman king in Ireland, one who knew all the tricks of 'modern' warfare and who, if once established, would have at his disposal the resources of a country known to be rich and with man-power almost equal to that of England.

Thus, the English reasons for that first 'English' invasion of Ireland—it was really an Anglo-Norman invasion—are clear enough. They can be summarized under three headings:

(1) Ecclesiastical.
(2) A struggle for power on the part of Henry II.
(3) The promise of wealth.

From the internal Irish point of view, there were reasons why an Anglo-Norman invasion by Henry II should be encouraged. There were the important Church reasons, and we have noted Dermot MacMurrough's activities which, incidentally, left him with the popular title of 'Dermot of the Foreigners' and a name that has been execrated in Ireland until today as that of a 'Quisling'. Henry went himself to Ireland in 1171, when nearly all the kings submitted to him and agreed to pay tribute, the exceptions being the northerners and Rory O'Connor the High King. The archbishops and bishops accepted Henry as their ruler and, in 1172, the Pope informed them that they must give Henry support. He told Henry to help the hierarchy to strengthen the Church and to work for the moral correction and reform of the sinful natives. Thus, if one desires to think in terms of blame or guilt in regard to the Anglo-Norman invasion of Ireland, the ruling class of both countries share it fairly equally between them; the ordinary people, the lower orders' on both sides of the Irish Sea were left out of the higher calculations except as vassals of the lords. Behind it in the background was the deep concern of the Pope for the souls of all the Irish.

"Seldom," writes Curtis, "has so great a country been thrown open to a race of gentlemen buccaneers as Ireland now was, and as it was again in the sixteenth century." We need not follow that Anglo-Norman conquest in any detail, but we must glance at a few of its aspects and their results for the country and the people. Before doing so, it is essential to note three things: *first*, that the conquest was never thoroughly completed; *second*, that it was consolidated to fructify only in certain places and among the native Irish ruling class; *third*, that the ordinary peoples shrank back into their old Celtic shells and, battered as those shells often were by the conquerors, they acted as armour behind which the conservative nature of the Irish was able to go on surviving —until it was the conquerors who changed more than the Irish! This is a fate which Ireland seems always to have imposed upon invaders.

The Anglo-Normans exploited Ireland and the Irish and, in the Norse tradition, they were not gentle with any opposition to their rule. We may draw a veil over a bloody and ruthless business. The native Celts were easy-going, somewhat unstable, emotional, with the 'discipline of indiscipline' allied to a great love of life for life's sake. When aroused they could be formidable warriors, but they were (and still are) far less easily aroused than some writers would have us think.

Thus, they were fair game for the Normans, who were predatory, acquisitive and calculating and could keep their emotions under control and, in contrast to the Celts, kept their heads out of the clouds and their feet very much on earth: a brave, stubborn, vindictive race, as predictable in their acts as the Celts were unpredictable. They brought these qualities with them to Ireland; and also some benefits that are more easily definable. Into politics they introduced new tricks of which the Irish ruling class took advantage. They made the Irish better acquainted with classical and continental literature. In architecture they brought a revolution to the country. From that period architectural masterpieces—abbeys, churches, castles, keeps and so forth—arose in all directions and nearly always on sites which showed genius in the choice. Ireland is dotted with Norman edifices which survive mostly as ruins, but of which there are some beautiful examples in a good or fair state of preservation. For a full account of them the reader must be referred to the works of experts.[1]

In regard to large-scale architecture, the Norman contribution to Ireland is artistically striking and distinctive, as the visitor in our own time soon sees, however little he may be interested in the technical aspect of the subject. To Ireland the Normans brought a heavy contribution in that, to the widely dispersed native people who showed little or no inclination for living in populous agglomerations, they introduced the advantages of town and civic life, of civilized order in living; of what we call 'civilization' as distinct from 'culture'. They gave Ireland good roads, towns, ports. The Normans were *civilized*; the Gaels, notwithstanding the many crude and rough features of their way of life, were *cultured.* The Normans were organizers. The Gaels disliked and, one suspects, were suspicious of organization based on authority, in which they resembled some modern anarchists. These differences between conquerors and conquered, considered in terms of the centuries which followed, showed a

[1] *Ecclesiastical Architecture of Ireland,* by George Petrie; *Norman Castles in Ireland,* by Goddard Orpen; *Notes on Irish Architecture,* by Lord Dunraven. Frank O'Connor in his rollicking books, *Irish Miles* and *Leinster, Munster and Connacht,* shows a sensitive appreciation for architecture and is always entertaining.

strange outcome: the civilization of the Normans stood hard and upright for a time and then began to crumble until it fell into ruins to be absorbed into the landscape and, in parts where it was most vigorous, by the people. We find Norman pockets here and there in Ireland, where signs of surviving Norman influence can be observed in the appearance of the people and in certain aspects of local life. Outside these pockets the most that we can find visible of that considerable Norman intrusion, and of the final fusion, are architectural specimens and ruins.

On the politico-religious plane a point was reached at which the Normans—Catholics like the Irish—found themselves in spiritual conflict with the Protestant Reformation in England, which had this effect on them that, willy-nilly for survival, they must fraternize and become close friends with the native Irish, whom they had mostly hitherto avoided. Thus a great fusion took place, a physical, psychological and even economic assimilation in which the distinction between the two 'races' of Anglo-Normans and Celtic Irish vanished in the melting-pot of common adversity. The amalgam strengthened Ireland and frightened England. We may fix the date of this as about the middle of the sixteenth century: nearly five hundred years after the first coming of the Normans. A vast, complex and intensely interesting human experiment, in which there is enough history to fill a library, had taken place. All we need record here is that it took place and, in its climax, had the effect of turning the eyes of the hitherto otherwise occupied England on a flourishing Ireland which threatened to become strong, and was therefore regarded as a real or potential menace to the power of the English king. The idea that Ireland could possibly be a threat to English power may now seem strange. It must not be forgotten that in population there was little difference between the Ireland and England of the sixteenth century, and in essential resources Ireland was also almost equal. In one respect Ireland had a distinct advantage in that she had more continental friends than the English king. All that Ireland needed was organization, discipline and unity and, if this were achieved, there was no knowing that the next step would not be Irish-continental alliances. Far better, from the English point of view, to take all the precautions necessary to prevent these things from happening. The work must be done thoroughly and nothing left to chance. At this point what is today known as capitalist imperialism began to work. For Ireland the consequences were tragic. We must briefly consider them, if only for the reason that they put one more layer over the face of that country and represent another contribution to a palimpsest of history on which were already many writings.

2

English Plantations and Settlements: 1553–1653

A new and terrible phase of Irish history now opened. The full story is a complex one, but it is possible to sum it up briefly. It consisted in a long-term English policy calculated to eliminate the possibility, not only that Ireland could ever be any sort of menace to England, but that England should also use the policy to exploit Ireland to the utmost for her own benefit. It is easy now, looking back on what happened, for English and Irish to be wise after the events. We now see clearly enough that the root cause of Ireland's weakness was the time-lag between the moment when she was attacked and that at which she was sufficiently roused to discipline herself to the point of striving for unified, concerted and well-organized action against the attackers. As it was, there were all sorts of disunities in Ireland added to the easy-going inclinations of the Irish. Religion played a strong part in it all. In Ireland, when this new phase of history began, the people were all Catholics, and the menace to their religion aroused deep passions and stimulated fierce resistance. The new union between the Norman-Irish ruling class and the Gaels meant that England faced an Ireland which could be united on a religious basis if on no other, and this notwithstanding the end of rule by the Norman earls. As it happened, the threat not only to religion, but also to the land which provided for their very existence, had a result which, considering the nature of those people, need not have been unexpected by any competent political observer. It was inevitable. Hence began the English attack and the Irish defence and counterattack which, with many complications and many side-issues, both with and in the wake of violent clashes, wrought general havoc in Ireland. Some of this story cannot be omitted, because it helps to explain the Ireland of our own times.

Pope Adrian's grant to Henry II gave the English king the 'Lordship' of Ireland. King Henry VIII, who began the new policy in Ireland, dropped this hitherto satisfactory title, and in 1541 arranged for himself the title "King of Ireland". Henry VIII, one must remember, was already engaged in a struggle to throw off papal power and had declared himself Supreme Head of the Church of England: which made his Irish position ridiculous. For, how could he claim a 'Lordship' of Ireland depending on a papal grant! He had destroyed the Pope's power in England. Now he set about doing so in Ireland, his first move being to induce Parliament to make him Supreme Head of the Church in that country also, where he forbade the payment of money to Rome. This roused the ire of the Irish clergy. Henry then tried to win the Irish chiefs to his side by promising them lands and new titles; and he often succeeded in dividing and ruling. It is curious how, from the Anglo-Norman invasion onwards, invaders of Ireland always found some Irish ready to work with them and share spoils. Ireland has no monopoly of this propensity, which is as old as history and is to be found almost everywhere. At the time of which this is written, O'Neill became English Earl of Tyrone, Burke became Earl of Clanrickard, O'Brien became Earl of Thomond. In this deal, the Irish aristocrats obtained an English grant in lands which in Irish law were not regarded as their property. That law provided that lands ruled by a chief—excepting his own personal land—was the collective property of the clan. The old Irish law of 'heredity and election' still applied, and by it the Irish had a right to elect from the chief's relatives the successor to the title. This conflict of laws caused widespread trouble, for Henry's new policy meant that English law, with descent to the eldest son, now applied. Henry's next step was direct attack on the Irish Church. He closed all the monasteries in Ireland, seized the monastic lands, and granted some of them to his new Earls. The Church refused to accept his supremacy, the people refused to accept his laws, the dispossessed monks took the people's side. All Ireland turned in anger against English encroachment on the old rights, customs and religion. In the reign of his successor, Edward VI, resistance became stronger.

To us now, a curious feature of all this was that, although the attack was on papal power, the doctrines of the Church had not been changed. This shows it to have been a political and not a religious matter. Edward was followed by the Catholic, Mary, who did two things which seem to us contradictory. She abolished the changes made by Henry VIII and initiated what, from the Irish point of view, was a far more devastating policy, one which appealed so much to successive rulers of England that it was continued for a century. This policy was called 'Plantation'. The idea behind it was simple: to confiscate Irish land and settle English people on it. The natives must abandon two-thirds of their land and give it to the English settlers, retaining one-third for themselves. The settlers must have English servants, English soldiers for defence, and be an English garrison. Mary began by confiscating the territories of Leix and Offaly, which were renamed Queen's County and King's County. This much happened on paper, but in practice it did not work out so easily. The Irish put up an uncompromising resistance—one so strong that, in the next reign, the Plantation had to be modified and some Irish chiefs were even given back their lands. Two Irish leaders provided a foretaste of what the Irish could be capable when their land was threatened. One of them, O'Connor, went on resisting for years until the O'Connors were wiped out. Another, O'More, fought until only one O'More survived; and he was to have a famous son who continued and intensified resistance. This sort of life struggle, one which continued from generation to generation, developed into a fighting tradition, a permanent Resistance Movement. At times the Irish were beaten to the point of exhaustion. They rose again from their ashes and again fought the invaders; until they were again beaten—or, as happened on several occasions, until they won a victory. A pattern of a struggle was thus established which marks itself through Irish history from then down to our own century. Sometimes it was violent; sometimes peaceful and constitutional; but still *struggle*. Many patriotic Irish historians assert that, strictly speaking, the country was never completely subdued in this 'Reconquest of Ireland' as it has often been called by English historians. We need not argue about that, but what cannot be disputed is that, from Mary onwards, Ireland suffered as she had never before suffered and as few countries have ever suffered, even considering what has happened around us in Europe in our own appalling times.

Queen Elizabeth continued and added variegations to Mary's policy, with the main difference that she devoted more attention to politics and less to religion, for although she was a Protestant, she was never an ardent one. In Ireland, she had to face permanent unrest and three serious rebellions during her reign. The English became more ruthless as Irish resistance became fiercer. In Elizabeth's time a new idea was applied: the deliberate devastation of the country in order to weaken Irish resistance through hunger and famine. Crops were burned, cattle taken from the people. This worked better than battle. In 1586 Elizabeth confiscated nearly a quarter of a million acres in Munster which were given to English gentlemen called 'Undertakers', because they 'undertook' to import into Ireland tenants from England, to have no Irish tenants, and to prevent intermarriage with the wild and barbarous natives. It was not a successful scheme, for English people hesitated to settle in a country with such a reputation for turbulence, disregard for English law, and a lack of proper respect for those who seized their land. The English Undertakers then took Irish tenants, but Elizabeth was so disappointed with the financial results and indeed with the whole experiment that she never tried another Plantation. She did overcome the three great rebellions and, a few days after her death, the last great Gaelic leader Ireland produced, Hugh O'Neill, Earl of Tyrone, was defeated. He had a valiant and brilliant collaborator in resistance in Red Hugh O'Donnell, a kinsman by marriage. O'Neill achieved something in which no Irish chief had hitherto ever succeeded before or since Brian Boru. He *united* the country in that struggle.

The defeat of O'Neill resulted in profound changes, some

of which went to the roots of ancient institutions. It meant the abolition of the old Gaelic Law which had survived from pre-Christian times and had later been modified and codified by the Brehons (judges and jurists) who, by the very antiquity of their office, represented a tradition. The still older *filidh,* who from the dawn of history had been the carriers of culture and of the old Gaelic literary traditions: they also disappeared. The old Gaelic divisions were abolished and the country was divided English-fashion into shires. Finally, English law and law courts took over justice. The first two of these changes struck at the roots of Irish law and culture; the others, to which was added the disarmament of the defeated, were to help in consolidating the conquest. From 1603 onwards more and more Irishmen fled abroad. In 1607 the new Earl of Tyrconnell (Red Hugh O'Donnell's brother) and the great Hugh O'Neill, Earl of Tyrone, fled to the Netherlands and thence to Rome. They never returned to Ireland. The Irish refer to this incident as "The Flight of the Earls". To those who care for the past, it marks a twofold tragedy: the end of an awful and devastating struggle; the virtual end of the satisfying old Gaeldom in which the people had lived.

These tragedies were merely forerunners of others which quickly followed. A new Plantation was projected, one which took advantage of mistakes of the past in order to avoid failure in the future. King James I of England, a shrewd man behind an unprepossessing exterior, the first of the Stuarts, confiscated the territories of the two absent Earls—Tyrone and Donegal (Tyrconnell)—and, on lighter excuses, also confiscated Derry, Armagh, Cavan and Fermanagh: six great counties which had long been in the forefront of resistance. He calculated that, if these 'difficult' territories could be efficiently settled, there would be no more serious trouble in Ireland. He was wrong about the latter, but he planned a thorough Plantation of Ulster. County Down he did not plant, as many Scots—Presbyterians—had settled there already; Antrim was dominated by the Scottish MacDonnells of the Glens; and poor Monaghan he left to the natives. The Plantation of Ulster was efficiently done, for it made Ulster largely Presbyterian, that is, a Protestant territory. It was so successful that other Plantations followed. The Plantations were organized by Undertakers, who by now had little difficulty in persuading people to come from England and Scotland to a prostrate Ireland on the very favourable terms that were offered. The Undertakers were Scots and English, and there were also Scots 'Servitors' who got less favourable terms because they were allowed to take Irish tenants, which the Undertakers were not. Finally, there were the "Meritorious Irish", namely, those who had not taken an active part in resisting the invasion. Altogether, out of over half a million acres planted, some 58,000 went to native Irish who got little or none of the good lands. All sorts of Anglo-Irish enterprises developed rapidly. In London an Irish Society was formed to organize and supervise the Plantation of Derry, which was renamed Londonderry; a part rich in woods, fisheries, good land and attractive for trade generally. England grew richer out of these Plantations, and the planters and "Meritorious Irish" also benefited by the new trade and the money which went into Ulster. Ulster began to prosper. The native Irish in other parts did not do so well: they were left to recover by their own strength. They were for a time subdued, but discontented, and then, in 1641, infuriated by a number of measures and decisions causing them great hardships, there was a general rising in Ulster following one which had failed in Leix. Thousands of Undertakers, Servitors and their fellow-planters were massacred. The native Irish overran the whole province of Ulster and took a terrible revenge on those who had settled on the confiscated lands. In a few weeks the Plantation was all but ruined, except in Enniskillen and Derry, which remained in the hands of the newcomers. The whole of Ireland was affected, for soon the English began to pour in troops, the Irish chiefs joined in alliance with Anglo-Irish Catholics to form the Confederation of Kilkenny (1642), and armed Irish rebels sprang up in all directions. Presbyterians who objected to Episcopalian attempts to crush their religion joined with these malcontents against the English Parliament. The execution of Charles I in England encouraged this unity, yet the alliance was unsatisfactory and nothing very exciting happened as a result of it. Meanwhile, a new figure had risen to despotic power in England: a man whose name, however estimated in England, is immortal in

Rock of Cashel—Co. Tipperary
ITA

Glengarriff—Co. Cork ITA

Blarney Castle—Co. Cork ITA

Ireland. This was Oliver Cromwell. He decided that hitherto there had been far too much vacillation, far too much incompetence and general nonsense about English rule in Ireland. Hence, as soon as he could find time to do so, he turned his great military and political ability to that country.

We may pass over Cromwell's military campaigns, which are usually described as brilliant. They had clearly defined objectives: to crush all rebellion and in a way that there could be no recurrence; to bring all of Ireland under the control of Parliament in London; to stamp out Roman Catholicism; to punish the Irish for violence on certain occasions and against settlers or garrison. All we need note is that, against superior generalship and the hard-disciplined and well-organized soldiers of Cromwell, the Irish forces, though one-third greater in number than those of the attackers, were defeated. Ten years of uninterrupted warfare had weakened the country, of which the population is estimated to have gone down to about half a million.[1] Cromwell and his soldiers faced not only disunity but physical weakness. A few scattered bands of last-ditch guerrilla fighters kept up the struggle and held out in the west for a couple of years. But there was no collective surrender, and comprehensive peace terms were never signed. Ireland was now helpless; and she was devastated. Pestilence and famine came to add to the military defeat. On all sides there were extremes of misery and desolation.

Parliament in London now considered that the "Irish Question" was settled for all time; and that Ireland could be considered as forfeited. Legislation was necessary to round off the military victory, so in 1652 an Act of Parliament was passed at Westminster, of which the gist is all that we need here. The Irish working people, tradesmen, craftsmen, labourers and small farmers whose worldly wealth could be valued at less than £10 would be pardoned and would remain where they were to be of service to the 'Ascendancy'. All of the people above the poor or the useful in status—

[1] *Note on Population:* The first Census of Ireland was in 1821, before which there are only estimates. A notable estimate (1687) was that of Sir William Petty: 1,300,000. The population question is involved and important. See T. W. Freeman's *Ireland,* Chapter VI, and *The Population of Ireland 1750–1845,* by K. H. Connell, both published in 1950.

gentry and landowners whether of old native or of Norman-Irish stock—were ordered to move themselves and their families across the River Shannon into the County Clare and the desolate territory of Connacht—"to hell or Connacht"—where they were to be granted little allotments of waste land. They must remain there—on penalty of death. Parliament also took all lands belonging to the Church of Ireland; and all Catholics must leave garrisoned towns. Three other factors helped to complete the arrangements made for the Cromwellian Settlement. First, the Irish soldiers who had fought against the invaders were allowed to leave the country and some 30,000 went abroad, mostly to Spain; second, the cost of the English campaign had, before it started, been underwritten by men called 'Adventurers'—we should call them 'speculators'—and now they were paid with lands confiscated from Irish leaders; and third, Cromwell's conquering soldiers must also be given a share of Irish land.[1]

These clear-cut decisions brought about a new influx of settlers, this time consisting almost entirely of English: the Adventurers and their friends; the Soldiers and theirs. The transference of Irish lands was, says Prendergast, to "an overwhelming flood of new English settlers, filled with the intensest national and religious hatred of the Irish". We need not pursue this story nor dwell on the state of physical and mental misery to which the native Irish and the Norman-Irish were reduced, more than to say that two further settlements followed, one called the Restoration Settlement, the other known as the Revolution Settlement. Nor is there any important point to be achieved by cataloguing the measures —Penal Laws and so forth—applied by the State in support of the new settlers, and backed by the full strength of the State, to exploit Ireland and the Irish for the full benefit of those settlers. Yet in spite of everything, these settlements were none of them a complete success, for the curious alchemy of the island had never ceased from working. In spite of all their misery, the native Irish lived on. Intermarriage and intercourse with settlers began to play their powerful parts. To cut that story short, before many years elapsed large num-

[1] For the full story see *The Cromwellian Settlement of Ireland,* by John Prendergast.

bers of settlers became indistinguishable from the natives—often "more Irish than the Irish themselves". This is one of history's greater ironies.

3

Anglo-Ireland: Seventeenth, Eighteenth and Nineteenth Centuries

Two Irelands evolved out of it all, one of which was an Anglo-Ireland with strong Scottish elements in the north and north-east. The other, a Norman-Gaelic Ireland now comparatively quiet: poor, proud, patient, tough and still holding fast to its old Gaelic language and traditions, nursing its religion and its imagination.

Gaelic Ireland was a discontented Ireland. That wonderful eighteenth century came in which there was a miserable peasantry—the mass—and beside them the now increasingly cultured descendants of the Adventurers and Soldiers who, with the earlier Undertakers, Servitors and Meritorious Irish, high and low, were the 'Ascendancy' and its hangers-on. This was a prosperous and contented Ireland: the Ireland from which sprang those delightful pictures of the hard-drinking, hard-riding 'Irish' gentlemen who, very often, lived well in England on incomes from confiscated Irish land supervised by agents, and came to Ireland only for a holiday or to recover from one form of dissipation and start another. But it was also civilized and cultured. It was the Ireland of many great Anglo-Irish names: of Swift, who was not blind to the two sides of the picture. Swift did not like Catholics; Presbyterians he detested. To him the Irish Episcopalians, equivalent to low-church English, should rule the country from their own Parliament in Dublin and in accordance with their own ideas. It was an arrogant point of view, but it was that of the Ascendancy, whose members regarded themselves as a class privileged by wealth and culture to rule the 'Descendancy'—that is, the oppressed and impoverished malcontents who, it would seem, only by the grace of God, survived as hewers of wood and drawers of water. Or, as very often happened among those individualists, by eking out a mere existence from a patch of land which nobody a few generations back had thought good enough even to confiscate —but from which a rent, increasing as the holding improved, could now be extracted by the others. Time had its effects on those of the 'Descendancy'. They began to recover some of the lost strength; and their numbers increased. One of the most difficult tasks of anybody who attempts to write about seventeenth- and eighteenth-century Ireland is to form a moderately accurate idea of the number of the population, for there are no reliable statistics. After the passage of those terrible Penal Laws at the end of the seventeenth and beginning of the eighteenth centuries which, as Burke said, "divided the nation into two distinct bodies", large numbers of the younger and more vigorous Irish left Ireland—the "Flight of the Wild Geese", it was called—to look for any sort of livelihood abroad. There was no future for them at home, and they went to France, Spain, Austria, Italy, even to Russia, and in these countries offered their services to rulers and others. One estimate gives half a million as the number of those expatriates, and their story is a remarkable one which has never yet been adequately written. After the various Settlements, which brought large numbers of Scots and English to Ireland, and the decrease of the Irish population through war, famine and pestilence, and the further loss in "Flying Geese", there is no knowing what the population may have been, though at one moment it is reasonably believed to have sunk as low as a total of half a million people of Irish and Norman-Irish stock. What we do know with fair certainty is that, when the nineteenth century opened, the population had increased to four and a half millions; and that it was fast and steadily increasing in the Catholic areas and among Catholics generally. A new social pattern was evolving as that new century dawned.

English was the mother tongue of the Ascendancy; Irish of the others. So many of the Irish learnt English that the country became largely bi-lingual. The English which those Irish learnt was that spoken by the settlers, some of whom had retained their manner of speech from the time of Mary and Elizabeth, others from Scottish settlers, others from the Cromwellian settlers and from others among the limited number of newcomers from across the water during the eighteenth century. Furthermore, many of the Irish who learnt English not only learnt a vigorous and racy colloquial language, but they carried into their English speech many grammatical, idiomatic and phonetic characteristics of the rich Gaelic. New forms of English were thus evolved in the north, south, east and west of Ireland, each with its own idiosyncrasies and accent, of which much survives to this day with minor modifications. A curious feature of that "Irish-English" was that it quickly became a settled speech and remained so while English in England went on developing and changing. This language question is of importance from many points of view. Some Irish writers began to write in English and some descendants of settlers who had "become more Irish than the Irish" and whose mother tongue was Irish, also began to write in English. (Note that what has been said does not include the speech of the topmost 'upper class', for that always remained close to the English of England, as most of those people received their education in England.) We have, in the works of William Carleton (1794–1869), a perfect example of the Anglo-Irish literature of that period. Here was a man of the cabins, a man of peasant stock whose first language was Irish, but who used English like a master and left us, in his *Traits and Stories of the Irish Peasantry,* a work which can never be surpassed for its accuracy, beauty and strength. It is a social document and literature. The reader who wishes to know what life was for most Irish people outside the towns in the first half of the nineteenth century need hardly look farther than these and other writings of Carleton. He will look elsewhere for life among the Ascendancy, and for an account of the reviving consciousness, the politics, the many rebellious movements of the Irish against land laws and oppressive measures. And he will not have to read between the lines to realize that, if the culture to be found in the Big Houses (the beautiful country residences of Ascendancy gentry) was often of a high standard, the political outlook and behaviour were more often abominable: narrow, reactionary, oppressive and intolerant. Yet one must be fair, for among those very same people there were some who were ashamed of the politics of the others, and from these more liberal-minded members of the Ascendancy arose leaders and organizers who made themselves active in and out of Parliament on behalf of the exploited and down-trodden peasantry. We must needs pass over a long and embittered period of political history which is almost as much a part of English as of Irish history. But the reader must never fail to keep well in mind that, from the Ascendancy, came some of the greatest benefactors Ireland has ever had.

Certain great events have left their mark on Ireland and are still spoken of with awe. Irish history is not lacking in ironies, but of them all perhaps the greatest is that the man who planted the most fruitful of the ideas to work against English rule should have been a descendant of a Cromwellian planter. Theobald Wolfe Tone (1763–1798), a Presbyterian barrister for whom English law had few attractions, became the prototype of Irish revolutionary leader and out-and-out separatist. His great achievement was to unite Protestants and Catholics, not only for the cause of Catholic emancipation, but on behalf of the Rights of Man. His ideas were those of the French Revolution applied to Ireland; so that separatism for Ireland, and Catholic Emancipation, were merely items in a wider programme based on 'Liberty, Equality, Fraternity'. Although his attempted *coup* (1798) with French aid failed, and he died by his own hand when the Government refused to execute him by shooting as a soldier (a court-martial sentenced him to be hanged and disembowelled), Wolfe Tone succeeded in planting ideas from which the Irish drew strength for generations. One of these was for a Republic of Ireland, and only in 1949 was that achieved. Republicanism with a lively 'Liberty, Equality, Fraternity' picture inspiring it is not yet dead, and the hero of 1798 is still the hero of many today. In one branch of their struggle the Irish were successful: in 1829, after one of the most extraordinary campaigns in political history by the Irish leader Daniel O'Connell, the English Parliament passed the Catholic Relief Act. The last two disabilities were lifted from those of the Roman Catholic religion, which meant three-quarters of the population of Ireland. From now, Catholics could sit in Parliament and hold all offices but three—that of Lord-Lieutenant of Ireland, of Lord Chancellor and Regent of England. This was a great step forward. O'Connell became a national hero, and was called 'The Liberator'. From then the Irish began to make themselves felt in the English Parliament, which they had never been able to do hitherto. A highly significant feature of the situation in Ireland was that the population increased steadily from the beginning of the century, and by the 1840s amounted to over eight millions, a figure never before known. In spite of their poverty, the Irish were alive and, if there was nothing else, there was growth among the people, a reviving vigour, more interest in life and the world; and less of the hopeless feeling which had marred the lives of their forefathers in the eighteenth century.

Then came The Famine—suddenly, with devastating, catastrophic effects. It was as if Nature herself decided that Ireland must be depopulated. The mass of the people, now grown into a very poor peasantry, having lost all their lands, were compelled by the land laws to exist (*exist* and no more than that) on small patches which they worked to the best of their ability. Their main food was the potato, without which gift from Heaven the greater part of the peasant population might long previously have died out. The potato grows where other crops cannot be cultivated; and with it the Irish made the best of their situation. They survived, even multiplied. A savant of our own times, who has made an exhaustive study of the potato, tells us that, because the potato is easy to cultivate, this made the Irish a lazy people! That professor has never seen the amount of work which must be done by the Aranman or a man of Connemara before a few potatoes can be taken from a surface which, until they have laboriously put it right, would not, as they say, provide "grazing for a gander". In other parts, the potato grows easily. But never where a man has no land in which to plant it! In Ireland of the 1840s the circumstances of the social system compelled the peasant population to rely on this plant; and glad they were to have such a godsend. An epidemic disease popularly called 'blight' attacked the potato and, as a consequence, the crop failed in Ireland in 1845 and 1846. In the years 1846 and 1847 hundreds of thousands of people died of starvation, hunger-typhus and cholera. An interesting side-light on the imposed economic system is that Ireland was then producing enough corn and cattle to feed the whole country, but these and other foodstuffs were exported for profit to the English market in order that rent might be paid to landlords. The net result was that about one-fourth of the population of Ireland died in the two years 1846 and 1847: two million men, women and children out of a total of eight. Such a calamity in time of peace had never been recorded for any other people. The Famine—the Great Hunger—and its trail of sorrow stamped itself on the minds of the Irish and it is never likely to be forgotten.

The Famine changed the face of Ireland in more ways than one, and it affected the whole country. After it, the Irish turned their eyes to fix them on America, a land which promised great things. Emigration began on a scale which in 1852 reached the astonishing figure for one year of nearly a quarter of a million. It continued in an unceasing stream almost until the outbreak of the First World War. The emigrants went to the United States from every part of Ireland, hundreds of thousands of them. In lesser numbers they went to other countries, some to Scotland and England, some to Canada, many to Australia, and a fair number to Argentina. The present writer is old enough to remember what even the tail-end of the exodus to America meant to families and individuals. On certain fixed days in every month the vessels of the great English shipping companies called at Irish ports to take on the passengers, who left their home railway-stations always on the same days and by the same trains to catch their ships. To be in good time for the train, they would be waiting at the station perhaps an hour or more before the time of departure. Relations and friends came there to see them off. The emigrants—mostly men—were dressed in their best clothes. Few took with them any luggage bigger than a small handbag or, more often, a bundle with maybe a collar or two, a spare shirt, a couple of pairs of socks, shaving-tackle, a piece of soap and a towel. That would be the whole kit. Fine men they were, many of magnificent physique, upright, and with clear blue eyes calmly containing the misery of the past, the hope for the future. They stood around talking quietly with parents and brothers and sisters.

Suddenly there might be a slight commotion around the platform as some well-known 'boyo' arrived in a state of elation from having wet his leave-taking in a pub. The chances were that he would be singing one of the many old songs the departing Irish emigrants used to sing. His music usually inspired some of the others, for melancholy songs would now come one after another. But often their sad notes would change suddenly to something the complete opposite, with a fluter to accompany, and a merry dance—jig, reel or hornpipe—would start. The merry side of that leave-taking was far more affecting than the sad, for it covered—and was intended to cover—a state of heartbreak never far from hysteria. It often had such an effect on my old nurse that, unable to bear it for long, with tears in her eyes she would drag me away—only to take me once again to the railway-station on the next day that a group was leaving for the New World, to share in the sorrows of the partings. Those people emigrated entirely at their own expense, passage money being scraped from the soil, the family often going without necessities to help the prospective emigrant. When the latter reached paradise on the other side of the Atlantic, the ties with the old folk in Ireland were not severed, for no sooner was Pat in a job than he would work like two men to save money to be sent home, to pay the expenses of another member of the family who planned to leave the Old Country, or to help the parents. In this way, some millions of Ireland's best sons and daughters left her to become new leaven in a new life. In Ireland today there are just over four million inhabitants. How many descendants of Irish people there are in various parts of the world it is difficult to compute. I have seen one estimate of thirty-five millions, on which I am not able to comment. But the number must be many times that of the present population of the mother country.

Deserving of note among the many Irish movements which followed the Famine is one which survives to our own times and, curiously enough, first revealed itself during the American Civil War. It was called Fenianism, and behind it was the Fenian Brotherhood (from the *fianna,* the legendary warriors of Finn MacCool, a hero capable of fabulous achievements). Inside the Fenian movement grew the Irish

Republican Brotherhood, a select body of trusted leaders founded in 1858. Their endeavour was to resume the work of Wolf Tone's United Irishmen. The Irish Republican Brotherhood became a stable, enduring political force which guaranteed to every generation a continuing separatist tradition. It is certainly one of the most remarkable of all political secret societies, and one of the most enduring in political history. From it sprang the outward popular manifestation known as *Sinn Fein,* of which more will be said in a moment. But meanwhile it is worth noting how long-memoried and tenacious the Irish can be, though it is not uncommon to hear them described as fickle-minded! Here we have a set of ideas carried forward from Wolfe Tone to the Fenian Movement of the nineteenth century, then on to the Sinn Fein Movement which, only the other day, so to speak, achieved its goal of an Irish Republic. And the Irish Republican Brotherhood is still there in Ireland, a faithful watchdog over sacred interests.

4

Northern Ireland and the Republic: Today

From the newly evolving pattern of life in Ireland during the years following the Famine, a hitherto important feature of life began to disappear: the Irish language and with it the old Gaelic tradition. In 1895 Douglas Hyde could write: "Not that the history of mankind is not full of such instances (as this disappearance), but it has nothing of the kind to show in modern times so startling, so wholesale, and so rapid, as this suddenly extinguishing of one of the finest, most perfect, and best preserved of the great Aryan languages. It has gone—this most important of those units which go to constitute the nationality of the *Clann-na-nGael;* gone, as a day in the late autumn sometimes gives way to night with scarce any interweaving twilight; gone with its songs, ballads, poems, folk-lore, romances and literature."[1] It is largely to the credit of that Protestant gentleman, a product of the Ascendancy, that from his initiative and work came a revival

[1] *The Story of Early Gaelic Literature.*

in the language, which, when he wrote those words, could be heard only in a few western parts and was spoken by only some thousands of Gaels who survived—remote, mysterious Celts who eked out a poor life in the impoverished and neglected *Gaeltacht* or Irish-speaking districts.

If that element all but disappeared and had to have artificial respiration to bring it to life again, another mark of an old pattern of Irish life began to reappear with an increasing strength which caused many headaches and much heartburning to the English Government. This was nothing less than an agitation for complete separation: complete political independence for Ireland. From the agitation for Catholic Emancipation, and then long and persistent agitation for reasonable land laws, there grew, in the nineteenth and early twentieth centuries, a strong Irish Nationalist Party which for two generations worked in accordance with constitutional methods and, within those methods, played a fair but vigorous political game in the endeavour to win a moderate measure of 'Home Rule' for Ireland. The English people but not their Government were sympathetic to the Irish cause. The Irish Nationalists won the political game in Parliament by 1914 and a Home Rule Act reached the Statute Book in that year. England's time of war was not considered by the Government to be the moment to introduce so revolutionary a measure in Ireland; and so it was shelved. Meanwhile, another and far more vigorous movement had started in Ireland, that of *Sinn Fein* ('Self-Help') which, from the moment that the English Government refused to implement even a moderate measure of Home Rule, never looked back. Sinn Fein was organized as no Irish movement had been organized since the days of Wolf Tone. It had even some of the all-embracing spirit of the Great O'Neill, the last of the great Gaels. This is not the place for a retelling of the story of the deeply symbolical Rebellion which took place in Easter Week 1916, nor of the methods used to crush it: more than to say that the executions of the rebel leaders after quick trial by court martial aroused in Ireland a spirit of revolt which had been dormant though never dead since the Fight of the Earls. A struggle began between the Irish, fighting for their independence of English rule, and the English

Government, fighting to impose English law and order. Once again Ireland was in the throes of internal war. The Irish were now facing a powerful nation which played a great part in the winning of the First World War and was, if not at the peak of its military strength, not greatly below it. It is an episode in history beyond our scope here, but it deserves to be read if only for its political lessons.[1]

For a century and a half, English Governments, one after another, had again and again shown themselves to be either extraordinarily blind or extremely callous about Ireland. Half the time there seems to have been present at all England's councils on Ireland a demon of mismanagement, a *deus ex machina,* turning, so it now seems, even well-meaning effort into one of stupid or criminally short-sighted misgovernment. The English methods of dealing with the new situation of Ireland in those years from 1916 to 1922 were the apotheosis of the work of this demon, which has often done far more harm to England than to Ireland. The English ruling class, whose mastery of style in political technics had hitherto enabled it to surmount colonial, imperial and other difficulties all over the world, now, after more than three centuries of "Ascendancy Rule" in Ireland, was to experience its first real failure in that strange and incalculable little country. We must let all that pass. On 6th December, 1922, a Treaty was signed by which an "Irish Free State" was recognized as a self-governing Dominion, but leaving to Great Britain the control of certain harbours for purposes of defence. Furthermore, to a newly created political unit called Northern Ireland, and consisting of six of the nine Ulster counties, was given the right to exclude itself from the political entity that was to be known as the Irish Free State. Advantage was taken of this by the northern dominants—Ascendancy and supporters—and so we have today the Six County enclave known officially as Northern Ireland. The rest of Ireland did not settle down immediately on the signing of the Treaty. A sad episode followed in the form of an internecine struggle reaching at times the dimensions of

[1] For the history of the movement and the outcome see *The Victory of Sinn Fein,* by P. S. O'Hegarty, and *The Irish Republic,* by Dorothy Macardle.

civil war, and arising out of the signature and interpretation of the Treaty. But even that ended, and there remained to be cleared only a few points which a considerable section of Irish public opinion regarded as matters of principle. What seems to have been the last but one of these was cleared up in 1949, when with a characteristic gesture what had been the *Irish Free State* under the Treaty (and then became known as *Eire,* the old Gaelic name of the country) was changed to the *Republic of Ireland,*[1] the name by which the Twenty-six County area is now known. The major political problem now remaining was that of the Partition which had come about. The position as this is written is that neither England nor Ireland is satisfied that the division of the island into these two political units is an ideal state of affairs. The Government of the Twenty-six County Area in Dublin would like to see Ireland a united country—a nation of thirty-two counties. The Government of the Six County Area have not until now shown any inclination to take part in an all-Ireland Government. Meanwhile, a Border was established between the two areas with Customs and all the State machinery, rules and regulations on each side which such a frontier demands. The Border irritates those on both sides.

We must go to the 1609 Plantation to seek for the basic explanation of this modern Partition. A great anglicization, with a strong Scots element in the north, then took place. Beginning with those Plantations, Irish history was a tale of struggle between two ways of life: the old Gaelic way with its loose-knit political system, and a vague sort of inter-clan federalism which could at moments be evoked; the other an evolution of feudalism into modern capitalism, organized and close-knit. The Plantations were *intended* to be the consolidation of a conquest for the two clearly defined purposes of (1) eliminating for all time any 'Irish danger', and (2) establishing English and Scots planters—Episcopalians and Presbyterians—as a wedge among the Catholic Gaels in such a way that those planters could never again be disturbed by the natives. The struggle between the old and the new way of life had its ups and downs: in some places the old wiped out the new altogether; in other places there was mutual

[1] *Poblacht na h-Eireann* in Gaelic.

assimilation; in others the new could not be displaced, by whatever efforts the Irish might exert; in a very few the old remained intact. Such was the general strength of the various efforts exerted by the Norman-Gaels, often with the strong support of the Anglo-Irish, that by 1914 all of Ireland, excepting the fast-declining Ascendancy and a part of Ulster, was thinking in terms of a new nation, an idealized unity, a native collectivity independent of rule by the Parliament at

Westminster. If we consider those two political units into which Ireland is now divided—*Northern Ireland* of the Six Counties, *The Republic of Ireland* of the Twenty-six—and observe the differences in religion, culture, economic basis of life, social outlook and origin, it is not difficult to note divergences. One might add two further factors: the politico-economic ties of Northern Irish industrialism with British capitalism, and the ultramontanism of influential elements in The Republic of Ireland. When we touch the 'Border Question', we touch a subject of controversy, and one with deep roots. The reader might not thank anybody for a disquisition on the involved politics thereof. But he should at least be warned of the existence of ground which, especially for the stranger, must be marked DANGEROUS! If any opinion is to be expressed about it at all, my own is that something in the nature of an overriding, compelling motive or force has yet to appear before the Partition can give place to a united Ireland, with the lions and the lambs of The North lying down with the tigers and the lambs of The Republic. Here we must be content to leave Partition for the future to decide.

5
The Resultant Miracle

If what has been written in this sketch has done its work, it should show that Ireland is a country with a long and involved history, and that the Irish of today are, to say the least, a very mixed product of at least half a dozen peoples themselves already mixed. There were first the aborigines—the inhabitants of the country before the arrival of the Celts. Speculation about their racial origins and strength is simply guesswork. Second, the Celts—now recognized as a people, not a race: various tribes and clans without a state, and held together loosely by a common language and a particular way of life and culture. They have left their mark on Ireland: one that is unmistakable. Third, the Norsemen who left little of importance, though we must not forget that a few important communities at river-mouths, including Dublin, started as Norse forts. Culturally, the Norsemen had little influence. Fourth, there were the Normans or Norman-English, whose influence was great and who contributed enormously—advantageously—to the country and the race. Fifth, there were the English who, as we know, were an ethnic mixture into which had entered the ancient Britons (Celts) and the western Teutons—who were not without a touch of Celtic blood—well leavened by Norman-French and less important stocks. Sixth, in the North there was the largely Scottish but partly English influx which planted Ulster. Of the six elements which may constitute an 'Irishman', three dominate: the old *Celtic,* the mediæval *Norman* and the modern *English* (often replaced by Scottish in The North). Thus, it is about as sensible to speak of a 'pure' Irishman as it is of a 'pure' Englishman, and whoever wished to satirize the 'true-born Irishman' would have as much material at his disposal as Daniel Defoe had when he wrote *The True Born Englishman.* There is, however, what may fairly be regarded as an exception to this generalization: in some parts of the west, Connemara, Donegal, in the north-west, and Kerry in the south-west, the Celtic element still predominates. All the rest of Ireland, excepting these thinly populated parts, has lost in Gaelic tradition and language, which has necessitated a long-term educational scheme to revive. Such a scheme is gallant and worthy. Time will measure its success.

Climate and the nature of the landscape as well as the long history of often desperate struggles for existence would have to be added to the complex mixture of ethnic elements if one were to dare produce even a rough formula which might explain 'Irish psychology'. When we look back over that long history, we cannot help feeling that, although at times it has been as sad as that of any people, it has also been as inspiring as any; so much so that, considered as a whole, it has been not short of the miraculous. Like England, Ireland was conquered by the Normans, and assimilated them so effectively that she conquered them; she was almost killed by the English Plantations and Settlements, and came to life again to absorb the invaders into her soft landscape; she was weakened by famine, pestilence and emigration, but lived on to

Close View of the Rock of Cashel
ITA

Dublin—O'Connell Street

Cork—General View

ITA

rise in what seemed a hopeless rebellion against the might of the British Empire and to succeed in establishing her own distinctive place in the world. Any one of these achievements can be regarded as remarkable, but their sum represents a miracle in terms of survival and human strength; and this applies to all Ireland, if we think in long-term human values, and not in those of the politics of the moment. We know that struggle can develop virtues; and that it can also leave vices behind it. The Irish are not alone in having a right to boast of their virtues. Their natural modesty does not go so far as to permit them to claim to be without vices. Or not often. What they are not inclined to dwell upon is that *culturally* the Ireland we now know is, whatever else it may be, an Anglo-Irish phenomenon. For good or ill, Ireland and the Irish are firmly established as a part of the English-speaking world; and a part which, though the homeland is small geographically and in population, is not unimportant. English is the language of all Irish people excepting a very few: the number of Gaelic speakers who cannot also speak English is negligible. And also, for good or ill, Ireland and the Irish are inextricably intermixed with the two great branches of the English-speaking world: with Britain and the British Commonwealth and with the United States of America. In Britain there are hundreds of thousands of Irish. On the other side of the Atlantic there are millions of Irish descent. The Irish have fought, fought well and at times brilliantly, for both branches of the English-speaking world.

What seems very extraordinary, when we consider the history of the parent island, is that this curious amalgam of mixed peoples should have shown such persistent virility and liveliness down to the present moment. Perhaps, after all, the old legends were right! And, if we are to look for the explanation of the unique nature of those whom we call Irish, we shall find its source in the fabulous Parthalonians, Fomorians and Túatha Dé Danann of the myths and legends!

CHAPTER IV

LITERATURE AND FOLKLORE

> Beyond, beyond the mountain line,
> The grey-stone and the boulder,
> Beyond the growth of dark-green pine,
> That crowns its western shoulder,
> There lies that fairy-land of mine,
> Unseen of a beholder.
>
> From *Dreams,* by CECIL FRANCES ALEXANDER.

1

Tradition and Return to Tradition

LIGHT readers—and they are more numerous than the heavy ones—are not deeply concerned with order. Too much chronology distresses them, so perhaps the less we have of it the better, even if philosophers hold that time moves in one way only: forward, as we say, and not backward. In attempting to sketch complex human activities of wide scope such as those touched on here, it seemed more desirable to pick out and dwell upon those which best indicate an Irish way of thinking and without too much regard for the chronological order in which they may have happened or have been recorded. However they are ordered, one is struck again and again, first, by a *sameness* that is strangely constant in the working of the Irish mind, and second, by facets or aspects of it which vary in the literary pattern from age to age by seemingly disparate superficial and minor changes—all of which duly re-form and settle down to end in a marked resemblance to what went before.

The old racial theories concerning the Celts are, we now know, so much sounding brass and tinkling cymbals. That there is a Celtic and especially an Irish way of thinking can be shown beyond much doubt from the records of nearly two thousand years of history. In nothing is this more clearly proved than in precisely that department in which we might expect to find it—literature.

As we have seen in Chapters II and III, the ethnic face of Ireland has changed many times from the coming of the Celts onwards; and it continues to be in a state of flux. But consider this poem:

I am the wind which breathes upon the sea,
I am the wave of the ocean,
I am the murmur of the billows,
I am the ox of the seven combats.
I am the vulture upon the rocks,
I am a beam of the sun,
I am the fairest of plants,
I am a wild boar in valour,
I am a salmon in the water,
I am a lake in the plain,
I am a word of science,
I am the point of the lance in battle,
I am the god who creates in the head the fire.
Who is it who throws light into the meeting of the mountain?
Who announces the ages of the moon, if not I?
Who teaches the place where couches the sun, if not I?[1]

The poem is attributed to Amergin, one of the Milesian princes who in that fifth invasion (see page 44) colonized Ireland. If Amergin composed it, that is to say, if it is a poem which came down by oral tradition from the period of the 'Milesian' invasion, then it must be well over two thousand years old. Douglas Hyde writes: "No faith can be placed in the alleged date or genuineness of Amergin's verses. They are, however, of interest, because as Irish tradition has always represented them as being the first verses made in Ireland, so it may very well be that they actually do present the oldest surviving lines in any vernacular tongue in Europe except Greek."

The first thing one notices about this poem is the pantheism which pervades it throughout. One is struck especially by the emphasis on Nature: sea, ocean, billows, sun, rock, plants, water, plain, mountain, moon. Then the reference to combat and to the 'lance of battle'; and to thought —'the fire in the head' of man. Having noted these fairly obvious elements of the poem—the pantheism (*religion*), the great attention to *Nature,* the references to *valour* and

[1] Translation by Douglas Hyde.

physical beauty, and finally the 'fire in the head' or *ardent thought*—as one proceeds from that very early Amergin poem onwards through Gaelic literature and that written in English by the Irish and Anglo-Irish, one finds that these themes constantly recur. It is interesting to turn back to this old poem after one has read other branches of Irish literature, for then it is possible to realize that Amergin—consciously or unconsciously, and it does not matter which—gives us a picture of the Celtic mind. One finds the picture confirmed by even a bald statement of what has survived in the considerable *corpus* of literary material in Gaelic which has not been destroyed by tumults, invasions and wars. Omitting what cannot be considered truly Irish—translations into Gaelic of classical and foreign literature—here is a summary of what survives:

1. *A mass of Story:* heroic and romantic and in prose and verse, developing from mythological and heroic sagas towards the long story (novel) and short story or *conte*.

2. *A mass of Poetry:* narrative, lyrical, mournful, gay; and nearly always with strong emphasis on Nature.

3. *A mass of Folklore:* in songs, old epigrammatic wisdom, proverbs, ballads; as well as throughout the prose.

These three groups include the greater part of the *corpus* of pure literature surviving in Irish, much of it not yet thoroughly scrutinized. Lest anybody should think from what has been said that this is the whole of the surviving literature, it may be added that there is also an abundance of miscellaneous annals, histories, clan records, typographies, lives of saints, devotional works (Catholic) and a great body of 'technical' works on old laws, mediæval science, medicine and philosophy. It should perhaps also be noted that in all this literature there is *no drama* such as that of ancient Greece; *no autobiography; no science* that matters; *no 'travels'*, and *no 'criticism'* as we understand the words. What will perhaps surprise those who approach this subject for the first time is to discover how great is the quantity of Irish literature still surviving. How much it would be if it included all that was destroyed by Norsemen, Normans, English and by careless or ignorant Irish, is not entirely a matter for conjecture, for that which survives contains innumerable references and glosses to items, many of great interest, which disappeared in the conflagrations or otherwise.[1] What is certain is that, even with what remains of Gaelic literature, its position in Western culture is one of which any country could be proud.

This brings us to a branch of ignorance which is very common among English-speaking people outside Ireland, and not only among ordinary, average people, but even in the ranks of those who are educated, cultured, enlightened and sophisticated. It is nicely exemplified in a question put to me a year or so ago by an English poet who had made his mark before the First World War. His work is in almost every anthology of note published since the 1920s. This good poet said to me one day: "Tell me, is there any such thing as Irish literature—I mean, literature in Irish Gaelic? I am told that there are lots of old annals and so forth—but is there anything which a civilized person could regard as *real* literature, real *poetry*?" The question took me aback, yet I succeeded in making the physical effort to nod and say, "Yes—there is." I was afraid to expand on my reply, well knowing that I might hurt his feelings.

Nearly all of the old literature survives in the form of manuscripts. I have not attempted to find the most up-to-date estimates of how many old Irish manuscripts have been catalogued, and of how much literary material they represent in terms of modern printed books. We can rest content with E. O'Curry's estimates, to be found in his *Lectures* published nearly eighty years ago, as they suffice to give an idea of the considerable volume of the material. O'Curry states that the five oldest manuscripts if printed would represent 9,400 quarto pages. Other vellum manuscripts dating 1300–1600 would fill another 9,000 quarto pages. Another batch, mostly early eighteenth century, would fill 30,000 printed pages. And the French scholar D'Arbois de Jubainville in 1883 published a catalogue of 953 Irish manuscripts preserved in libraries in these islands, to which were later added 56 in Continental libraries. Since then, the late Robin Flower spent

[1] For further information on this subject, see Douglas Hyde's *Literary History of Ireland,* Eleanor Hull's *Textbook of Irish Literature* and, most up to date, *Gaelic Literature Surveyed* by Aodh De Blacam. To all these I am indebted.—C. D.

a great part of his life in the British Museum working on a new and more detailed catalogue of manuscript and other literature in Gaelic. The work of cataloguing continues, and will continue for nobody knows how long. The point of mentioning these quantities, irrespective of their nature or qualities, is to show how much work remains to be done in this interesting field, not counting what yet remains to be discovered. For all that, it may be said that since the Gaelic revival, which began in the last decade of the nineteenth century, a great volume of extremely interesting material in the Irish language has been printed in scholarly editions, often with an English translation beside the original. We cannot here examine more than a fraction of what is available. The most that can be dared is to select from it enough to show in rough outline certain peaks in which, as in a sketch of peaks in the Irish physical landscape, some of the main features can be appreciated.

Story, poetry, folklore: one or the other and often all three are found from the earliest times down to our own, from the successors of Amergin to the successors of Yeats. Throughout will be found as constants one or other or all forms of the characteristic Irish emphasis: on paganism or pantheism in the early literature (the Mythological Cycle), and on religion in Christian terms when the early phase has passed; on Nature at all times; on physical valour, beauty, and on what an Irish peasant of today would call 'decency' and others could with reason call chivalry; and on the 'fire in the head', which as often as not proves to be in the heart or to spring from it.

This may seem to be over-simplification; and perhaps it is. The most that can be claimed for it is that it may help as a rough kind of chart in a sea full of rocks for the person who is unacquainted with it, and that it may ease the bewilderment which usually besets those who venture on it for the first time. The consistency, the *conservatism* if you will, in the working of the Irish mind is striking. For we must not forget that the latest flowering of that mind, as manifested in what is known as the Literary Renaissance or Revival which dated from the 1890s to the 1920s, was the result of an inspiration which largely came from the return to those stories, poetry and folklore of the old Ireland. Although the language of the Literary Revival was English and the main activities were related to contemporary Irish problems, there can be no evading the fact that W. B. Yeats, the leader, the man who more than any other made the Revival, drew the early inspiration which gave him his great power and impetus from translations of the heroic cycles, the Sagas and the Nature poetry of that other Ireland which used its own language. The Revival virtually ended with the Treaty of 1921, but some of the best Irish writers of the years following remained in the tradition of the Revival. Irish literary talents were concentrated on Irish themes and Irish life, and at long last the writers—the good ones, that is—got rid of the false values and overworked stage Irishman of Charles Lever and inferior authors who had discovered that there was nothing the comfortable English loved more than to sit back and laugh at the absurdities in behaviour and speech of the ignorant, laughable, ragged Irish. The poor Irish peasant had become fair game for a host of Irish writers who consciously or unconsciously seized on what the English regarded as his 'picturesque' and 'amusing' qualities, but in reality were nothing but a manifestation of various aspects of a grim philosophy of survivalism. It was a philosophy of fatalism, of Stoicism, of making the best of the very terrible circumstances created for him by the conquerors of his country and the robbers of his land. In order to survive those circumstances, the poor peasant in Ireland relied, not only on his great powers of physical resistance, but on his innate good humour and on his wit as well as on his wits. He developed a rich technique of resourcefulness and, because even his manner of speech was 'funny' to English ears, all this combined to make "Paddy and his Pig" the stock comics in a mass of literature which, if it pleased the English market, too often brought poor Paddy into ridicule if not contempt. It was, to say the least, undignified, and even at its best (as in Sommerville and Ross's *Irish R.M.*) this literature, in which the main theme was a harping on the relations between the Ascendancy and the Descendancy, with emphasis on the great fun of it all, did not serve the best interests of the Irish. When the Literary Revival evoked the spirit of ancient Ireland, it showed up the "Paddy and his Pig" stuff for what it was. It meant a return to dignity. And it not only swept away the greater part of that false and derogatory set of values, but it canalized an overdue awakening of the people. For a moment it seemed as if the mystical Ireland had become the real Ireland. It was not until long afterwards that even the closest observers realized that what was a literary reawakening and the birth of a new drama were closely intermingled with the social and political movements of that period. And even to this day there are people —James Joyce was one until his death—who maintain that there was much shadow but little substance in what they prefer to call the 'so-called' literary renaissance. The facts are against them. The Irish Literary Revival added many names to the list of those whose achievements in English literature have a permanent value.

It seems strange that this grand clearance and fresh outlook in the beginning of the twentieth century should have sprung from sources that were already old more than one thousand years earlier. But it is so, and hence there is no need to emphasize the importance for our own times of the stories, the poetry and the folklore of Gaeldom. Their spirit is alive, not only in the works of many modern Irish writers, but in the mind of a considerable section of the Irish people today. Nobody can say that the same source of inspiration cannot produce a further and even more unpredictable revival.

2

The Great Cycles

The principal source or sources of this inspiration are to be found in three great Cycles, each of which is a group or groups of stories that are the work of writers many of whose names are either unknown or a matter of speculation. The cycles are:

I. *The Mythological* or *Pagan Cycle*—deals with events B.C.

II. *The Red Branch or Ulster Cycle*—events about A.D. 1.

III. *The Fenian or Ossianic Cycle*—events A.D. 200 onwards.

This is the logical order by contents, though it does not represent the chronological order of the documents, which contain the earliest written statements of the Cycles, writings which represent an oral tradition coming from a much earlier period. In the latter sense, the Red Branch (seventh century) comes first; next (twelfth century) the Fenian; and last (twelfth century) the Mythological. For the present purpose it may be better to consider them in the order of the periods to which their contents refer. These old Sagas are mostly in prose, but sometimes they are interspersed with poems or incantations of varying length. The narrative and descriptive parts which constitute the bulk are in prose; and here and there in metre are eulogies, rhapsodies, laments, dramatic dialogues and the high spots of rhetoric. The older poems are often in a form resembling that with which we are acquainted in the Book of Isaiah (especially in the English Authorized Version), and although their themes bear little or no resemblance to those of the Bible—they come closer to Greek mythology—there is often an Old Testament power in their language.

In Chapter II an account was given of the various invasions of Ireland which are said to have happened in prehistoric times and recorded in the *Book of Invasions*. Those invasions are the main themes of the Mythological Cycle, but the telling of the stories and especially the embroidery and digressions bring us at the same time into realms of the imagination and lead us through worlds of magic and of the weird and wonderful. The *Arabian Nights* represent a more ordered body of story-telling, but the Orientals do not go farther in magic or imaginative range than these occidentals of the Irish Sagas. Presumably because they are pagan tales, because in terms of 'scientific' history they are demonstrably nonsense or not far removed from it, and possibly because our hardened modern minds are directed towards such stirring actual achievements as atomic fission, solar rays, stratosphere flight and the possibilities of inter-planetary communication as demonstrated by our fabulous 'flying saucers', we are not always able to appreciate those old tales at their full worth. There can be no denying their great and inspiring charm, the loveliness of their descriptions, or their far-away other-worldly sweep.[1] Here is escapist literature worthy of gods and supermen: supermen of that prehistoric age, who bear no resemblance to the super-yahoos of our times who may one day be written into another Cycle for the contemplation of a saner posterity. The Mythological Cycle contains the Irish pantheon and that old 'history' already referred to. It is also the fount of Ireland's poetic and literary traditions, as well as what may be the concealed core of her pre-Christian religion. For these, if for no other reasons, this Cycle must be our starting-point. The heroic tales of the Red Branch and those of the Fenian Cycle may have attracted greated attention and possibly also provided greater inspiration to the upsurge of the modern revival. But then the Red Branch and Fenian tales often hark back to those of the mythological age.

The fact that these old Cycles provided inspiration for the modern revival and Yeats is reason enough for us to pay attention to them. But there are other reasons not less important. It is in the Cycles that we find set out for our contemplation the various elements which combined to make up the old culture of Ireland. Rolleston deals with them under five convenient heads which amount to this. There were, first, a mass of popular superstitions and magical observances which varied from place to place. Secondly, there was a thoughtful and philosophic creed which had as its central object of worship the Sun and as its central doctrine the immortality of the soul. Thirdly, there was a worship of personified deities somewhat similar to those of the ancient Greeks; and of others conceived as representing the forces of Nature or man's social laws. Fourthly, the existence in the druidical religions of ancient Ireland (brought there with the Celtic, that is, the 'Milesian' invasion) of a body of teaching of a quasi-scientific nature about the constitution of the universe, natural phenomena and so forth, the details of which have been lost. Fifthly, the prevalence of a priestly and caste organization which administered all learning and tradition, and kept all this very carefully within the privileged

[1] See the work of De Jubainville, translated by R. I. Best as *The Irish Mythological Cycle and Celtic Mythology* (Dublin, 1908). Also T. W. Rolleston's *Myths and Legends of the Celtic Race* (London, 1917).

caste. In regard to this, it will be remembered what was said earlier about the *filidh,* who were at first a branch of the Druidic order. This caste achieved an intellectual and, up to a point, also a moral supremacy which, among the Celts everywhere and including Ireland, brought with it what amounted to sovereign power: social, political and religious. The caste had a widespread organization which, apparently, gave itself over willingly to Christianity. This explains, not only why it was that Ireland became so rapidly christianized, but why it is that even to this day we sometimes find a curiously surviving item of the old paganism. And there are those who see in the influence of the priest today a survival of the power of the old priestly caste. It is part of a tradition.

Of the Mythological Cycle few of the romances remain, and of them the most interesting are those about the *Túatha Dé Danann,* the People or Tribe of (the Goddess) Dana. These tales are the heritage of the Celtic peoples of Ireland, Wales and France; the Dé Danann stories are not known traditionally among the Scots Gaels. The Cycle is too long and complex for detailed examination here, but some of its features and characters deserve mention because of their constant recurrence in Irish thought and record. There was Ogma, an interesting deity who was patron of Eloquence and Literature. We do not know much about him, but what has come down is not without significance when we think of Ireland and the Irish. The Greek writer Lucian describes Ogma (*Ogmios*) as attired like Heracles but, what is odd for a patron of Eloquence and Literature, with a lion's skin and club. Ogma is pictured as a bald old man who drew after him a complacent crowd of people who were fastened to him by slender golden chains of which the ends passed through the god's tongue. A Celt explained to Lucian what this meant: the race—the Celts, that is—believed that power lay, not in the physical strength of the body, but in the eloquence and ready wit of the tongue, which accordingly drew men after the speaker, whose face smiles on his captives. This might be said to represent the attitude of the Celts towards eloquence and literature: the well-known Irish love of words, oratory and eloquence. It is at the opposite pole from that of the sophisticated Chinese, which is to regard oratory, especially eloquent oratory, as an impure art and suspect in accordance with the degree of the eloquence. Perhaps it is that the Irish like to be taken in, providing the deceiver is an artist in words; or as is more likely, they love almost any sort of eloquent appeal to the emotions. Whatever is the reason, there for us all to think about is Ogma—a two thousand years' old god who symbolizes something that still has a great appeal to the Gaels. It is said that Ogma's name survives in the word Ogham, for he it was who invented that ancient form of writing.

The goddess Dana was also called Brigid, and by this name she was held in great honour in pagan Ireland. This Brigid was a daughter of the supreme being of the *Túatha Dé Danann,* known as the Daga Mór. Dana or Brigid was the greatest of all those Celtic goddesses; an early text calls her the "mother of the Irish Gods". Like the Dagda, she was associated with fertility and blessing, but she was also the goddess of Wisdom and Knowledge and of the Arts and Crafts. And that is what makes her interesting, for here is the old Irish equivalent of the Greek goddess Athena and the goddess Minerva of the Romans: the personification of the thinking power, and to the Irish the "female sage or mistress of wisdom, the goddess whom poets adored on account of the greatness of her protecting care, whence she is called the goddess of the poets". Brigid had two 'sisters' of the same name, one of them a medical doctor, the other a supreme craftswoman in metalwork: a good example of the old Irish custom of making mythological personalities into triads. Here it is to be understood that the Brigid who was goddess of Wisdom and Knowledge presided over the three great departments: poetry-philosophy, medicine, metalcraft. All this implies a high respect for culture in pagan Ireland, and it is not surprising that the Christian Irish took over what their old pagan Brigid represented, or that a great Abbess of Kildare, Saint Brigid, should have been named after the highly respected deity. This is a fair example of the sort of transfusion from paganism into Christianity which occurred again and again, not only in Ireland, but elsewhere. It was generally a transfusion of *power* in some form; and, for this reason, it aided greatly in the success of the new religion.

There were many of these goddesses and gods, and very wonderful were their activities and achievements. Of them all the Dagda Mór, the Good, the All-knowing One, was the most important. He knew all the wisdoms and was so huge that he could hardly move about. His club was so big that it had to be drawn after him on a wheeled car pulled by eight men, the vehicle leaving tracks which served as dykes to mark the boundary between two provinces. He had a feeding cauldron to hold eighty gallons of milk and the same amount of fat and meat, to which were added whole goats, sheep and pigs, all of which made a stew from which he drew nourishment. The Dagda seems to have been the Irish equivalent of the Greek Cronus, youngest of the Titans, Saturnus of the Romans, and known to us as Saturn. In the Mythological Cycle there is an account of the struggle between the People of Dana and their predecessors, the Fomorians, and in the story of the Second Battle of Moytura we read that the Fomorians filled the cauldron and commanded the Dagda to eat the whole contents on pain of death. "Each bit," said Eleanor Hull, "as he brought it up was half a salted pig or a quarter of beef, and he ate it with a ladle big enough to hold a man and woman lying in the trough of the spoon. He possessed, too, a magic harp, into which he had so bound the melodies that they sounded forth only when summoned by his call, and the harp would move of its own power from the wall to his hand when he summoned it, overthrowing all that stood in its way. He played on it the three strains known to the perfect musician: sleep-strain, which brought slumber on the hosts and on invalids in pain or trouble; the wail-strain, which made men and women weep; and the laughing-strain, on hearing which all who listened to it laughed aloud." All these old deities and many other great figures took part in battle. Each represents some human quality: the Dagda was All-knowing; Brigid was Poetry and Philosophy; Ogma was Eloquence; one named Diancecht represented the Art of Medicine; and one known as Goibniu was the smith who made spears which killed when they pierced a man's skin. In later times Goibniu became known as the Gobhan Saer, a mysterious wandering smith, a craftsman and architect to whom popular tradition attributed the invention and erection of the first Round Towers.

A formidable monster who took part in the Battle of Moytura was Balor of the Evil Eye. The eye was opened only on a battlefield; it required four men using a polished rod to lift the lid. But the effort was worth while: a whole enemy host could be killed by its envenomed glance. The god Lugh is deserving of note also. Lugh was a younger god, being the grandson of Diancecht and son of Cian, and we find his name recurring often in differing forms and in places widely dispersed. Lugh—in Latin Lugus—was the Celtic god of Light, and his cult was widespread throughout the Celtic world. The names of Lyons, Laon and Leyden come to us from it (Lyons in Latin is *Lugdunum,* from the Celtic words *Lugh* and *dún,* the Fort of Lugh); no doubt these were centres of the cult. Lugh is well known in Welsh literature as Llew, and always as the god of Light. The Welsh married him to a girl made of flowers; and sent him heavenwards in the form of an eagle. Lugh came against Balor of the Evil Eye in battle, and we read that the one-eyed monster said to his henchman, "Lift up mine eye-lid that I may see this babbler who is talking to me." When the lid was raised from Balor's single eye, Lugh let fly a stone from his sling. The stone, we are informed, carried the eye right through Balor's head and, when it reached the other side, its poisoned glance fell on Balor's own host, whereupon they all fell dead before its venom. These struggles, in which fabulous figures took part, culminating in what is called in the Cycle the Second Battle of Moytura, can be read as stories of marvellous adventures in which we are given the full play of magic and the miraculous. As such they are exciting; but behind the stories there is always something more. The contests of the great figures usually symbolize something. We find then that, for example, the Second Battle of Moytura symbolizes the struggle between the forces of Enlightenment and Knowledge on the one hand, and the powers of Ignorance and Darkness on the other: a struggle as old as man, and one which recurs again and again in human history. And will recur. In the myth we see man advancing, progressing against the forces of Nature; and enlightened man wins the battle. In this there is encouragement and inspiration. There is a great spaciousness, almost a sense of infinity, about the Irish story.

In the Irish pantheon there is an Adonis, known as Aengus Óg, *óg* meaning 'young', and so Angus the Younger. Angus symbolizes love, youth and beauty. He cannot be forgotten, because his name is associated with one of the greatest and most interesting of all the pagan survivals there are in Europe: the great range of tumuli known as Brug na Boinne on the left or northern bank of the River Boyne about five miles from the town of Drogheda in County Louth.[1] Here are to be seen by the interested visitor three great tumuli, those of Dowth, Knowth and New Grange, with several smaller structures and some standing stones and earthen enclosures, one of the latter being regarded as of great archæological importance. The "Palace of the Boyne" (from the Gaelic *Brug na Boinne*) is the name given to this burial-place for important personalities of pagan Ireland. Aengus Óg became better known as Aengus na Boinne, "Angus of the Boyne", and his name in the old literature and even in fairly modern folklore is associated with this great burial-place, of which he is sometimes said to have been the builder. Angus is conceived as inhabiting the original palace, which is taken to have been adorned with flowers and decorated with splendour. Macallister says: "It is no undue straining of probability to see here a lingering memory of the king who once ruled this palace and was buried in the neighbouring tumulus, his earthly divinity enhanced by the mystery of death." It should be noted that in New Grange we are confronted with a wonderful and altogether remarkable signpost in history. On the one hand, we have the myths and legends of the Cycle; on the other, we have this great mass of surviving solid material which, if it can be read and co-related with what is to be found in the three Cycles—what is in one is sometimes carried over to another—a solution may be found of many problems that are at present complete mysteries. What is already happening about all this old material surviving from ancient Ireland is similar to what is happening in regard to similar material elsewhere in the world. As

[1] Macallister's *Archæology of Ireland* gives an account of the tumuli and of what has been found there to date.

scientific investigation progresses, the basic truth of some of the old myths and legends is confirmed; and some of the others are proved to have been little else than the work of some imaginative person or persons who, for one reason or another, decided to leave a mystery in one form or another for posterity.

Of the Palace of the Boyne, we read in the old cycle that originally it belonged to Elcmar, foster-father of Angus, his real father being the Dagda Mór. Manannán Mac Lir, son of the Sea-god, and himself a god of changing moods and places symbolizing the unstable ocean, requested Angus to plead with Elcmar that he be allowed possession of the Palace for a night and a day. The request was granted, and Manannán then refused to give up his place, arguing that all of time was made of nights and days. The god surrounded himself with an invisible wall and remained in splendour in the Palace, eating the flesh of pigs which never failed and drinking the ale of immortality. And so, one by one the old deities and chiefs found their final resting-places. When the pagan gods retired and had lost their hold on the minds of the people, tradition, as recorded by later writers, says that after a battle at what is now called Teltown in County Meath—the country of the Sagas—in which the Milesians defeated the hosts of the Túatha Dé Danann, the latter retired into the hills and valleys and set up new kingdoms underground. They gave sovereignty to another son of the Dagda, one Boab Derg, and they settled in their hosts with their chiefs as new beings. In this we have one version of the beginning of fairyland, of fairy dwelling-places, of fairies. But was it really the beginning? P. W. Joyce, the scholar and historian, tells us: "It is very probable that the belief in the existence of fairies came in with the earliest colonists that entered Ireland, and that this belief is recorded in the oldest of native Irish writings in a way that proves it to have been, at the time treated of, long established and universally received." We find in St. Patrick's time a record that a belief in a world of fairies existed in the High King's household. And then comes Christian disapproval or at least discouragement of the belief, and there is an explanation to the effect that the fairies were "angels cast out from heaven for their unworthiness, yet

Connemara Turf Carrier
ITA

not evil enough for hell, and who, therefore, occupy intermediate space here on earth".[1]

So we can make for ourselves a line which runs from the mythology of the earliest Cycle down to the fairy-story which the visitor may hear any day and in many places from one end of Ireland to the other.

3

The Red Branch and Fenian Cycles

When we leave the Mythological Cycle and consider that called *Craobh Ruadh*—the 'Red Branch' or Ulster Cycle—we find another and somewhat different manifestation of the Irish mind. The stories in the Red Branch are the heroic tales and lore of the Ulidians, the people who ruled the northern part of Ireland until early in the fourth century of the Christian era. In them we have the concrete and realistic in contrast to the nebulous and other-worldly of the myths. Because of this concreteness the Red Branch Cycle is regarded, apart from its literary value, as a storehouse of reliable information on a great variety of the everyday things and affairs of an ancient period. Although these tales must have been transmitted orally for nearly a thousand years, they were finally committed to writing during the period dating approximately from 1100 to late in the fourteenth century. They were an important part of the material relied upon by the *seanchaidhe* (pronounced shanahy) or storyteller—an entertainer on all great occasions such as festivals and banquets, as well as at minor social events such as a *céilidhe* (pronounced cailey), which might be an evening's entertainment in a private house or nothing more than a friendly little gathering of neighbours around the fire for talk and mutual entertainment. The *seanchaidhe* and the *céilidhe* have come down to our own times.

The *Táin*—already mentioned in Chapter II—the work which in English is called 'The Cattle Drive of Cooley', with many introductory stories and sequels, makes up the Red Branch Cycle, so called from the name given to the Ulidians (Ulstermen) who were its principal characters and quasi-

[1] *The Irish Fairy Book,* by Alfred Percival Graves.

Connemara
—Bringing Home the Turf
ITA

Achaen heroes. Myths brought forward from the older Cycle find their way into the Red Branch. The chief heroes of the latter trace their origin to the gods of the vanished past; and thus preserve from the prehistoric period the continuity in Irish story. Before we look at these tales, a word of explanation is required in regard to cattle drives, of which that of Cooley was to become so famous. In the Ireland of that period, cattle represented not only wealth but currency. Wars between kings or clans were always preceded by raids to take possession of the enemy's cattle and drive the beasts to the home pasturage. This preliminary preparation served the double purpose of depriving the enemy of the live-stock required to feed his men and, if successful, make provision for the army which the raider would use in the major campaign. With the raids there was often burning, depredations and the carrying off of women. Horses, cattle, sheep and swine were then more important than land itself, and the possession of great numbers of these animals represented power in a form more useful than that represented by land: the sum of a man's wealth was reckoned by the amount of his live-stock plus his household utensils, ornaments, female slaves and, in the case of a chief, the fighting men on whom he could count. In comparison with the items comprised in this inventory, the extent of territory owned or the number of its inhabitants was of less importance. Thus, a cattle drive in ancient Ireland was an event of some importance (of fairly frequent occurrence in most parts of the country), and sometimes it would amount to a large-scale expedition. There are many stories of such events, but in 'The Cattle Drive of Cooley' we have one of the greatest raised from the level of a tribal episode into one of epic grandeur. It rises to warfare in which heroes are gods and gods heroes, all taking place in the pastoral setting of the country, and all conceived in such a way that we feel, with the creators of the epic story, that it has a spiritual significance far above the simple events with which it deals. The framework of the story is simplicity itself. Queen Maeve, the domineering Queen of Connacht, having decided to capture a famous animal, the Brown Bull of Cooley, organizes and directs a campaign with this object. The men of the North, because of some strange debility or mental state, are unable to mount a defence—all except one, Cúchulainn (pronounced coohoolinn), who is Lord of Cooley and becomes the hero around whom the whole epic revolves. It is a tale of invasion, the resistance to it and final victory for the Ulidians, the men of Ulster. In this alone we can see why the poets and others of the Literary Revival found in it inspiration for their nationalist campaign. It is as if they realized that the people of their Ireland were not unlike the men of the North in the *Táin* and needed some such example to inspire them against the invader of their natural rights.

There are two versions in the Gaelic of this epic, the Irish *Iliad,* the first of them dating from the seventh, the second from the fourteenth century. Theme and general outline are substantially the same in both, but whereas the earlier version is spare, rather abrupt in parts and more starkly prosaic, the second is exuberant, more elaborate, and is considered to be the finer work of art. Perhaps the principal difference in tone between the Irish and Greek epics is that in the former we have constantly recurring a note of native chivalry, one that is often highly pitched, but Homer either overlooked the chivalry of his heroes or he may not have had good material to draw upon. The Irish heroes always behave like great gentlemen, like the best of the aristocratic knights in the European age of chivalry. The Prologue of the *Táin* sets the theme. The strong-willed Queen Maeve of Connacht has a 'pillow-conversation' with her husband Aillil, a man of weak character, whom she informs arrogantly that she could have married many a better man but chose him because she was confident that he was not the man to interfere with anything she did. There is a gay, carefree humour and whimsicality in the preliminary part of the tale that is a recurrent characteristic in Irish literature. As the drama develops, this changes into an altogether more serious and elevated mood and manner. The pillow-conversation ends in Queen Maeve's decision to collect her cattle and spread out her household wealth for comparison with the corresponding possessions of Aillil in order to see which of them owned most. The wealth of husband and wife was seen to be exactly equal except in one item. A bull of Maeve's, it seems, had gone over to Aillil's cattle because he thought it unbecoming in a bull to be managed by a woman—one of the many satirical touches in the work. When the Queen learned the facts, she was deeply annoyed to discover that she was even to this small extent poorer than her husband. From this annoyance her jealousy and pride rose to inspire action. She determined on an expedition to Cooley to capture the greatest and most famous animal in all Ireland: *an Donn Cuailgne,* 'The Brown Bull of Cooley'. The *Iliad* starts from the beauty and frailty of woman; the *Táin* from woman's pride and jealousy. For Homer, as for the anonymous Irish storyteller, woman could be a good starting-point, as lesser literary artists have since then noticed. From the Prologue we go on to the preparation of the expedition, the mobilization and first movements of the Queen of Connacht's army, and at this stage she became aware of a formidable foe whom she would have to face, the great *Cú-Chulainn,* offspring of Lugh the god, whose divine powers he inherits, and so called because at the age of six he had slain *Cú,* the fabulous watchdog of *Culann* the smith, this giving him the unusual name which means 'Hound of Culann'. Maeve is curious to know all about her potential adversary, and makes enquiries of her court adviser, Fergus, who duly relates in great detail the 'boy-deeds' of the mysterious Cúchulainn, warning the Queen that, although he is but a youth of seventeen, she may find him more than a match for her forces. Next come accounts of the long series of Cúchulainn's single-handed combats, some trivial and gay, some highly bombastic, becoming more serious as the telling proceeds and culminating in his great fight with an old comrade Ferdia. This is followed by a rout of Maeve's whole forces at Magh Murthemne, the district of Dundalk in County Louth. After this battle the warriors of Ulster awaken from their mental depression, shake off the spell of feebleness that was on them, rouse themselves from their lethargy. Whatever miracle happened was due to the inspiration of the god-like Cúchulainn. From it the northerners became different men, taking on many of the qualities of the Great One who had inspired them. They gathered, group by group, clan by clan, on the Hill of Slane, and then comes a final struggle in the Battle of Gairech and Ilgairech, the ultimate rout of Maeve's beaten army, and the wonderful climax of a desperate and noble fight between Maeve's bull, Finn-benna, and the Donn, 'The Brown Bull of Cooley', with the triumph of the latter. But the Donn also had suffered in the fight and the *Táin* logically ends:

> *At the hour of eve*
> *The women and young lads and little folk*
> *Within the beautiful, high-mountained cantred*
> *Of Cooley of blossomful sweet-watered glens,*
> *Were wailing for their Donn of Cooley. Then*
> *They saw him where he came approaching them.*
> *But there was on him blindness and great ire,*
> *Because of his sore wounds. He, storming on,*
> *Stormed up amongst them; and full many there,*
> *Of women and young lads and little folk,*
> *Fell on that hill-slope of high Cooley, slain*
> *By their own Donn of Cooley. He lay down*
> *Against the hill, and his great heart broke there,*
> *And sent a stream of blood down all the slope;*
> *And thus when all this war and Táin had ended,*
> *In his own land, 'midst his own hills, he died.*[1]

The men—and women, for there were some great ones—of the Revival did not and could not all turn to the Gaelic texts for their inspiration; nor did they have to. A born storyteller and Irish scholar, Standish O'Grady, wrote in English the whole story of Cúchullainn in his own words in three volumes [2] which, I should say, have had almost as much political as they have had literary influence. O'Grady caught the spirit of the Red Branch cycle, and he wrote his interpretation of it in a vigorous and effective prose. His work was popular, but it remained for young George Russell (Æ) to find in it the key to a new attitude towards life which this far-seeing man thought essential for Irish nationalism. Here are Æ's words, quoted from his Introduction to the first volume: "When I close my eyes, and brood in memory over the books which most profoundly affected me, I find none

[1] Eleanor Hull's translation.

[2] (1) *The Coming of Cuchullain;* (2) *In the Gates of the North;* (3) *The Triumph and Passing of Cuchullain.* By Standish O'Grady. Published by The Talbot Press, Dublin.

which excited my imagination more than Standish O'Grady's epical narrative of Cúchullainn. Whitman said of his *Leaves of Grass*: 'Camerado, this is no book: who touches this touches a man', and O'Grady might have boasted of his Bardic *History of Ireland,* written with his whole being, that there was more than a man in it, there was the soul of a people, its noblest and most exalted life symbolized in the story of one heroic character. . . . When I read O'Grady I was as a man who suddenly feels ancient memories rushing at him, and knows that he was born in a royal house, that he had mixed with the mighty of heaven and earth and had the very noblest for his companions. . . . That is what O'Grady did for me and for others who were my contemporaries. . . ."

O'Grady's trilogy must be strange reading for the non-Irish person, and I have heard more than one English friend say that they could not understand it and therefore could not read much of it. The themes, the treatment, the ideas are far more remote for the average English reader than Homer, because there is a tradition of classical education in England, the ideas of Rome and Greece having permeated English literature, and Latin and Greek continue to have effect on the language. If there was an English tradition in regard to Ireland, it was based on a conqueror's attitude, which included a great contempt for and ignorance of all things truly Irish. It even included a policy calculated to make the Irish forget their own language and ancient culture and almost to despise themselves. That a mere cattle-drive should be the subject of an epic seems comic to those who do not realize that cattle-drive in that Irish sense merely meant a campaign to gain wealth and achieve power. It is anything but comic. O'Grady realized very thoroughly that his task was a difficult one, because he was writing for an Ireland which had all but forgotten its old self after centuries of foreign rule, exploitation and misery. In presenting his work he says: "I have endeavoured so to tell the story as to give a general idea of the Cycle, and of primitive heroic Irish life as reflected in that literature, laying the Cycle, so far as accessible, under contribution to furnish forth the tale. Within a short compass I would bring before swift modern readers the more striking aspects of a literature so vast and archaic as to repel all but students." O'Grady felt that what he was doing was important; even he could hardly have foreseen the consequences. To George Russell and many other intelligent men in Ireland it was a beacon. To some it was even more, for it made them think that beneath a surface which promised little and seemed to be set hard, there might be remaining some of the fires and strength of an apparently extinct volcano. From that it began to set them thinking of how to release and guide that strength in the long-term interests of the people, in the cause of national pride and dignity. It disinterred and revivified what had seemed to be a corpse. From such beginnings came the Literary Revival that, although not so intended, seems miraculously to have been conceived to be a natural propaganda in tune with and on behalf of the political and national resurgence which showed itself in the language revival, in the Sinn Fein Movement, in that deeply symbolical Easter Week Rebellion of 1916, and in the campaign and struggle for Independence which ended with the Treaty of 1921.

The Red Branch Cycle was, because of its compactness, power and unity, the principal source from which the impelling inspiration was drawn. The period of its events would be that of the birth of Christ. But the Fenian or Ossianic Cycle cannot be placed below it in importance, and in the opinion of many is to be preferred as literature. The name is given to a collection of tales in prose and verse dealing with the exploits of the great Finn MacCool[1] and the *Fianna Eireann* or body of 'Fenians', picked men of remarkable physical prowess who were often poets and philosophers and who flourished in the third century A.D. To these stories is added a collection of very beautiful Nature poems and lyrical poetry. From the name of Oisin, their traditional writer, they have been called the Ossianic tales and poems, especially since James MacPherson's travesty of them in English during the eighteenth century. Much of the literature of the Fenian Cycle cannot be dated—it is not certain when it was either begun or completed—but the tales and poems, having been a tradition for hundreds of years, came strongly into favour among the poets and intellectuals of twelfth-century Ireland

[1] In Gaelic *Fionn MacCumhaill.*

and continued to be elaborated for almost another five hundred years.

As the Red Branch is a contrast to the Mythological Cycle, so the Fenian is a contrast to both. One reason why it is so highly esteemed is because the spirit is democratic and we do not find in it the aristocratic, superior and often pompous strain, not to mention the blood and violence, of the Red Branch. Some of the old magic and many of the myths reappear in the Fenian tales, but perhaps their greatest claim to favour is that they cover all Ireland and are not, like the Red Branch, limited to one province.

The 'Fenians of Erin' (*Fianna Eireann*) are presented in the tales as a select military order or Samurai devoted in service to the high king and to the repulsion of invaders from abroad. The name reappeared in the Fenian Order which came into existence in the nineteenth century; and today there is the *Fianna Fáil,* the name given to the political party of Mr. de Valera. The leader of the ancient Fenians at the time of their greatest power and renown was Finn MacCool, whose son Oisin—called Usheen and Ossian in English —is the traditional poet-author. Finn and the Fenians were regarded as realities by the later annalists who put the stories in writing, and the stories as sober history. But this need not be taken too seriously, because for one thing there were no invaders during that period and the Fenian tales have no resemblance to history as now established. They are, in most senses, tales of fairyland; but that does not render them the less effective. The storytelling and poetry, the rich imaginative qualities shown in the tales endear them to the Irish and also to the Scottish Gaels. Finn MacCool, like Cúchullainn, had an ancestry which dated back to the gods of the mythological age, of the Dé Danann. Finn (the 'Fair One') at an early stage of his career, we are told, went to an ancient sage and Druid named Finegas, who lived on a bank of the River Boyne, to learn from him science and the art of poetry. Rolleston recounts: "Here, in a pool of this river, under boughs of hazel from which dropped the Nuts of Knowledge on the stream, lived Fintan the Salmon of Knowledge, which whoso ate of him would enjoy all the wisdom of the ages. Finegas had many a time sought to catch this salmon, but failed until Finn had come to be his pupil. Then one day he caught it, and gave it to Finn to cook, bidding him eat none of it himself, but to tell him when it was ready. When the lad brought the salmon, Finegas saw that his countenance was changed. 'Hast thou eaten of the salmon?' he asked. 'Nay,' said Finn, 'but when I turned it on the spit my thumb was burnt, and I put it to my mouth.' 'Take the Salmon of Knowledge and eat it,' then said Finegas, 'for in thee the prophecy is come true. And now go hence, for I can teach thee no more.' After that Finn became as wise as he was strong and bold, and it is said that whenever he wished to divine what would befall, or what was happening at a distance, he had but to put his thumb to his mouth and bite it, and the knowledge he wished for would be his." With such an ancestry and so auspicious a start, we know what we may expect of the hero; and we are never disappointed. Adventure follows on adventure. Life generally, we realize, is altogether gentler and less violent in the Fenian stories than in those of the Red Branch. The Fenians often show themselves as real poets and have a philosophy expressed in timeless maxims:

> Without a fault of his, beat not thy hound; until thou ascertain her guilt, bring not a charge against thy wife.
>
> In battle meddle not with a fool; for, O mac Luga, he is but a fool.
>
> Stand not up to take part in a brawl; have naught to do with a madman or a wicked one.
>
> Two-third of thy gentleness be shown to women, to little children and to poets; and be not violent to the common people.
>
> Utter not swaggering speech, nor say thou wilt not yield what is right; it is shameful to speak too stiffly unless that it be feasible to carry out thy words.
>
> Be more apt to give than to deny, and follow after gentleness.

The code of behaviour was chivalrous, elevating, and on the whole seems to be far above that which we read of as prevailing among other European peoples of the period. It is true that the members of the Fenian Order were not average men; and one must make allowance for that. But the mere fact that they had such a noble code of behaviour, and in a period usually regarded as primitive if not barbarous, is an indication that a deep moral and ethical sense was not lacking. We look in vain for anything approaching it in contemporary literatures.

Usheen the poet and traditional author of the tales was Finn's son, born of Saba, the fairest of women, who was changed into a deer by the stroke of a hazel wand held by a phantom enchanter in Finn's form. When Finn returned home from his travels and adventures, Saba was gone, and he sought her in the glens and forests. One day on Ben Bulben he heard the bay of his hounds change to yelping, and discovered the cause of this to be a boy who lay under a great tree. This boy, he learnt afterwards, was his son, and Finn called him Usheen (Oisin), which means Little Fawn. Later, Usheen meets Niam of the Golden Hair, daughter of the King of the Land of Youth, and she asks him to go with her to the land of her father. They go together, and from that story we have the beautiful *Wanderings of Usheen,* one of Yeats's early poems.

The Fenian Cycle is much more elaborate and covers far more ground than the Red Branch. As already stated, it gained in popularity in the eleventh century, in the period after Brian Boru's victory over the Norsemen. One appreciates why it should gain in favour when it was a question of dealing with invaders; why it should maintain its hold on the mind of the people after the defeat of the Norsemen and during the Anglo-Norman invasion; during the later Plantations; and during the resurgence of the late nineteenth century. Those who are interested will find an outline of the tales in Rolleston. More need not be said of them here, except to add that with them goes that collection of Nature and lyrical poetry which must be left to speak for itself. The Cycle includes some fine narratives of Irish patriotism, and the long and beautifully told story of Diarmuid and Gráinne. Perhaps the best story of all is that of Usheen in the Land of Youth, *Tír na nÓg,* the ancient Irish land of dreams, heaven of all delights, which has about it a great gaiety and vigorous good health, an enchantment and carefree happiness to make it compare well with any other conceptions of heaven which men's minds have formed. The conception of *Tír na nÓg* captures the heart. The Fenian Cycle has not only a great charm. It represents the Irish genuis for imaginative storytelling at its best; and its short poems and lyrics are as lovely as those to be found in any other literature.

CHAPTER V

THE MODERN MIND

Ill fares the land, to hastening ills a prey
Where wealth accumulates, and men decay:
Princes and lords may flourish, or may fade;
A breath can make them, as a breath has made;
But a bold peasantry, their country's pride,
When once destroyed can never be supplied.
From Goldsmith's *Deserted Village.*

1

The Irish Mind and the Ascendancy

THIS is not intended as a history or even as a sketch of Irish literature, nor as a critical evaluation of the literary tradition or writing. What has been dealt with in the preceding sections is intended merely to show in the broadest strokes the way of thinking and attitude towards life as manifested in the Cycles. A careful analysis of that way of thinking is not necessary to discover, as many observers have noted, that although there is a persistent conservatism in the Irish mind, it also often runs to extremes. This shows itself in almost everything. There has always been, for example, and there still is a tendency among the Irish (as among the Spaniards) to see things in terms of black or white and seldom of grey. One finds that when there is goodness in the Irish, it can be very good; and when there is badness, it can be very bad indeed. Furthermore, both extremes are not unusual in the same person. We find the extremes of violence; and of gentleness and piety. Extremes of passion; and of coldness. Great gaiety and laughter; and a sadness to touch any heart. We find many manifestations of ruthlessness; and as many or more of soft-heartedness. The list of opposites can be extended almost as you wish, and to include almost all the qualities of the human being. The happy medium of the English is rare. There is, however, one feature of all these extremes and extremisms in which the Irish excel, and that is in their capacity for what most other peoples would regard as a lightning change from one frame of mind to its opposite. This remarkable capacity has often won for them the reputation of being unpredictable, which is largely nonsense; and as unreliable, which indicates a wrong assessment on the part of the observer. What it amounts to is that what seems to be a change of mind may be shown in words which, when it comes to action, need not indicate any change of mind so fundamental as to become the opposite to what it was a moment previously. Enough is not known about the early invasions of Ireland for us to be able to say that all the invaders fell into this error, but the English of the Plantations, those who were to become the Ascendancy, were thoroughly mistaken about the mentality of the Irish, and in nothing except in one thing were they more completely wrong than in believing the Irish to be unpredictable and unreliable. This one thing was the effect of the Irish mind—of the Irish people, that is—upon those who had chosen to live in constant contact with them. The English and Scottish planters in a couple of generations became transmogrified into other beings who were, so to speak, infected with the Irish virus. Those planters grew into what a Freudian might call new 'psychological types' which differed from their original types but were not to be 100 per cent. Irish. They might try to hold themselves aloof from the Irish, but in many ways they began to have an Irish way of thinking and in many respects to adopt an Irish attitude towards life. This often made them run to those extremes noted above as characteristic of the Irish. In combination with what they may have inherited as characteristics from English or Scottish ancestors, or acquired by their environment in Ireland, it was to have far-reaching effects on Irish history. What is of particular interest is that even those very effects showed the same tendency to run to extremes, good and bad. One would look far, for example, to find worse oppressors or exploiters than some of the Ascendancy landowners. One would go just as far to find better, more humane or more intelligent men than many who by birth and upbringing were members of that same Ascendancy. The very bad were counterbalanced by the very good.

There is another point worthy of notice: the surviving

Anglo-Normans imbued with the Irish spirit must have influenced the Planters, and passed on to them many Irish traditions. Furthermore, it required only a generation to create among most of the newcomers the feeling that they were more Irish than English. There was increasing intermarriage between them and the Irish. But it was an *Ascendancy* and it remained an Ascendancy until the present century, and it was this Ascendancy plus what I have called elsewhere the 'Descendancy', the 'real Irish', from which has come the Ireland of today. In matters of culture the Ascendancy lost none of its influence until the Treaty of 1921, and even since then, when it ceased absolutely to have political power, the cultural influence remained fast. Whatever may have been their political and social sins, or their failure in other respects, Ireland owes much on the credit and creditable side to those Anglo-Irish.

For some time after the first Plantation the sons of Ascendancy gentlemen were either educated privately or they were sent to English schools and universities. But the Ascendancy duly began to found schools and, in 1591, under a charter from Queen Elizabeth, they founded the College of the 'Holy and Undivided Trinity', to be known as Trinity College, Dublin, or Dublin University, the greatest of all the Ascendancy educational establishments. T.C.D., as it was popularly called, in its long and honourable history, proved itself to be a work of genius in the sense spoken of by Heine when he says that "a work of genius goes farther than genius itself". In some mysterious way T.C.D. imparted to those who became its students a humanist, rational outlook with a tendency to judge things from a rather cold, intellectual standpoint while maintaining high standards of scholarship. It can reasonably be argued that nothing could have been better for the sons of a ruling class scattered over the face of the country, comfortably off as regards money, but often by their isolation and easy circumstances tempted into excesses. Or for those young men who, not being so well provided with this world's goods, could enter the College as 'sizars' with certain relaxations of fees, and thus obtain the same benefits of liberal education as those available to the more fortunate financially. But if these advantages were good for the minds of the young men of the Ascendancy, they were to prove of inestimable all-round advantage to Ireland, to the Ireland of the ordinary people and exploited. The University of Dublin became a receiving-station for progressive ideas, for those of English and continental literary, intellectual and political movements. From this it became a nursery of ideas which went so far as to include the liberation of Ireland from Ascendancy and English rule. And so it was that Anglo-Ireland nourished within itself the seeds of its own destruction.

Trinity College, Dublin, created and nursed to maturity the genius which made the eighteenth century a Golden Age for the Anglo-Irish Ascendancy, an age which, among its other creations, gave to Ireland the very beautiful city of Dublin with its spacious planning and wealth of fine architecture, lovely old houses and pleasant atmosphere. Outside of Dublin and from one end of Ireland to the other the Anglo-Irish country gentlemen built for themselves fine mansions in worthy settings. Theirs was a cultured society in the classical spirit; a society apart from that of the native Irish. When the Anglo-Irish began to produce literature it was largely in the English and not the Irish tradition, though there was often to be found in it a spirit not found in the English literature of that or of any preceding period. There were three main influences at work: England and its traditions and literature; Ireland and its people and their traditions; and that of the University of Dublin. In T.C.D. the 'intelligentsia' of the Ascendancy had a crucible, a melting-pot, an educational and cultural apparatus from which Irish causes and Irish ideas were not excluded and by its very nature could never be excluded. Nearly all the great writers of the Ascendancy in the eighteenth century passed through T.C.D. and, even when they did not pass out with a degree, they always brought with them into the world a good measure of its rational, humanist urbanity; its aloofness and avoidance of sentiment; its respect for scholarship; and its cultivated wit, which was often well mixed with a satirical or cynical outlook. What a list of writers that is! Swift, Burke, Berkeley, Goldsmith and Sheridan wrote classics which have become part of the European cultural heritage.

In that Ireland were men who left their mark, not only on literature, but on philosophy, science and scholarship in general. Modern physics leading to the 'Atomic Age' began with Robert Boyle, a son of the Earl of Cork. His work, *The Sceptical Chemist,* is a landmark in the evolution of modern science. William Molyneux, a Dubliner and T.C.D. man, not only distinguished himself in astronomy and optics, but wrote a little book calling for Irish economic independence which politically inspired, not only a later generation of Irishmen, but also the makers of the American Revolution. Sir Richard Steele, of the famous *Essays* published originally in the *Tatler* and the *Spectator,* was a Dubliner. Laurence Sterne showed in all his works, but especially in *Tristram Shandy,* distinguishable Irish characteristics; he was born in Clonmel. Richard Brinsley Sheridan, another Dubliner, was the best dramatist England had since the death of Shakespeare; and his work still lives. The Protestant T.C.D. man, Theobald Wolfe Tone, another great Dubliner, best known as an Irish patriot and as the founder of Irish Republicanism, was also a distinguished man of letters who left in his *Autobiography* and *Journals* works in which the style is delightful and vivacious like that of Goldsmith.

Among the writers of the period, Swift stands in isolated grandeur, a solitary figure, a genius whose writings include, not only the greatest satire, *Gulliver's Travels,* but in the *Drapier's Letters* the greatest political polemical writing in the English language. As a pamphleteer he is unsurpassed. He it was who wrote telling the Irish that they must "burn everything from England except her coals"; and, if he did not implant, he at least inspired ideas which came strongly into those of Irish patriots from his time onwards. In more than one respect Swift was an original spirit, but there is one aspect of his humour in which this Anglo-Irishman of the Ascendancy provides us with examples of a kind that hardly existed, if it existed at all, in English literature before him and has been comparatively rare in English, though not in Irish speech and writing. The Germans call it *Galgenhumor* ('gallows humour'), and the French *l'humour noir* ('black humour'). There is no phrase for it in English, and that fact speaks for itself. It is the flippant or whimsical treatment of

Glendalough—Co. Wicklow
ITA

Creamery—Dingle, Co. Kerry ITA

Fair Day in Killarney ITA

a serious or even grim subject, in which the light and seeming detachment of the humour has behind it a deep feeling of unhappiness in regard to the subject referred to. A perfect example of it is Swift's 'Modest Proposal'. No writer has ever used this powerful weapon of the malcontent to greater effect than Dean Swift. The English did not always understand what was behind it, but the Irish knew and fully appreciated the profound spiritual misery and rage from which it sprang, for these feelings were their own and the grim, whimsical humour a part of their nature. This endeared Swift to them, so that they overlooked his shortcomings; to them he is and always will be a great Irishman, though his origin was English.

A strong sense of the macabre is an Irish characteristic; and so also is flippancy in grave circumstances. The sense of the macabre is shown in the work of many Irish and Anglo-Irish writers from Swift to Maturin, Le Fanu and Bram Stoker, and in that of Edgar Allan Poe, an American of Anglo-Irish origin. The flippancy is well exemplified in the works of Oscar Wilde and George Bernard Shaw. Shaw's family originally came from Scotland, settled in Hampshire, and one of them (a William Shaw) went to Ireland in the army of William III duly to receive a grant of forfeited land in Kilkenny, on which the Shaws lived for generations as members of the Ascendancy. Shaw, so far as I can find, had in him a Celtic strain from his remote Scottish ancestors and no more; the rest was English and Anglo-Irish. Where could one find a more Irish spirit than in his work? But I need not pursue this course farther, for I think that enough has been said to indicate a truth in those words I have already quoted which Shaw puts into the mouth of Broadbent the Englishman: "Ireland, Sir, for good or evil, is like no other place under heaven; and no man can touch its sod or breathe its air without becoming better or worse." It was from those alien settlers who, regarded from the Irish point of view, became *better* that arose the movement which was to change the face of Ireland. But not its mind.

2
Renaissance

It is interesting now, thirty years or so after the events leading up to the Treaty, to read some of the things said about the Irish by those who disliked them and their campaign for political freedom. One English writer paid this tribute: "Now," says he, "you can beat the Irish in battle, you can beat them in industry, you can beat them in scholarship, you can beat them in statesmanship, you can shame them in art and dwarf them in letters. And when I say 'you' I mean any breed, whether paltry or noble of mind, whose will has raised it to the status of a people. But you cannot beat the Irish in propaganda. In the hands of an Irish apologist, not only is white made black and black made white, green made purple and orange made red, but pale pink, at one swift gesture and the briefest of incantations, becomes all the bloodier colours of the spectrum." [1] That is high praise, coming from such a source; though I wonder where an Irish apologist is to be found, as that kind of Irish person must be as rare as the black swan. Nevertheless, one cannot but sympathize with this splenetic commentator's observation about propaganda. The great Hubert, in his work on the Celts, noted that from the earliest times they distinguished themselves as expositors, teachers, missionaries and persuaders. It is equally true that the Irish in most things show a strange obstinacy about being moved to action, but when they are moved they can become tirelessly active and energetic, a latent dynamism springing into life. In Ireland this became abundantly evident in the nineteenth-century campaigns for Catholic Emancipation, Land Reform, and in the Literary Revival which began in the 1890s and became allied to the political campaign which ended with the Treaty of 1921. In all these campaigns the Irish proved themselves remarkable propagandists. And among the greatest of the propagandists who worked hand in hand with native Irishmen for the conservation of the language, traditions and old Irish spirit as well as for national freedom,

[1] *The Impossible Irish,* by Tom Penhaligon.

were men and women of the Ascendancy. The collaboration existed from Wolfe Tone, Robert Emmett, Thomas Davis and Parnell onwards to Douglas Hyde, a Protestant who founded and inspired the Gaelic Revival. This Anglo-Irishman, a product of Trinity College, Dublin, was to become President of the New Irish Free State from 1938 to 1944; but it was in the field of culture rather than of politics that he most distinguished himself. Hyde was the man who set the Irish on the way to a return to their language and traditions; and that, with what is called the Literary Revival which began about the same time, helped greatly to bring about the transformation from which has come the contemporary Ireland we now know.

There is no need to tell in any detail the story of either the Gaelic Revival or of the Literary Revival. Those stories have been adequately told again and again. But it is necessary to stress the strongly romantic element that combined with nostalgia and sentimentality to provide both the driving force and the appeal of the Literary Revival. The work of scholars on the old literature, the work of popularizers (such as Standish O'Grady in retelling the stories of the Red Branch), the vision of men such as George Russell—all this began to affect the younger generation in the nineties. And in that younger generation the most important figure to appear was William Butler Yeats, a man who was to become, in the opinion of many critics, the dominant poet of English literature during the first half of our century, and whose influence and importance seem to be firmly established. But it is not as a poet that Yeats had most influence in Ireland, though that influence need not be underestimated. It is as an inspiring personality and in his suggestiveness. Yeats very largely *was* the Literary Revival, in that he inspired, stimulated, and in an odd and mystical sort of way kept organizers and writers to their work. His was the restless, dreaming spirit which pervaded their activities; and in those activities he was also the leader. We ought therefore to look for a moment at this man and his achievement, for in Yeats we have the apotheosis of the Anglo-Irishman at his best and most beneficially influential. The very qualities and achievements which Yeats, a man of the Ascendancy, regarded as the ideal to be aimed at by the Irish were among the most powerful of those forces which brought the Anglo-Irish Ascendancy to its end. Yeats helps us to understand modern Ireland.

John Butler Yeats, father of the poet, was the son of an episcopalian rector. His mother, Susan Pollexfen of Sligo before her marriage, has been described as a deep, instinctive woman who would at any time rather hear a ghost story or a fairy-tale from a peasant than listen to the finest flight of abstract theorizing by a good thinker. If the poet inherited or acquired this same propensity from his mother, he himself and many who followed his career closely seem to be agreed that his father's influence not only shaped his youth but continued until the old man died in 1922. John Butler Yeats was in every way an exceptional man. The son of a clergyman, he became a sceptic. Brought up in the Ascendancy as a Unionist, that is, as a Conservative, he became a strong Irish nationalist. The scepticism and nationalism were nursed to become a part of him while he was still a student at Trinity College, Dublin, and reading law with the intention of becoming a barrister, the career planned for him by his father. At this time he was a member of the Law Students' Debating Society, in which a student took one or the other side of a 'case' for practice in the art of advocacy. We can form some idea of the way John Butler Yeats must have been thinking even then, from a remarkably iconoclastic speech he made propounding the shocking suggestion that, instead of concentrating on rhetoric for the sake of effect and to win a case, the real aim of debate and argument should be the honest pursuit of truth. One year after he was called to the bar, the law had seen the last of him; having inherited some money, he decided to become a painter. He was a competent and sympathetic though never a great artist, but happily for posterity he was, with all his many foibles, intensely honest, widely cultured and a clear thinker on fundamental things. In his letters to his son William, there is throughout a humanist spirit, an individualist philosophy and a sane, intelligent attitude towards life. To William Butler Yeats those letters received in adult life from his father took the place of a university education, for the young man feared that he could not pass the entrance examination and therefore could never enter T.C.D. His mother always regarded him as backward; his father thought that he needed special intellectual care; and his schoolmaster had pronounced him 'hopeless'. From his strange and not too promising background in the worldly sense came the great poet of modern Ireland.

He read the work of Standish O'Grady on the advice of George Russell, and from that stirring account of the Red Branch Cycle he went on to the Fenian and other stories of ancient Ireland. Yeats was at this time writing lyrical poems, delicate, beautiful poems well in the tradition of Allingham and other Anglo-Irish poets. But now from the old Cycles he drew an entirely new conception and, from a stage of groping and fumbling with ideas and with life, he emerged almost overnight to become a man with a mission which was to begin with what seemed to his friends a visionary project: to make Irish myth the theme of a new art and new poetry. It so happened that the ground was being prepared for this by scholars and enthusiasts—Douglas Hyde, Eleanor Hull and Father Patrick Dinneen were their leaders—who were toiling night and day to revive, edit, translate and order the mass of forgotten or half-forgotten and greatly neglected works in Gaelic: the folk-lore, tales, songs, proverbs and traditions of that Ireland which had almost disappeared. Here was a series of fortunate coincidences of which Yeats took the fullest advantage. His was the romantic, the heroic approach to the revival. He threw himself into it with great energy and, as regards his poetry, with a single-mindedness which never wavered during the rest of his life, but in which the themes widened and his power increased as the years passed. The curious feature of all this is that in some way (which friends explained as due to his studies in esoteric Buddhism) this man Yeats penetrated deeply into that world of Gaelic magic—the world of the Mythological and of the other Cycles—and from it transmitted by his own magic an astonishing and infectious inspiration. The material was there, the moment was right, and in Yeats the man of that moment appeared.

It was now, around the turn of the century, that the Irish

Literary Theatre was conceived and came into being. By this time Yeats had written his great poetical play 'The Countess Cathleen', Edward Martin his 'Heather Field' and George Moore his 'Bending of the Bough', Alice Milligan, 'The Last Feast of the Fianna', and Douglas Hyde surpassed them with a *tour de force* in Irish, the first Gaelic play that was ever acted in a theatre. To Yeats the stage appealed as the best platform for his poetry, and the theatre as the best apparatus for propagating the new ideas. Yeats, Martin and Hyde were joined by that remarkable dynamo in human form, Lady Gregory, who brought to the group, not only her energy, but her influence with moneyed people ready to support the venture, and also her considerable organizing ability. The Abbey Theatre was founded in 1904, combining all these talents and embracing many others. In the Abbey Theatre 'ham acting' was not permitted, and here, at last, Irish actors were able to find plays worthy of their great natural ability—in the rich and musical 'Irish-English' of the dialogue, in the dramatic poetry of Yeats, and in the extravaganzas of John Millington Synge. The latter's 'Playboy of the Western World' caused a riot in the theatre. Some members of the audience thought that the 'playboy' idea was carried a little too far by the author, and therefore travestied Irish character. Synge was a Yeats product, if such a term can be applied to a playwright. Yeats found him wasting his time in Paris trying to turn himself into a literary man on the French model; and told him to get back to Irish-Ireland and study the peasants, their speech and life. Synge went to the Aran Isles, learnt Gaelic and the English of western Ireland, and wrote his now famous plays. But for Yeats he might not have done so, and literature would be so much the poorer. Yeats had an influence on every Irish writer with whom he came into contact. He had a capacity for divination which enabled him to tell a puzzled writer wherein his strength or weakness lay; and such was his personality that he could do this without giving offence to the most sensitive, though he never tolerated literary or other fools, bores or vulgarians. In this way he provided inspiration for innumerable works of poetry, drama and prose by Irish writers during his lifetime. Not all the writers who benefited by his advice have acknowledged the fact, but those who have done so leave us in no doubts about its value. Yet, in all the good things that Yeats did, perhaps the greatest was that, by precept and example, he made Irish writers realize that Ireland was rich enough to provide them with all the material they could ever require, and that by keeping to their own people and their own native soil and atmosphere, they could produce better work than by looking elsewhere. To the Irish, his early work still has a greater appeal than his later, which is very different and greatly influenced by ideas which came from Ezra Pound.

The Gaelic Revival, the Literary Revival, the Irish Literary Theatre—these three elements were all part of a veritable Renaissance, a 'renaissance of wonder' on a small scale no doubt, but of the greatest importance to Ireland. The story of the growing national spirit of which this renaissance was an integral part requires only the story of the political developments of the same period to round it off. Politics, Literature and Theatre helped one another in the national resurgence. It was never a *littérature engagée,* never a literature based on a political ideology or co-ordinated and controlled by authority. The spirit was free, as free as it has ever been anywhere; freer than in the Ireland which came from that great movement. When politics and the physical effort rose to play their part, the ground was already well prepared. Ireland, Anglo-Ireland side by side with Irish-Ireland, won in the struggle—of which the year 1921 marks the end.

From then on we have a new Ireland with its uneasy geographical division, new people wielding power, many new ideas. The North retained its own Ascendancy; in The South the days of the Ascendancy had ended. Because of the political division, the new Ireland is not entirely at ease. But this is not the place to pursue that story.

We have come to modern Ireland, and with that we must deal.

3
Changing Face and Unchanging Mind

The term 'Modern Ireland' can be misleading if it conveys the idea that all Ireland is a modern country. It certainly is not, at all events in 'The South'; and only Belfast in The North can claim to have caught the modern spirit. The period referred to in these remarks is that from the end of the Second World War onwards. This is written in the spring of 1951; the mid-century is a convenient date for such rough estimates and valuations as follow.

As I see it, and from all that I can hear or read, that part of the country known politically as Northern Ireland (and popularly as the 'Six County Area', or simply as 'The North') has been affected since Partition in a variety of ways, often to a considerable degree, and mostly with a definite tendency in one direction. Outside of Belfast it is becoming more and more like an English agricultural area; say, like the West Country counties of Somerset, Devon and Cornwall. In this I mean the way it strikes a first-time visitor who is not looking deeper than the surface. Belfast grows more and more like an English industrial city. Here there is modernity: on all sides one can see evidence of a fairly straight line of progress as the word is now used. In Belfast you will find machinery, manufacturing, business (even big business), up-to-dateness in those little things of the surface which show both a desire and alertness not to get behind the times. The visitor who goes from England and enters Ireland by Belfast will not see much to surprise him merely by looking at the city or its people. He may feel that he is at home. But, when he begins to talk to the inhabitants of that northern city, he will know immediately that he is dealing with a mind which is anything but English, one that is narrower, sharper and tougher. When he leaves Belfast, goes into the country and engages in conversation with the people there, the difference in mentality is more striking. There is more 'Irishness' than 'Englishness' about the northern country folk, and the visitor will often find what he can easily recognize as a Scottish strain. When Ulster was 'planted' by English and Scottish settlers in the seventeenth century, the Plantation was thorough in most places though not complete anywhere. There remained pockets, enclaves of people who might be regarded as survivors of the Ulster Gaels. Even these were not quite the same people as the Gaels in the rest of Ireland: in some parts of Ulster there had been considerable communities of the old race of Cruithne or Picts, an extraordinarily tough people, perhaps not very brilliant intellectually, who must have mixed with the Celts—to tone them up in some ways and down in others. Maybe that early mixture of Cruithne and Celt explains the starkness of parts of the Red Branch tales; and later contributed towards the distinctive dourness of the contemporary Ulsterman that is often intermixed with a Celtic waywardness, an English sense of the practical or a Scottish canniness. Nothing could be more interesting—or at times more difficult—than to trace these strains and influences, ethnic and cultural, which contribute towards the make-up of the Ulster countryman. We can, however, see the final product; and it is a good one.

But to return. Has the Northern Irishman changed much since 1921? I do not think so, and I should say that, in mental make-up and general outlook, there has been as little fundamental change in the people of The North as in the people of The South. Changes in Ireland, when we examine them closely, are nearly always to be found on the surface or not far below it. The 'personality' of Ireland is like an iceberg: the greater part of it is concealed beneath the surface, and what is visible looks different from every angle and in every change of light. This curious personality floats on through time, through storm, mist and sunshine. Such changes as may happen are on an exposed surface, which is merely part of a hidden mass that changes, if at all, only imperceptibly.

Whoever would wish to test the truth of this should observe the attitude of the Irish mind towards time. I have said that the Irish mind has defeated time in the long-term sense. To it the past can be present, the present future; and by another stroke of the invisible wand, the present changed to the past. There are no difficulties in all this. But one might think that the vast influence of modern civilization, with its speeding up of life and sharp observance of time in terms of calendars and clocks, would have had effect on the Irish mind: to make it, say, a little more punctual, a little sharper in regard to keeping appointments, catching a train and so on. It has to be almost a matter of life and death before the Irish person will show the slightest concern about time in relation to such things. I have before me an Irish local newspaper in which there is a report of a function which upset the inhabitants of a good-sized town because, instead of beginning half an hour or an hour later than the hour advertised, it began punctually at that hour with not more than half a dozen people present. The full audience did turn up—an hour or so later! This does not happen in cities, or not too often. But it is the sort of thing happening every day in rural Ireland, has happened as far back as I can remember and will go on happening, no doubt. The stranger, accustomed to life in Britain or America, must be prepared not to be exasperated by this lack of concern for time; and, as it cannot be changed, make his allowances accordingly.

The surface change that has taken place in the Twenty-six Counties is greater than that in The North. But in spite of that, there is one thing the Republic of Ireland has not become: a modern country. This is not due, as many English and American people think, to sheer apathy and backwardness, but to a *choice of a way of life* which those Irish, rightly or wrongly, believe to be better for them, body and soul, than the way of life resulting from what the nineteenth century called progress. The French Revolution gave Wolfe Tone and the United Irishmen the idea of a free Republic, and there have been and still are Irishmen who are attracted by the broader ideas of Liberty, Equality and Fraternity which Tone and others learnt from France. Otherwise Ireland has ignored all social revolutions—the French, the industrial (except in Belfast), the Russian and even that mild reformism now being worked out in England and known as the Welfare State, though Northern Ireland gains something from this. The only social revolutionary Ireland produced since Wolfe Tone was James Connolly; and Connolly willingly sacrificed himself in the nationalist struggle, as Tone had done before him. If there could be a formula to represent what the present rulers of the Irish Republic are trying to do, it might be expressed thus: to achieve a stability based on their own ideas. If there is any other ambition, the signs of it are lacking. If this is near the mark, we are reminded of Hubert's observation to the effect that the ancient Celts liked that which pleased themselves. The modern Irish seem to think similarly; and they are indifferent to what others think of it. The stranger to Ireland can hardly fail to notice that the Irish care little or nothing about what others think of their chosen way of life. Their attitude is that of the English working man when he says of something that, if you don't like it, you can lump it! Sensitiveness to the world outside Ireland, and even curiosity about that outside world, do not disturb the dreams of the common man in this country.

To say that the Irish are indifferent to outside things is not to say that they are indifferent to people from outside Ireland whom they may meet. The visitor will pass under a close native scrutiny that has the object of discovering what he really is. This is judged more by the way he behaves than by the way he thinks or expresses himself in conversation. The Irish, being accustomed to their own flights of talk, tend not to take other people's talk too seriously; but they do take seriously how those other people behave. This has always been so; never has it been more noticeable than today. The Irish of The South have also strengthened the spiritual factor which separates them from two-thirds of the people of The North and from those of Britain. I mean their religion. Roman Catholicism is so fully accepted in The South that such a thing as religious discussion or argument seldom arises. The contemporary Irish Catholic shows respect and toleration for another man's religion, never proselytizes, but is deeply suspicious of any other attitude or behaviour in this respect on the part of that other man. Looking back on the Ireland of my time, it seems to me that Irish Catholicism has grown enormously in the secular power it has always held in the greater part of the country. This increase dates from the inception of the New Ireland in 1921. In this Ireland the non-Catholics get a fair, even a generous deal and, as they know their fellow-countrymen, those non-Catholics do not abuse the toleration they have so wisely been given. It is true there are many things which neither they nor, for that matter, many of the Catholics like. One of these is the literary censorship which (though understandable and in itself sanely conceived) tends in practice to produce results that are often incomprehensible either in Ireland or outside it. The Irish Censorship Board's primary function is to prevent the circulation of printed matter containing blasphemy, information on contraception, also obscenity or indecency, and this includes the vigorous branch of literature not always correctly defined as pornography. Nobody need take exception to the censorship's aims, if the principle is accepted. For all that, the Board consists of human beings and, no doubt, of human beings with a keen sense of their duty and therefore more inclined to suppress a borderline work than to allow it a circulation which might lower the high standard of morality and chastity that is deemed, by those best able to judge, to be essential for the good of the people. The Board cannot be accused of not being active and conscientious if we are to judge by the list of censored books which, I see, contains more than 2,000 titles, including those of works by the best writers of modern Ireland as well as of works by authors with an international reputation. The list causes surprise to whoever reads it, for it is often difficult for the person, Irish or English or American, who is not initiated, to understand why some of those books and authors are listed. No doubt there must be a reason. What is even more surprising and more inexplicable, if this were possible, is that the Censorship Board allows to circulate freely many books that are neither obscene nor indecent, but which most of us would regard as poisonous and pernicious. No doubt there must be a reason for that also. The subject is mentioned, not in a spirit of criticism, but rather in one of bewilderment, not only to inform the possible visitor to The South that the Censorship is a sore point with Irish writers (who are thereby often barred from their home market), but at the same time to explain why he may not always find the publications he may wish to read. It is nevertheless true that in Ireland most people find a way to obtain the books they really want, as they do everywhere else.

The new Ireland, North and South, is strongly against

Marxist Communism, and dislikes the ideology which is known as Nazi-Fascist. In the struggle for power that is taking place as this is written, with its division of the world into two camps facing one another uneasily, the whole of Ireland is in sympathy with the Atlantic Powers. It has been noted elsewhere that Beatrice Webb said that the Irish do not know the beginning of Socialism, and that every one of them is an individualist to the backbone. Her statement was made nearly half a century ago, but it is as true to-day of The South as it was then. The North tends to move with England; it moves slowly. Compared with either, England is an advanced country. The stranger may think as he or she pleases about this, but the less said about it to the Irish the better, for in The North it might be resented and in The South it would be taken to indicate that, whoever thought this, had not the slightest conception of their way of regarding what modern peoples call advance or progress, which most of those southerners do not want at any price. And, after all is said, the Irish have some strong arguments on their side in this, for it may be better to be a little 'backward' in other people's eyes than run the risks of becoming contaminated with some of the evils and unpleasantnesses that accompany or spring from what we call progress.

For the rest, Ireland remains—outside of Belfast—an essentially agricultural country: as before. The machinery and methods of agriculture have improved, marketing is better organized, and there have been all sorts of surface-changes, including that great one which has made the country one of peasant and yeomen farmers owning their land. The mind of the farmer has changed very little, North or South. It is true that there is the Irish language which is now taught in schools throughout The South, and that it is now an official language. One sees the beautiful Gaelic letters on official documents, in street names and so forth. Outside the few remaining far-away districts where the people retain their old speech, the visitor may not hear a word of it spoken. But it may be as well for him to realize that the teaching of the language to the rising generation must have *some* effect some time or other. It is not easy to calculate what the main effect will be, assuming that the teaching improves, and in the next generation the work now being done to intensify the dissemination and learning of Gaelic comes to fruition. Yet there is this to be said about it: the old language and its literature compel those who know them to think back with pride. That in itself can produce one of two possible effects. It might lead to general intellectual retrogression; or it might one day provide a new sort of inspiration. This last can hardly be expected in the present half-way stage, at best one of transition. Until the new inspiration comes, one waits and hopes. The revival and widespread teaching of Gaelic is an intensely interesting experiment, but, even although it is not yet a completely successful one, it need not be judged harshly or dismissed as just another Irish dream. One of the most disquieting things said by some critics is that the teaching of other subjects through the medium of Gaelic is having a serious effect on the general standard of education in The South. If this is true, the country is the loser.

A wit has said, "Ireland has a great future—and she always has had". The irony carries a half-truth. Nationalism has largely achieved its purpose and might now cool down but for Partition which helps to keep it alive. It is still strong in The South. Most southern Irishmen are consciously nationalists and, if they no longer parade their nationalism as they did before 1921, it takes little to rouse it to open declaration. In this also there is no deep change. Nor has there been any great change in literature. The writers now active come under two broad headings: those who are survivals from the Literary Revival and maintain many of its traditions, and those who have not been deeply affected by that Revival—even to react against it—and have not yet found a new and original conception of their work, or, if they have, there is not yet behind it the power or enthusiasm which enabled the writers of the 1890–1921 period to achieve such marvels. One thing the revival did—and did thoroughly. It brought about the disappearance of the 'Paddy and his Pig' school of literary exploiters. And after the Revival had done its main work, a new school of realistic writers came, and in their work showed that they had finished with the romantic and heroic conceptions behind that great creative episode in Ireland's history. If, as some critics believe, the new writers represented an inevitable reaction against the old, those new ones brought further honours to Ireland. Their work came like a blast of wind to blow away many cobwebs. O'Casey in the drama, O'Flaherty, O'Faolain, O'Connor in the short story, and Peadar O'Donnell in the novel, all showed that they had little to learn from the best of the Russian realists. James Joyce in *Ulysses* encompassed all the traditions, and to the writings about Dublin by Dubliners added his sombre, Rabelaisian masterpiece to provide one more Irish surprise in the list. If we think of Shaw, established as the greatest living dramatist and polemist in English, of Yeats as the dominant poet of the century and of Joyce's astonishing virtuosity as a prose-writer, we get some measure of what this small country is capable in the field of literary achievement.

The present is a period of transition in all the arts. The poetry remains, and the storytelling; but much of the folklore is now being forgotten, except in the Irish-speaking districts. The moment is approaching for something new and, if most of the Irish are indifferent to alien thought, this does not apply to all the writers, many of whom are sharply conscious of literary trends outside their own country. Nevertheless, it seems to be that, if you look at the main things which occupy the 'average' Irish mind—life, death, religion, politics, the market price of live-stock and farm produce and so forth—there has been no fundamental change of outlook. Inside this simple horizon, the people want to be and to remain themselves. The face of the country changes but not the mind.

One must, however, always allow for the incalculable and unpredictable in Ireland, for there is an indefinable freshness and sprightliness about the people of this old country which often makes them behave as if they were inhabitants of that 'Land of Youth' of the old myths. One sees and almost feels a freshness about them that is not to be expected of a country with such a past. And there is in this country of individualists a permanent element of surprise, or perhaps I should say more accurately of ability to astonish. That seems likely to remain and from it anything may come.

Minawn Cliffs—Achill, Co. Mayo

ITA

The Shannon Hydro-electric Scheme ITA

Loading Guinness's Stout in Grand Canal Harbour—Dublin ITA

PART II

SEEING IRELAND

It has been said that the Irish, notwithstanding a deep susceptibility of sorrow, are a light-hearted people; and this is strictly true. What, however, is the one fact but a natural consequence of the other? No man, for instance, ever possessed a high order of humour, whose temperament was not naturally melancholy; and no country in the world more clearly establishes that point than Ireland. Here the melancholy and mirth are not simply a proximate state, but frequently flash together, and again separate so quickly that the alteration or blending, as the case may be, whilst it is felt by the spectators, yet stands beyond all known rules of philosophy to solve it. Anyone at all acquainted with Ireland knows that in no country is mirth lighter, or sorrow deeper, or the smile and the tear seen more frequently on the face at the same moment. Their mirth, however, is not levity, nor is their sorrow gloom. . . .

WILLIAM CARLETON: Introduction to *Traits and Stories of the Irish Peasantry.*

CHAPTER I

CONVENIENT CENTRES AND EAST COAST

One morning Tim was rather full,
His head felt heavy which made him shake,
He fell from the ladder and broke his skull,
So they carried him home his corpse to wake.
They rolled him in a nice clean sheet,
And laid him out upon the bed,
With a gallon of whiskey at his feet,
And a barrel of porter at his head.

Finnegan's Wake.

1

Convenient Centres—Central Plain—Coastal Fringe

VISITORS to Ireland may be roughly divided into three categories, excluding those who are rich. We shall not greatly concern ourselves here with the rich, because, wherever they go, they live in a world of their own, all sorts of people being ready and eager to serve them with information and guidance of a nature to help them spend their money without having to think too deeply about what it is spent on. The rich are highly esteemed and carefully nursed by the commercially minded Irish, who are no different from commercially minded people elsewhere. That little homily completed, we may consider our three broad categories of visitors.

First, there are those vigorous and restless people, the young and others, who like to be always on the move, seeing much and with a constantly changing scene before their eyes as if looking at a film.

Second, those who like to settle in one place in order to take life easily in new surroundings, and whose main idea is to break the monotony of their normal home existence.

Third, there are those (I confess I come into the category) who prefer to pick upon some place as a 'convenient centre' or headquarters which may or may not itself be of exceptional interest, but (*a*) which provides reasonable amenities, and (*b*) to and from which one can move easily and quickly and thus have a number of really interesting places and scenes within a workable radius. By workable I mean that transport is available to enable the visitor to leave his 'headquarters' for a day and be back the same evening or night. Nearly all the popular Irish seaside resorts are of this nature. They have the usual disadvantages of popular seaside resorts everywhere: for example, in that rooms must be booked ahead, these are not always available, and once a seaside town has become popular, there is a tendency on the part of its inhabitants to regard all visitors as open to exploitation. If a comparison is made with England in this respect, the Irish seasides come out fairly well. Hotel and guest-house prices in the Six County Area are less than in England. In The South they are controlled on a basis which seems very reasonable to the visitor from across the water, and ridiculously cheap to Americans. Donaghadee, Portrush, Bundoran, Rosses Point, Salthill, Bray and Tramore may be cited as well-developed and typical seaside resorts which provide nearly all the amenities the average holidaymaker is likely to demand. None of these pleasant places is remarkable, but they are all convenient centres and well placed to be headquarters from which trips can be made by road, by rail or on foot across-country, to places and scenes which the most exacting visitor would have to admit as interesting or impressive. And there are many other 'convenient centres', as we shall note as we go along.

If the reader agrees with me that, as one cannot hope to see all of Ireland in one visit, and that this method of approach is at least practical and likely to be rewarding, it is useful at the outset to have in mind the main Convenient Centres in Ireland which can serve as holiday headquarters. In this way, by visiting one of the Centres and working from it into the surrounding countryside, much can be seen and something pleasing and not easily lost can be brought away in the mind. At the very least the possibilities of Ireland will be revealed. My own experience in recent years is that, having recommended to friends in England one or other of the convenient centres I am about to list, those people go again and again to the same place, and refuse even to consider one of the other

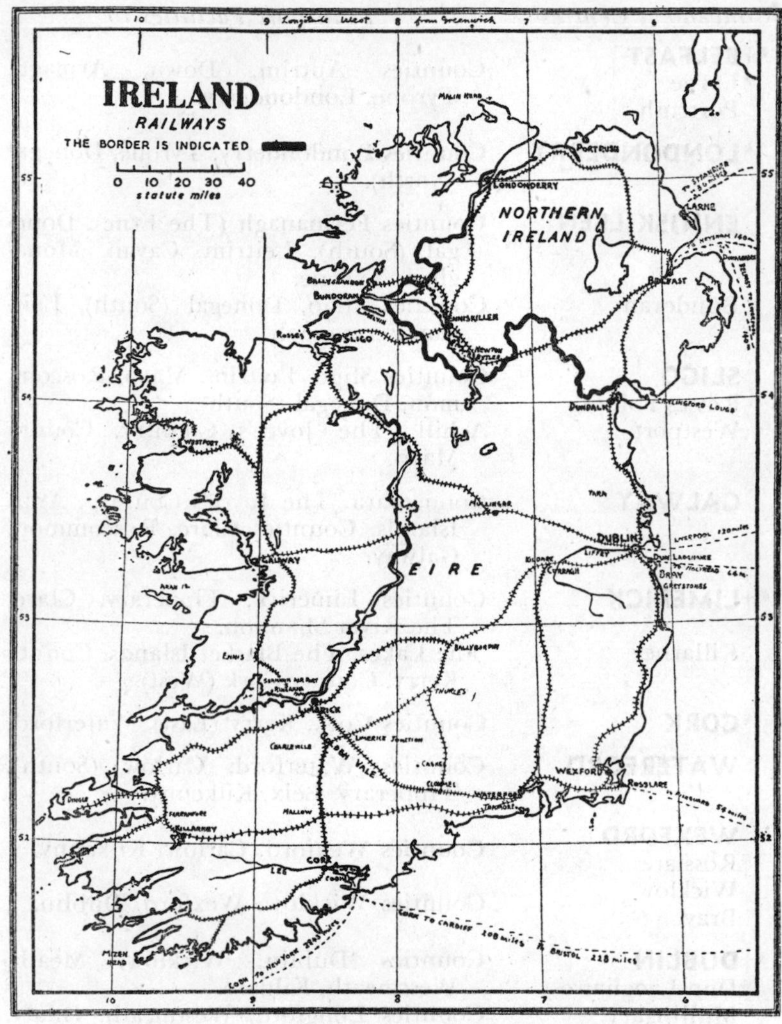

places in my short list as capable of providing an interesting change.

Let us first have our list, and then we can go on to consider how to use it.

The maps will show that those places in heavy type in the list given are not only geographically but in other ways Centres on which the visitor would be advised to concentrate

Convenient Centres	*Transport Facilities to*
*†**BELFAST**, *Larne, Portrush	Counties Antrim, Down, Armagh, Tyrone, Londonderry.
***LONDONDERRY**	Counties Londonderry, Tyrone, Donegal (North).
ENNISKILLEN	Counties Fermanagh (The Erne), Donegal (South), Leitrim, Cavan, Monaghan, Tyrone.
Bundoran	Counties Sligo, Donegal (South), Leitrim, Fermanagh.
SLIGO, Rosses Point	Counties Sligo, Leitrim, Mayo, Roscommon, Donegal (South).
Westport	Achill, The Joyce's Country, County Mayo.
GALWAY	Connemara, The Joyce's Country, Aran Islands, Counties Clare, Roscommon, Galway.
*†**LIMERICK**	Counties Limerick, Tipperary, Clare, The River Shannon.
Killarney	The Lakes, The Blasket Islands, County Kerry, County Cork (West).
***CORK**	Counties Cork, Kerry (East), Waterford.
WATERFORD	Counties Waterford, Carlow (South), Tipperary, Leix, Kilkenny.
WEXFORD, *Rosslare	Counties Wexford, Carlow, Kilkenny.
Wicklow, Bray	Counties Wicklow, Wexford, Dublin.
*†**DUBLIN**, *Dun Laoghaire	Counties Dublin, Wicklow, Meath, Westmeath, Kildare.
Mullingar	Counties Longford, Westmeath, Offaly, The Central Plain.
*Dundalk	Counties Louth, Cavan, Meath.

attention if he wishes to get 'the hang of things' in Ireland and some general idea of the 'lie of the land'. Those marked * are ports of landing. Those marked † are Air Ports or are near them. The transatlantic *Shannon Air Port* is near Limerick. *Cobh* (pronounced Cove), in Cork harbour, is a port of call for transatlantic liners. The visitor from the United States lands here.

If the prospective visitor should be one of those fortunate people who has his own means of transport, whether a car, a motor-cycle or a bicycle, and is ambitious to do a circular tour of Ireland, he has merely to start at one of the places marked in heavy type and, in the order given, go to the next one in heavy type and continue on round the list. If he starts at, say, Dublin, he can either go to Belfast and thence to Londonderry, Enniskillen, Sligo, etc., or he can take the list in reverse order and go to Wexford, Waterford, Cork, etc. Such a circular tour would omit the Central Plain. Although this is very different from and less exciting in scenery than the seaboard country, especially in the west, it is of considerable historical and archæological interest, also for its flora and fauna, and not least for the very good-natured and racy people who live there. This Central Plain consists mostly of either rich fields or of bog and, as its name implies, it is mostly flatland. It is on a limestone base. There are in it some delightful lakes as well as beautiful though not very big rivers; and the Curragh, which everybody interested in horses must visit.

As more than one-fifth part of the surface of Ireland consists of 'bog', and the great Bog of Allen covers a considerable area of the Plain and the greater part of Offaly, the word demands some explanation. It comes from the Gaelic *bogach*, bog, meaning 'soft'. A bog is a tract of sometimes water-logged but generally spongy ground, of which the composition consists of vegetation, mostly mosses, in various stages of decomposition. At one stage in the process of decomposition it forms the substance known in Ireland as 'turf' and in England and elsewhere as 'peat'. As 'turf' is an excellent fuel for domestic purposes—it is quick-burning and therefore not so good for factories or locomotives, though it is used when coal is not available—a piece of bog is valuable in accordance with the quantity and quality of turf it yields. In all parts of the Irish countryside in the summer months, men can be seen cutting turf with spades specially shaped for the purpose. It is cut in blocks of convenient size for household use and laid out to dry in the sun, remaining there for some weeks until thoroughly dry, when it is stacked and later carted to the cottages, villages or towns to be stored for use in the winter months. Turf is an industry in Ireland, and an important one, as there is little coal to be found in the country, and the best is inferior to English or Welsh coal. Although turf suitable for domestic use can be found in most parts of Ireland, there are many impressive tracts of soggy ground or marshland—also known as bogs—of little use for any purpose but often dominating a landscape. The great Bog of Allen occupies a considerable part of three counties—Meath, Kildare and Offaly. The train from Dublin to Galway cuts across it. Bog makes a rich contribution to Irish landscape.

The town of Kilkenny is in the Plain, and a very pleasant town it is, being exceptionally well laid out. Those who built it gave much attention to the architecture and used a local limestone of distinctive colour. The result is a surprise to the visitor who has become accustomed to the sameness of the towns in the Central Plain. Tipperary, with its Golden Vale, and Cashel, with its historic rock, do not deserve to be overlooked, and out of historical respect one should visit the Hill of Tara in Meath, though there is nothing extraordinary about its appearance. The visitor who stands on it can contemplate its past glories, or, at the very least, he who is there on a fine day will enjoy a long and inspiring view which he will not easily forget. These are the principal places in the Central Plain to which the attention of the visitor must be directed. After reading what is said in tourist literature about Longford, Westmeath, Offaly and Leix—Mullingar is a convenient centre for them—he may decide that some or all of these places are worthy of some of his time. I must be content merely to mention them, to give a general idea in the broadest terms what to look for, and always on the assumption that it is read by persons who do not know Ireland, but wish to gain some general ideas to guide them in their choice of what to see.

The general consensus of travellers' opinion is that the seaboard and places not far from the sea, with the interior lake and river districts—The Erne, The Shannon System and Killarney—are likely to be of most interest to the first-time visitor. Next, the northern, western and southern seaboards are likely to prove more interesting than the East or the interior. Finally, though some may not agree, the more you keep to what survives of the old, unanglicized Ireland, the fresher and more stimulating you will find it. All this fits with the history you have read, from which you cannot but conclude that the east coast, being nearest England, has been most affected by English influences; and the same applies to much of the Six County Area, with Scottish influence added. If you *must* see English things and the English way of life, you will see them better in England. If you want to see *Irish* things and the Irish way of life, you must go after them; and in this my suggestions will, I hope, be found helpful. Nobody need take offence at what I am now about to say.

Protestantism and prosperity will be found to go together in many, though not in all parts of the countryside, not only of The North but of The South. History provides the reason. In the Settlements and Plantations the Protestants were given the best lands and the Catholics had to be content with what was left over. That was the conquerors' rule of thumb. Time has modified the outcome, which explains most of the exceptions. One more point not irrelevant to this: look for the worst, most barren, least valuable and hardest-to-work lands in the whole of Ireland, and there you will find the *Gaeltacht,* the Irish-speaking parts. Native Irish speakers are survivors of great struggles. The more Irish an area is, the poorer it is likely to be. It is a curious commentary on the workings of Nature that it is in those poor, neglected areas, peopled by survivors of the former victims of the Ascendancy, one meets Nature's own gentlefolk and some of the finest people to be found anywhere in the world. In saying this I trust that nobody will regard it as a considered judgment intending to imply a slur on all the rest of the population of the country, for I think that most of those others will agree with me in what I have said of the *Gaeltacht* people, who have this quality: they win everybody's heart, and they do so without ever losing their sense of human dignity, their spirit of independence and a never-failing courtesy which the utmost poverty cannot impair. My advice, therefore, to the person who wishes to get the best out of a visit to Ireland is that, although the best is usually what he finds for himself, he will rarely be disappointed in a Gaelic-speaking area.

Perhaps the most difficult problem of all is to decide whether to begin your holiday with country or seaside and end it in one of the cities, or to begin with a city and end away from it. Although I greatly enjoy it, to me life in Dublin is likely to demand top-pressure living, because I meet so many old friends and make the acquaintance of so many interesting new ones. Having reached a little more than the half-way post in life, I decided a few years ago that it might be wiser to begin with Dublin and afterwards take advantage of some quieter place outside it in order to recover mental and physical equilibrium. It worked so well that on the next visit I reversed the process by way of experiment. And to my surprise *that* also worked remarkably well. So, who am I to say what is best? I have come to the conclusion that what the holiday-maker *wants* to do, however foolish, however irrational, is just as likely to be good for his mind and body as the most carefully and cautiously planned programme. There is always something stimulating about surprises, whether they come in the form of delights or disappointments. Begin and end an Irish visit wherever you please and as the mood takes you. Few countries yield better results by taking things easy.

2
Irish Language—Place-names

In the Six Counties of The North, the Irish language has disappeared for all practical purposes but one. In that area the only people who attempt to keep it alive are scholars and a few enthusiasts, most of the latter being attracted to it for political or sentimental reasons. The one practical purpose, if indeed it can be called practical, for which Irish remains in The North is in geographical and typographical nomenclature. Most of the place-names in The North are in the old language, as they are throughout the whole of Ireland. And although one can travel everywhere in Ireland and enjoy the country without a knowledge of Irish—perhaps one word demands to be known: *'Sláinte'*,[1] meaning 'Health' in a toast—because nearly everybody but a few old people can speak English, those who wish to look a little deeper than the surface cannot afford to ignore the significance of place-names. These often hold the key to interesting folklore or antiquities. Nor can any visitor to The South afford to ignore the fact that one of the two official languages of the Republic is Irish; that it is a compulsory subject in primary schools; and that all candidates for public appointments must pass a test in it. Nevertheless, unless he is more than superficially interested in the language, folklore and history of the country, the language problem need not cause the slightest anxiety. But the visitor should know what in Irish is called the *Gaeltacht*—the Irish or partly Irish-speaking districts. Here the language survives in its traditional forms. Travelling from North to South, these districts are to be found in certain parts of the counties of Donegal, Sligo, Mayo, Galway, Clare, Tipperary, Kerry, Cork and, thence to the East, in Waterford. Irish is also spoken in the western islands: Tory, Achill, Aran and The Blaskets. Throughout the *Gaeltacht*—which includes some of the loveliest, most interesting parts of the country—Irish is the sole medium of instruction in elementary schools, English being taught as a second or foreign language.

This brings us back to place-names in Ireland, those often very beautiful words you will see on the map or hear spoken as you mix among the people. How they roll off the tongue! Ardnacrusha, Ardnageeha, Ardnapreaghaun—I take some of them from a list opened at random—Ballaghaderreen, Ballinahalla, Ballinvreena; Cahirconree, Carrantuohill, Cloghineely, Cloghvoola, Clonmacnoise; Donaghadee, Doondonnell, Drumcondra; Labbasheeda, Lisdoonvarna, Lugnaquilla. One is tempted to continue; and how easy that would be, for the names cannot be numbered. There are many used locally for little rivers, townlands, even for fields and little hills which are not on the maps. I do not mention these names merely for their grand sounds, their sweetness or their guttural sonority—there is every sort of variation—but be-

[1] Pronounced shláunthĕ or sláuntĕ, in two syllables, with the stress on the first.

cause there is not one of them without meaning and hardly one which does not hold within it some old story, record, or interesting association. This can be illustrated by taking almost any Irish place-name, let us say Cork. The name as we now have it is the shortened form of the Gaelic word *corcach,* which the dictionary informs us is a moor or marsh, a low-lying swamp, and P. W. Joyce, who has written extensively on Irish place-names,[1] tells us that the city grew round a monastery founded in the sixth century A.D. on the edge of a marsh by St. Finbar: a part of the city is still spoken of as the Marsh. It is just as well to know this, or the new visitor might be misled into associating the name of this delightful city—'Sweet Cork' in a lovely song—with the familiar material used as a stopper for bottles. Let Joyce tell us about the name Dublin:

> DUBLIN. The name is written in the annals *Duibh linn* (Duvlin), which, in some of the Latin Lives of the Saints, is translated *nigra therma,* 'black pool'; it was originally the name of that part of the Liffey on which the city was built, and is sufficiently descriptive at the present day. In very early ages an artificial ford of hurdles was constructed across the Liffey, where the main road from Tara to Wicklow crossed the river; and the city that subsequently sprang up around it was called from this circumstance *Áth-cliath* (ah-clee), the ford of hurdles, which was the ancient name of Dublin. This name is still used by speakers of Irish in every part of Ireland, but they join to it Bally—*Baile-atha-cliath* (which they pronounce 'Blaa-clee'), the town of the hurdle ford.

So now you know that Dublin, itself an Irish word, is *Baile-atha-cliath* in Irish, and that this name, of fifteen letters in our alphabet and thirteen in the Irish, is pronounced 'blaa-clee', which, as you see, is only two syllables. For two syllables, thirteen letters! Although the thirteen letters may remind us of the far-distant past and have other values, this example gives some idea, by modern standards in linguistics and phonetics, of how remote from the practical is the system

[1] *Irish Local Names Explained,* a condensed version of his bigger work *The Origin and History of Irish Names of Places,* 2 vols., 1870. Most of the modern explanations of place-names are based on Joyce's pioneering work in this field.

of orthography in this fascinating language. You perhaps already know that when you see a name beginning with *Bally-*, you may expect it to indicate a town. From which point you may proceed, if interested, to learn from Joyce's books other simple Irish words used in place-names.

In Dublin the names of streets are shown in Irish and English. Scholars are aware that sometimes the Irish and the English equivalent given are not always easily to be reconciled in rational terms, but the delights of listing the inconsistencies with possible explanations need not concern us. What can hardly fail to strike the visitor who has not seen them before is the beauty of the Irish letters, and he may ask himself why the Irish should have an alphabet of their own and whence they got it. It is a modification of the mediæval Latin alphabet, brought to artistic perfection by the monks of Ireland's Golden Age. There are only eighteen letters in it, the capitals are the same as the small letters, but are now written a little larger, and the handwriting or cursive form is closer to the printed than our cursive is to our printed forms. This alphabet is used for Gaelic only in Ireland. Scots Gaels used the Latin alphabet for what they have preserved of the language which was brought to Scotland by their ancestors, Irish invaders, and survives in a form so closely akin to Irish Gaelic that it is classified with the latter as virtually the same language.

3
English as spoken in Ireland

Each of the four provinces of Ulster, Munster, Leinster and Connacht has dialectical, phonetic and rhythmical peculiarities in the English spoken by the people, but most of these peculiarities tend to disappear with the passage of time. There have been many changes in Irish-English during the last fifty years. Newspapers, increasing facilities of transport, increasing intercommunication and, in recent years, the radio, have all played their part in an almost uninterrupted elimination of the localisms and turns of speech which, at the end of the nineteenth century, made Irish-English a racy and rich branch of the English language, one which Irish and English writers have exploited in fiction and plays. Much of that Irish-English remains in the countryside, in remote districts and in the *Gaeltacht,* but one never finds it anywhere today in the richly poeticized form with which we have been made acquainted in, to name a repository, the plays of John Millington Synge. I must admit that it has never once in my lifetime been my good fortune to meet anybody anywhere in Ireland, from Fair Head in The North to Mizen Head in The South, who spoke so wonderfully as some of Synge's characters, and I have more than a suspicion that this playwright not only selected but often made up his language to suit his artistic purpose. This is not to assert that the Irish have not their own ways and manners of speech, or that these are not interesting or even fascinating for the visitor as well as for the student of dialect. The subject is one with far too many ramifications and pitfalls to justify here more than a few pointers which may help the newcomer to understand why Irish-English differs from standard English, why the English spoken in the Six County Area differs from that of the rest of Ireland, and why the English spoken in the West and in the *Gaeltacht* has its own peculiarities.

As we have seen in Part I, Chapter III, a large part of Ulster was 'planted' by settlers who came mostly from Scotland. They brought with them their Scottish dialect of English, and this is the basis of a great part of the everyday speech today of the people in the Six Counties and of many who live just over The Border. Variations in this speech are mostly due to English and not to Gaelic influences. Thus, in this area we have a form of English based entirely on English influences, for the Scottish English of the Planters had itself sprung from English sources. There are few 'hibernicisms'—turns of speech or idiom taken directly from the Gaelic—in the English spoken in Northern Ireland. And such peculiarities as exist not only sprang from Scottish and English sources, but there is another factor: the people retain from Plantation times many words and turns of phrase which have disappeared from contemporary standard English.

The Presbyterians and others who emigrated from Ulster to North America brought their speech with them, and it was a strong element in the nucleus around which has grown what H. L. Mencken calls the 'American Language' as we know it today. English as spoken in The North of Ireland is a rich, interesting and sharp dialect. Its pronunciation is distinctive to the point of being almost unmistakable and all but ineradicable. Belfast can claim to have an accent of its own, quite unmistakable, penetrating and as irresistible in character as that of the city's inhabitants. A friend who is a phonetician (not one of those people so useful to politicians, lawyers, actors and actresses in the eradication of an unwanted or vulgar accent and the imparting of another, but a university professor in the modern science of phonetics) informs me that a person who in youth acquires a northern Irish accent seldom fails to retain at least traces of it to his dying day. This phonetician also says that he has rarely met a Belfastman whom he could not identify as such after listening to his speech for a moment or so. There is much strength of character in that northern speech!

Outside Northern Ireland the English that is spoken is very different for different reasons; and it is often more difficult to explain. From the Anglo-Norman invasion onwards the eastern seaboard was settled by colonies of people from across the Irish Sea. In Elizabethan times, large numbers of English people went to Ireland and intermarried with natives, who then learnt to speak Elizabethan English in all its richness and rhythmic beauty. This was the language of Shakespeare. The Gaelic-speaking Irish learnt it as a second language. They also did something *to* that Elizabethan English, for very often they might not know the correct equivalent in it for something they wished to say, and then they would translate literally from their own Gaelic. Furthermore, when they could not translate, they would often retain the Gaelic word. There were many Gaelic words for which there was no exact equivalent, and so a number of those words were grafted on the rich English that had come to Ireland. This process continued throughout the Cromwellian Settlement, until the English spoken in Ireland, with its roots in Elizabethan English and with modifications in usage made by the native Irish, developed along its own lines up to the eighteenth century, when a point was reached beyond which few further changes were made until well into the present century. In the *Gaeltacht,* as might be expected, the influence of Gaelic idiom and turns of speech has been greater and more persistent than elsewhere, and this, one must always admit, helps to justify much of the language of Synge's plays.

Thus it is that, outside The North, we have a distinctive dialect of English—one with Elizabethan roots and sprinklings from Gaelic, with rhythms, accents and many words and turns of phrase varying almost from county to county and certainly from province to province, and again in Irish-speaking districts. In all this, note that I refer to the speech of the bulk of the population, of those who in this remain under their own influences, go to school locally and finish their education in the country. There are others, especially among the Anglo-Irish, who go abroad to England or elsewhere for education and lose much of their Irishness in speech and everything else. But apart from them, the visitor will hear everywhere a softer and often a richer English than he will hear in England or elsewhere in the English-speaking world. He will not fail to meet playboys who, taking full advantage of their dialectical superiority, will put on an act for his delectation, with extravagances and exaggerations in speaking that are helped out and encouraged by their Irish-English. Irish-English goes with Irish character, and has made itself a part of Irish nature. The person who tries to imitate it or reproduce it will sooner or later give himself away. Not that the Irish will mind. But in this they are not easily deceived; and it often raises a quiet laugh.

Like everything else in this world of increasing standardization, Irish-English is losing some of its old fascinations, its vivid and picturesque words and phrases, the rich idiom of the nineteenth century—its best period—and even in accent and rhythms. The polite and refined Irish-English of the Irish radio stations is having its effect, though it is not nearly so polite and refined as the English which the Irish hear from English stations, often with envy, believing that it is in every way much better than their own, and therefore worthy of emulation. These new influences often produce the strangest results in Irish speech. Yet, long before they came, I heard an Irish maid speak of 'clane pleets', believing that this was

Dublin—Port and Customs House
ITA

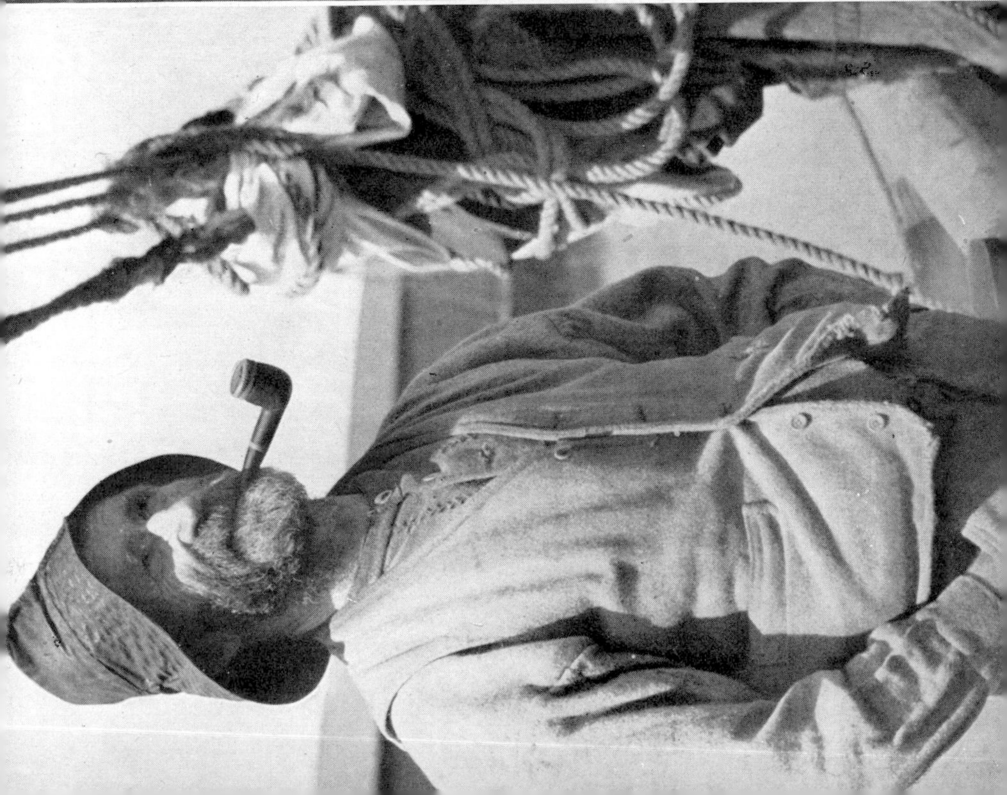

the correct and therefore the more educated, indeed more polite pronunciation of 'clean plates'! There is also the influence that is brought to Ireland by the large numbers of Irish who live in England, have their speech modified, and return to the old country from time to time for a holiday. This is not new. In an old song Terence says farewell to his Kathleen, who is going to England to work:

For Kathleen, you know, there's no knowing
When next I shall see your sweet face.
And when you come back to me, Kathleen,
None the better will I be off, then—
You'll be spaking such beautiful English,
Sure I won't know my Kathleen again.

The Irish-English Revival has yet to come.

4
Dublin and the East Coast

It is not a bad preparation for a visit to Dublin to read James Joyce's *Dubliners, Portrait of the Artist as a Young Man,* and *Ulysses*—in that order if you have not already read Joyce. On your second visit, or perhaps on some later occasion, you can have a try at *Finnegan's Wake,* which a Dublin friend assures me is best read by moonlight as you lean over one of the Liffey bridges, and preferably while in that state of imaginative gestation to which a reasonable consumption of the wine of the country—Guinness's Stout—is conducive. But you will not need any of this preparation to tell you that Dubliners are not always easy people to understand, and experience of Ireland can lead you to the conclusion that it is more difficult to grasp and analyse the mentality of the Dubliner than of any other kind or class of native. For one thing, Dubliners are a more mixed breed than you will find anywhere in Ireland, because Dublin has been a cosmopolitan community longer than any other in Ireland. This 'town of the ford of the hurdles' had its original Picts, Celtic Irish, its Norsemen, its Normans and then its English as the prin-

Young Irish Dancers
ITA

Fisherman—Atlantic Seaboard
ITA

cipal elements in its ethnic constitution. It has also had a generous sprinkling of the adventurous; and of the adventurers, military, political and commercial, who invariably find their way to promising territories. In Dublin you will find surnames which come direct or are derived from those of almost every country and race in Europe; one cannot say this of any other Irish city or town. Glance down a list of the street names, and you will see Aberdeen, Achill, Addison, St. Alphonsus, Anglesea, The Appian Way, Beaumont, Bella Place, Bellevue, Brighton, Brunswick, Cardiff, Charlemont, Costello, Darcy, De Burgh, D'Olier . . . but I need not continue, for this is enough to indicate the variety of influences that have moulded this lovely city. As you walk along the principal streets, it is interesting to look at the people and see whether you can pick out a dominant type. You will quickly perceive that there is a quality, expression, complexion, or perhaps all three, common to most Dubliners—for I do not include the many comparatively recent settlers who have found Dublin to be a good place after their own war-worn territories. Dubliners are of all sizes and colorations. The soft climate and absence of smoke and chemical fog permit them to enjoy fresh faces. They strike you as a cheerful, self-assured, good-natured and animated race of men and women: the men sprightly, the girls often strikingly beautiful. Good plain food has much to do with this, but the inborn philosophy of the average Dubliner may have more. No city in the world can so completely and so quickly absorb a foreigner; no city has more foreigners who can pass for natives. The Dublin accent, intonation, form and manner of speech all combine to account for this. I have stated these in the plural, for you will find that among those born and brought up in Dublin there are at least three varieties of speech. There is the way of speaking of those who remain of the Ascendancy or who wish to be regarded as forming part of an aristocratic survival: a cultured, smooth and altogether a superior delivery as clear and lacking in roughness as any in the English-speaking world. Then there is the speech of the considerable middle-class, often an attractive, sometimes an unattractive blend of 'Ascendancy' and 'ordinary'. And there is the 'ordinary' Dublin speech which, at its best, has a strong local accent, a characteristic rhythm and intonation, and a raciness in language not surpassed anywhere. And at its worst that 'ordinary' can be as unpleasant to the ear as any speech in the English-speaking world: an adenoidal delivery with a narrow epiglottal articulation of vowels and a slightly nasal intonation, all of which can be, to say the least, quite unmusical, but is almost invariably redeemed by the remarkable racy vocabulary and phraseology. There is as much difference between the speech of the Ascendancy survival and their imitators and the hearty Dublin bowser or jackeen as there is between that of the product of, say, Eton and Balliol in England and a Cockney spiv. The average visitor will find Dublin speech fascinating; the phonetician will often find it difficult to analyse. Nobody finds it difficult to understand. We have the word of Krupskaya, Lenin's widow, that when she and Lenin knew English only theoretically and could not yet follow the spoken language, they used to go to Irish political meetings in London to hear Irish, and especially Dublin speech, because they found it to be clearer and easier to understand than that of average English people. I have heard many foreigners extol the general clarity of Dublin speakers.

*

I should not like to attempt to describe the 'spirit' of Dublin, if it has one, my feeling being that it cannot be caught in words. It strikes me as a city of groups and of group-spirits, and the visitor will seek out and find whatever group he wants. *Literary Dublin*—once an important group-spirit—is still an interesting if uneasy and frustrated one. *Sporting Dublin*—a big and always lively entity. *Boosy Dublin*—not nearly so drunken as it used to be, but still very much alive and enjoying its drinks. *Scholastic Dublin*—not always as staid as the scholarship it represents. *Snobbish Dublin*—more snobbish than an English provincial city, but with a form of snobbery that yields more easily to human approach than that of any English provincial city, any London suburb or the Middle West. There is, of course, a money-snobbery in Dublin. Silly enough, it is, perhaps, sillier than money-snobbery elsewhere, for in this, as in other things, the Irish run to extremes. I think you will find more snobbery among the Protestants than among Catholics, though I am so doubtful of this suggestion that I offer it with trepidation. There is *artistic Dublin,* which I found to be serious, intelligent and hard-working—I refer particularly to painting, though I should like to include the arts generally. *Saintly Dublin* exists without doubt, but, poor sinner that I am, I have always been frightened of saints and more akin to sinners; and must leave it to those better qualified than myself to speak of Dublin saintliness. And one cannot mention Dublin without mentioning Dublin of the gombeen men and philistines. These villains operate mostly against Dubliners and native Irish; and try to win the favour of the visitor from abroad. They are an important element in Dublin life, and have a big say in what they call 'morality'.

There are as many Dublins as you care to look for.

Of James Joyce's Dublin, immortalized in *Ulysses,* there is much of the physical remaining, but the spirit of that Dublin is completely gone. I cannot better indicate the change than by taking as my example what was the really wonderful old pub known as 'Davy Byrne's' in Duke Street, off Grafton Street. It was in the old days an important strategic point in the defences-in-depth of a considerable legion of good drinkers, many of whose names are now on the roll of fame. That old tavern had an atmosphere unique in Dublin and in the world, for although its clientèle included men of the highest distinction and of a raggle-taggle disreputability, such was the strong personality of the pub that *bores* of any class or creed usually found themselves unhappy there, seldom stayed in it for more than a drink or two and, without apparently any need for open ostracism, took it to heart that the place did not suit their temperament. This rarely happens in the world of pubs, but in the golden age of Davy Byrne's, say from about 1900 until the 1920's, corresponding with the great days of the Irish Literary Revival, that was the sort of atmosphere it enjoyed. So far as my memory and experience of it goes, I cannot remember having been there in those days even once when it was uncomfortably crowded. In the 1940's the old place was completely reconstructed, and effectively so, in the spirit of the new age. It now has the appearance of an American film-set: glossy, modern, hygienic. The atmosphere is cocktailish, the seats are most comfortable, the carpets soft. I did not find the drinks or service any less efficient, nor, I must say in fairness, any more efficient than in the old days when, before Dublin was really awake in the morning, a kindly and sympathetic barman diagnosed your hangover and might prescribe, as he did for me on one occasion, a seidlitz powder, telling me not to drink anything alcoholic before noon, when he recommended a dozen oysters and a bottle or two of stout "to settle the inside and get back the feelings of a Christian". Today the atmosphere is convivial and friendly, and you will get a good drink there. But when you go out into the street you will not have the feelings *we* had after a session there. I think the main difference is that in the old days the drinkers in 'Davy Byrne's' had a higher opinion of one another than they have now. And in the old days you sat on any sort of old chair with a pint in front of you on a very plain table and *knew* that there was no other pub quite like this. It is almost ill-mannered to make the comparison, and perhaps unfair to the present house which, after all, is not responsible for the age in which we live. It is a popular pub—so popular in the tourist season that you will be lucky if you can find in it a place to sit down.

*

There are not many horse-drawn cabs in Dublin now, and fewer still are the jaunting-cars. The latter are kept for the benefit of the visitor, who can usually find one near O'Connell Bridge. And I can assure him that he can have a pleasant and instructive adventure by hiring one of these old vehicles for a drive round the Phœnix Park. The last time I was in Dublin I took one and drove through the streets north of the river by Oxmantown and Stony Batter to North Circular Road, into the Park there, then right round it, returning by the riverside gate, crossing the Liffey and clop-clopping slowly through the Coombe where Sean O'Casey found the characters of his great plays. You will get a far more intense 'feel' of Dublin in this way than if you take a taxi, for it is leisurely, and you will probably have an elderly jarvey who knows his stuff and can amuse and instruct you the whole way. The taximen are more hardboiled than the old cavaliers of jaunting-car and horse-cab. As for the horse-cabs, it is strange to think that Dublin once had more than seven thousand of them and now has hardly a hundred. And whereas the horse-cab was once an all-purposes vehicle which young men out for fun and the more spacious sort of pub-crawl would mobilize for their peregrinations, it is now a poor, drab, shabby and very sad survival which today seems to be used for only one purpose: to accompany a funeral. One still sees horse-cabs folowing hearses in Dublin; and the Joycean thinks of Dignam's funeral.

*

In the Phœnix Park is what I cannot but feel is one of the most delightful little zoos in the world. I do not like to see animals in captivity, but zoos are the only places we can see many of them, and, wherever I happen to be, if there is a zoo, I make a point of visiting it. I must say that I have never seen happier animals than those in the Dublin Zoo, or animals better cared for. It was founded in 1830, and has the double honour of having been the first place in Europe where lions were bred in captivity and, up to this moment, of breeding the finest lions to be found anywhere in captivity. The secret? I understand that it is because the Dublin lions are fed on the flesh of old goats and donkeys, these animals being nearest to the lion's natural food—deer and zebra. Dublin exports lions even to Africa, I am told—to improve the wild stock, no doubt, just as Britain exports bulls and rams to Argentina and elsewhere to improve local breeds. In the Dublin Zoo you will see snakes; though you will be told that they cannot live in Ireland since St. Patrick drove them out. It was in the Dublin Zoo that I saw a nightmare animal all alone in a little chalet painted green and marked 'Irish Independent'. Oh, what a creature! I asked somebody why it was labelled 'Irish Independent', which is the name of a national newspaper, and was indignantly asked, "*Why not?*" It seems that the chalet, and perhaps the animal also, was a gift from the newspaper to the Zoo. The animal I discovered later was a binturong. It was a puzzled-looking beast not unlike a cross between the Jabberwock and the Bandersnatch, and obviously had something on its mind—perhaps its own smell.

*

Lest omission to pause at the name of Guinness while we are in Dublin be regarded as *lèse-majesté,* I would have those who read these lines know that dark ale, black beer, porter, stout—call the wine of this country what you will—was well established as a popular drink in Ireland long before the Anglo-Norman invasion. My authority? No other than Sir James Ware, in whose *Antiquities of Ireland* I read that "the ancient and *peculiar* drink of the Irish was Ale". He quotes Latin verse of a Norman poet, who described its colour as Stygian, which is very dark—black:

Of this strange drink, so like the Stygian Lake,
Men call it Ale, I know not what to make,
They drink it thick, and pass it wondrous thin:
What store of dregs must needs remain within?

Apparently the dark beverage was good for them, even in that remote period. In the town of Leixlip, County Kildare, is a shuttered and barred little pub, without even a plaque to mark what ought to be cared for by the National Trust. It was there that a humble man, who knew about good drink, started the snowball movement which has grown into the still-growing fortune associated with the name of Guinness. On Guinness's Brewery is based the economy of Dublin. The drink is a great comfort, not only to Dubliners, but to visitors. They will notice that it is better here than anywhere else in the world.

*

A visit to St. Michan's (episcopalian) Church, situated a short distance from the river and near the Four Courts, is usually included in the visitor's round, but unless to see the interesting interior of the church with its quaint 'Stool of Repentance', movable pulpit, sprightly gilt cherubs and the organ on which Handel tried out his Messiah, or the churchyard which has what one school of opinion believes to be the grave of Robert Emmett, I should advise any friend of mine to give it a miss, and I must explain why. In the vaults of St. Michan's are some bodies which the peculiar quality of that atmosphere has mummified—without wrappings or embalming or other artificial treatment—to a state of mummification which I think can only be described as perfect. The air here seemed to be a natural antiseptic of unique powers. I say *keep away from St. Michan's,* because it seems to me to be an affront to the dignity of man to put on public show a collection of perfectly preserved bodies of what must have been human beings like ourselves, even if they were lords, ladies, statesmen, soldiers, notabilities and notorieties or, as many are, of unknown but assumed high social status. On the occasion when I visited the vault, I was invited to shake hands with a gentleman, the hand being worn to a polish by those ghoulish greetings. The texture of the flesh is that of tanned leather; the joints work; the expression on some of the faces is that of an achieved peace. There is the body of a crusader in the traditional posture of dead crusaders on tombs in many places outside Ireland, which gives an idea of how old some of these mummies must be: half a millennium or more, maybe. The only other denizens of the vault are a race of spiders which solve their subsistence problem by devouring one another. The vaults are spacious, and I do not know—and do not wish to know—how many of the sad survivals of humanity there are in this place, in their undignified attitudes which it would be more respectful to leave in their solitude. It needs, I think, a cold heart to look on those poor bodies without feeling enraged against whoever is responsible for putting them on show. Incidentally, you must buy a ticket to visit the vault. To me it is altogether an example of utter indecency and lack of feeling. But if you feel differently about it, go and enjoy, if you can, that chamber of natural horrors. Compared with it, the so-called 'Chamber of Horrors' in Madame Tussaud's in London is a fun-fair. I never want to see St. Michan's again, though I love the little church itself, which, I read, is in the place of a church founded by the Danish bishop St. Michan in 1095.

*

I would ask the indulgence of the reader for a digression

of little importance, but may be of some interest to those who collect scraps of Joyceana. I was for some years at school in Dublin: a hard school, ruled by an English headmaster with a whalebone riding-whip and Kennedy's *Latin Grammar*. Our only relief from institutional tyranny was on Sunday afternoons, when we boys were turned loose in the Phœnix Part to do as we liked. The delightful Zoological Gardens were out of bounds to us, otherwise the whole of this beautiful park was our playground. There was not an inch of it which we did not know. In the summer months a band played in the natural amphitheatre near the zoo. We found it very pleasant to sit on the grass and listen to the music. At one time (*c.* 1909) I was studying German and Italian with great enthusiasm, and it so happened that I made the acquaintance in the Park of a chocolate-seller with whom I could practise these languages. This was a sturdily built, clean-shaven native of Trieste, a young man with longish fair hair who used an engaging patter to sell his chocolates. I have a most pleasant memory of that good man for several reasons, one of which was that, if any of his friends among the boys happened to be short of cash, he would give us a bar of chocolate, "for luck" as he used to say, and refused to take the money for it when the donee came into funds. His kindness was not abused by many. Although Sunday afternoon was the busiest and most profitable occasion in his week, he would often sit down and chat with me, perhaps for half an hour, thereby losing a part of his small livelihood. One day he asked me if I liked the Moving Pictures. I said that I did. He then informed me that he had a friend (a relation, I think) who, in partnership with another man, ran the Volta Cinema in Henry Street and, if I cared to come along one day, he would introduce me to these friends, who would provide me with a free seat. This I thought marvellous. Myself and a schoolboy colleague went along to the Volta Cinema and were introduced to the Triestino's friend and to another man, a tall, thin Irishman with glasses and wearing a long overcoat which, in my memory, seems to have been most of the time turned up round the collar. This tall man usually kept his hands in the overcoat pockets, and took them out only when conversation in German or Italian demanded a gesture. My German was better than my Italian; his Italian was much better than his German. On the first occasion that we met, he accompanied me into the auditorium. The Volta Cinema was a plain, comfortless hall. The seats were wooden benches excepting a few rows in the front, which had hard kitchen chairs for the *élite* who could afford the top price—sixpence I think. There was no upstairs accommodation that I remember.

My friend in the overcoat took me to the front row, and we sat to watch those flickering old pictures to which the only sound-accompaniment was that provided by an upright piano. It was played by a gentleman who from time to time refreshed himself with Guinness's stout from a cup which, to complete the deception, had a saucer to go with it. Between times the orchestra slipped out of a nearby door, taking furtively an empty stout bottle. When our musician nonchalantly returned, he brought back in his pocket a full bottle, of which the cork had been drawn out of earshot. Thus fortified from morning to night, the pianist did his work; and did it right well. His music to horses galloping made us all move with the horses. Then the hall rattled.

My tall Irish friend, on the very first occasion that we met, took me after a time from those front seats to a position farther back from the screen, and asked me did I notice any difference. I must have told him that I thought the new position was better for seeing than the first, for he then took me to a place right at the end of the hall and farthest away from the screen. Again I must have approved of the change. Ever afterwards I always sat there when I went to the Volta Cinema, to which I had been given a permanent right of free entry for myself and another boy, whenever I cared to bring one along.

My new friend was the immortal James Joyce. I wrote to him in 1920 or 1921, outlining the circumstances, and asked whether he remembered the youngster at the Volta with whom he used to speak German and Italian. He wrote back a brief, politely worded note, saying that he remembered it all very well, and that he would very much like to meet me again; if I ever came to Paris would I let him know, and we should have a glass of wine together. The rest of the story is too long for this place, but something further might be recorded before we continue our journey. What remains most clearly in my memory of Joyce was his kindness to me, an awkward unknown schoolboy, who strayed into his life in the most casual way imaginable. I would be 14–15 years of age when this happened. Our common interests, it seems, were the Moving Pictures and the German and Italian languages. There may have been others, but I do not know them. Joyce often came gently to sit beside me when I visited the Volta (to do so I had to risk punishment for breaking school bounds, but he did not know that), and, sometimes when the programme of primitive films was finished, he might take me to a little tearoom nearby, where he treated me from his very light purse to a bun and a cup of tea. On several occasions his Triestino partner turned up to colour our simple conversations. It was the Park chocolate-seller, his relation, and above all, James Joyce who set me on the way to speaking Italian. It was from Joyce I first heard the wise dictum that "whoever cannot speak and understand a language when spoken does not know it". Kindness and humanity will always be associated in my mind with the name of James Joyce. Gone he is, but he has left his own monuments. Gone too is the Volta Cinema. Whoever wishes to see where it was should stand on the south pavement of Henry Street a couple of hundred yards from the O'Connell Street end and contemplate the business premises on the other side of the road.

*

The mention of Ireland at her craziest reminds me of a Dublin story. Just after World War II an Englishman went there on a holiday, taking his car with him. Petrol was rationed, but, as elsewhere, there was a black market for this essential product. The Englishman was complaining to a friend in a Dublin pub that even on the black market he could not get any petrol. When he had finished his tale of woe, he was tapped on the shoulder by a raw-boned man who commented: "I couldn't help overhearing what you said, Mister, and I feel sorry for you. Now then, you want some black-market petrol? Very well! Go down"—he mentioned a street—"and at the bottom of it there is a small garage kept by a friend of mine, Mickey Dooley. Tell him you've been sent by *me,* and you'll get all you want."

"That's very kind of you, and I'm much obliged," replied the Englishman. "What name shall I say?"

"Tell him," said the tall man, "tell him that Sergeant So-and-so of the Civic Guard sent you."

The Englishman was a little surprised, but, after all, was he not in Dublin, where anything can happen? So, thanking the Sergeant in plain clothes, off he went in search of the garage. He returned to the pub in ten minutes or so, and the Sergeant said to him: "Well, how did you get on?"

The Englishman replied: "No luck! He either had none or he wouldn't give it to me."

"But," said the Sergeant, "did you mention *my name and rank in the Civic Guard?*"

"Yes."

"And *that* didn't work?" The policeman was flabbergasted.

"No," replied the Englishman, shaking his head ironically, "even that didn't work."

"Well, now, did ye ever hear the like!" roared the Sergeant. "Ireland for ever! No damned respect for the law! Come with me and we'll see what we can do."

How it ended we are not told. Nor does it matter very much, the point being that, as every visitor quickly discovers, Dublin is above all else the City of Beautiful Nonsense. Here one moves from the sublime to the ridiculous—and vice versa —more quickly than in any other city on our planet.

*

No attempt can be made here to describe this historic city of half a million inhabitants and a thousand years of story. But do not miss St. Patrick's Cathedral for its memorials and records of Ascendancy Ireland, and Swift, that great soul who was great enough to have placed in the Cathedral a tablet to his footman. There it is, amid the memorials to those who were considered people of importance. But Swift thought that his manservant was as worthy as they of this honour; and who can gainsay his judgment? If you wish to make Dublin your Convenient Centre, you will find it a good one: not only for what the city itself has to offer—this you will find in the guide-books—but because from Dublin you can quickly reach Dundalk and the Boyne country with those wonderful antiquities of *Brug na Boinne*; or strike southwards into the Wicklow Mountains and take in their beauties; or, if you wish for seaside in the English sense, there are Dun Laoghaire (the English still call it Kingstown, and so do the older Irish) and Bray. Dublin city dominates that small County Dublin. Outside the city there is not much of architectural interest, though the whole of this little county is good for that great category of people who, once in a while, go all out for a *good time*. Whoever cannot enjoy life hereabouts must be incurably sad.

You must not forget that Dublin is also a Convenient Centre for Counties Meath, Westmeath and Kildare, and one of the pleasant things of life is to travel from Dublin by bus into the interior. It is only about fifty miles to Athlone, and that is approximately half-way across Ireland. Never forget that distances in this country are short, and that almost wherever you go you will find interesting landscape. And interesting people.

CHAPTER II

DONEGAL AND THE WEST

When first I came to Ireland,
Some pleasure for to find,
It's there I spied a damsel fair,
Most pleasing to my mind.
Her rosy cheeks and sparkling eyes,
Like arrows pierced my breast:
They called her lovely Molly O,
The Lily of the West.

Street Ballad.

1

From Derry to Bundoran

If I transport the reader from Dublin to Derry, he must not take this long jump amiss. I do so merely as a matter of expediency, treating Derry as a Convenient Centre in The North from which the next county, Donegal, can be approached, and thence down the western seaboard. It is merely as a Convenient Centre for northern Donegal that Derry is mentioned at this point. Because it is in the political division of Northern Ireland, I shall have more to say about the city later—in the chapter which deals with the Six County Area.

In Derry you can never forget that you are in the political division called 'Northern Ireland', but you can walk from there across The Border into County Donegal in The Republic, *Poblacht na hEireann* since 1949. As you know, The Republic is popularly called 'The South'. One of the peculiarities of Ireland is that Malin Head, the most northerly point in the whole country, is in County Donegal—which is in 'The South'! If you should ever get as far as Malin Head, you will have become accustomed by this time to such little anomalies. All this northern part of Ireland enjoys an invigorating atmosphere. Draw a line on the map roughly from Bundoran to Drogheda, and north of it is the area to which I particularly refer. The line so drawn will almost follow the Black Pig's Dyke, made by a supernatural boar which furrowed the land and swam lakes as it charged across Ireland! In this area the wind tends to come more from the east than from the west, there is not much heavy frost in winter, and summer days, even when there is rain, are very stimulating—especially to the visitor from austerity Britain. In this respect there is little difference between Counties Derry and Donegal, but in almost every other respect the differences are striking.

This county has its English name from the town of that name, *Dun na nGall* (the 'Fort of the Foreigners') anglicized as Donegal. In Irish the territory is called *Tír Conaill* (the 'Land of Conal') from one Conal, an ancient prince ('Niall of the Nine Hostages', A.D. 380–405) of the Hy Neill and kinsman of the Owen (*Eoghain*) who gave his name to *Tír Eoghain* which the English called Tyrone. The two most striking differences which you will notice between Donegal and Derry are, first, in the hilly, mountainous and in parts *wildly* mountainous landscape, the irregular coast, and the ruggedness of nearly the whole of Donegal; and, second, in the Donegal people. Some person better equipped than I may be able to give all the reasons why Donegal people are so different from those of Derry, which is beside them. The most I can offer by way of explanation is that, because of the wildness and bleakness of most of that county, the English Planters preferred to keep to Derry as much more promising from a business point of view; and they benevolently left Donegal to those native Irish already there, and also for natives who might decide that the planted areas of Derry, Tyrone and Fermanagh would from then onwards provide them with little more than a bare existence, if that. And so Donegal remains, like Galway, Mayo and Kerry, an *Irish* part of Ireland with its *Gaeltacht,* Irish-speaking districts, pockets and islands. In some parts of Donegal you are among a foreign people, and experience a way of life as different from that of Britain—or Derry—as you will find among the mountain people of Macedonia. Hence, for the visitor, there are two major attractions: landscape and people.

You do not have to penetrate more than a few miles into Donegal before you begin to feel the impression of both. From Derry you can enjoy very wonderful outings in the neighbouring county, to Glencolumbcille, where you will find both pagan cromlechs and carved stone crosses; or along the coast of Lough Foyle to Moville and thence to Culdaff and Malin Head itself—the most northerly point of Ireland. Or you can go to Buncrana, a delightful little resort on Lough Swilly. Cross from Buncrana to Rathmullan on the other side of this Lough, and from now onwards, if you keep to the coast, you will hear Irish spoken. Farther westwards are three places any one of which is ideal for a quiet, interesting holiday: Creeslough, Gweedore and Dungloe. A little place which remains fondly in my memory is Dunfanaghy (The 'Fort of the Fair Warrior'). It has Horn Head on a peninsula to the North, good amenities and a golf-course, with a seaboard walk along a great strand and scenery to take away your breath. Hereabouts you will be able to get a boat to take you to islands, to Inishbofin and Tory, the latter well worth a visit, and only about nine miles out in the Atlantic. The name Tory is pronounced Torry and means 'towers' —the island or place of Towers. Visit it if you can and, if possible, stay for a few days or a week or two on the island; for this is a wonderful experience. Tory Island and wreckage are almost synonymous terms. This bleak island seems to draw to it what is left of the ships which perish in this wild, almost desolate part of Atlantic seaboard. The people are Irish-speaking. All Donegal Irish-speakers are bilingual, and while you are in these parts do not imagine, if you do not always hear Irish spoken in your presence, that the people do not know the language. In the *Gaeltacht* it is an unwritten law of politeness not to speak Irish in the presence of anybody who does not know it. In practice, Irish is the language used among people who know each other, English being used with all others—unless the others take the lead and show a desire to speak Irish. There is a curious cross on Tory Island, the design of which is of Egyptian origin: no doubt accountable by virtue of the connection there was between the old Irish and the Coptic branches of Christianity. I cannot pretend to tell you all you should know of

River Moy—Ballina, Co. Mayo
ITA

Tory Island, for which you must refer to Mason's best of all books on the Irish islands.[1]

And, since I mention this book, I must also remind you that this north Donegal countryside and hereabouts is the homeland of Peadar O'Donnell, author of *Islanders, The Knife* and other works of fiction which are at the same time works of art and 'documents'. Read this author's works before or after your visit to this part of Ireland; but read them you must. In them are vivid pictures of the countryside and landscape and of the mentality of the people by one of them who is a native speaker of their language. In reading the beautiful prose of this writer I am always reminded of Oscar Wilde's remark that the Irish are too poetical a race to be poets. Peadar O'Donnell is the prose-poet of northern Donegal.

But we must some time go on to consider Bundoran, another Convenient Centre in the same county of Donegal—but rather a different one from most of the others. As its name indicates, Bundoran is 'the Foot of the Doran River', and here again old Ireland, Country of Beautiful Nonsense, lives up to her reputation for the eccentric. There is no such river hereabouts as the Doran; nor any record, sign or even a trace of one. Never mind! We must look to its foot, at the very southernmost end of Donegal on the Atlantic and on the border of County Sligo. Bundoran provides everything that you may wish in a popular seaside resort: good hotels and guest-houses, amusements, golf, surf and rock-pool bathing, a fine strand and a countryside and coastline with pleasant walks and interesting associations. Nearby in Donegal is Ballyshannon, birthplace of William Allingham, whom the English have kindly adopted as an English poet, though no poet writing in English had more of the Celtic spirit: just as Bernard Shaw has now been taken to heart as an 'English Dramatist', though before he arrived at the stage of fame, he was an 'impossible Irishman'! The Irish do not take such purloinings amiss, being long familiar with them and also of a most forgiving nature. But they do like, from time to time,

[1] *The Islands of Ireland,* by Thomas H. Mason (1936). This excellent work should be consulted, not only about Tory, but about the Aran, Blasket and other islands off the Irish coast. No other book provides more or more reliable information.

The Fiddle-Stone at Castle Caldwell—Fermanagh
UTDA

Farmer's Daughter
ITA

to draw attention to the facts. William Allingham was of Anglo-Irish parentage, and his family, like that of Shaw, came from Hampshire to Ireland, Allingham's in the reign of Queen Elizabeth. Ireland did the rest, and so we have in the poems of this gentle man, this close observer of beautiful things and poet of Nature, not one but many poems which might be translations from the *Fenian Cycle.* He achieves the miracle of the Celtic poet; that is, he can transport us to *Tír na nÓg,* the Land of Youth. Consider those Fairies of his who—

Down along the rocky shore
Some make their home,
They live on crispy pancakes
Of yellow tide-foam;
Some in the reeds
Of the black mountain lake,
With frogs for their watch-dogs,
All night awake.

No English poet could have written just like that.

When you are in Bundoran you can walk along its strand, climb some steps up a hill to a highland on which has been built a fine hotel with grand golf-links, walk along by the cliff-top and round by the sea, and you will come to—the Fairy Bridges!—with a natural wishing-chair of stone, in which you must sit and wish where, for generations visitors have sat and wished, as I have as a child on innumerable occasions. From practical experience, I can assure the prospective visitor that several of my wishes were granted: particularly one in which I expressed the wish to sail around the globe and see many strange lands and peoples. I doubt if it is much use wishing for *money*; and I can give a very good reason. Fairies do not think highly of money, and I would go so far as to dogmatize that they would not highly approve of those who put money in the forefront of desirables. No! Don't wish for money, but wish for the health of a salmon, land without rent, a wife without too much sense (if you are a male), a child every year if you are a farmer—and, as these are old Irish wishes, the fairies will understand them. If they take to you, your wish may be granted. And if none of your wishes is granted, this simply means that the fairies either don't understand you, or just don't like you! And that's all there is to it.

When you have wished and inspected those rough 'Bridges' of rock cut out by the Atlantic which, on occasion, beats in here even in summer with a force to make a maelstrom that is frightening to look at, walk on along the cliff-top, and you will come to a vast strand and sandhills. The strand is dangerous for bathers, though many a time I have bathed in the face of solemn warnings. On a summer's day nothing is more pleasant than to picnic on the top of the sandhills above Finner Strand—and sit there looking at the long range of mountains on the north side of Donegal Bay, or the coastline fading away towards Sligo and Ben Bulben in the south.

A few miles north of Ballyshannon is the little town of Donegal, of which the name and historical record are of greater interest than the modern town, pleasing as it is. On the seashore, and protected by a sea-wall, are the ruins of what was an important Franciscan Monastery, founded in 1474 by Hugh O'Donnell. The O'Donnells were the great people of this land. The name is known and respected wherever an Irish person has set foot. I have seen it stated somewhere that there are over three-quarters of a million people named O'Donnell now living on our globe, but am unable to vouch for the accuracy of the figure. Certain it is that O'Donnells were and are fine people; because, thanks to one of the princes of the family, Ireland has a record of her past such as few countries possess. This prince had among his followers a very learned family of O'Clerys, who were hereditary historians to the Princes of Tyrconnell. Those O'Clerys had from the O'Donnell's extensive lands in Donegal and a residence in Kilbarron Castle. In the years 1632–1636 three O'Clerys—Michael, Cucogry and Conary—assisted by Peregrine O'Duigenan, a learned antiquary and a Roscommon man, compiled from all available sources a very wonderful work giving, often in detail similar to Domesday Book, the history of Ireland from 'the year of the world' 2242 to the year 1616 (fifteen years after the defeat of the Great Hugh O'Neill, and the end of the old Gaelic Order in its last stronghold, Tyrone). The book is known as *The Annals of the Four Masters.* The principal author was Michael O'Clery. The four historians were assisted by two of the ancient O'Mulconnaires, hereditary historians to the Kings of Connacht. They made a fine team of scholars. *The Annals* are an indispensable source-book. One can almost say that without them the real history of Ireland would be unknown, for they contain accounts of not only great events but of the life and customs of the ordinary people. They were compiled either in the Franciscan Monastery at Donegal or in its immediate neighbourhood. East of the town is St. Patrick's Church of the Four Masters, a fitting memorial to those revered men.

Near the Fermanagh border, and five miles north of the Border town of Pettigo, lies Lough Derg ('the red lake'), to which thousands of Catholic Irish go on a pilgrimage each year in the summer months. I cannot say whether this is the most important pilgrimage of the Irish, but it is a deeply impressive one for reasons not all of which are religious. There is a bleakness about the whole surrounding country which strikes a chill into the soul to scare almost any human being, and Lough Derg itself, with its little islands, all situated in the midst of a mountain solitude, seems to be just the right kind of remote place that is made by Nature to assist contemplation. For centuries, ever since the days of St. Patrick, Lough Derg has been a place of pilgrimage. This pilgrimage is still a severe one, but there was a time towards the end of the fifteenth century when the religious excesses and extreme self-punishment of the pilgrims were such that Pope Alexander VI suppressed it. After a time the pilgrimage was again permitted by papal authority; and again suppressed. It was again restored in 1632, and since that year it has never failed to attract thousands of men and women, who, barefooted, devoutly go through the prescribed exercises and meanwhile observe a three-days' black fast. A special permission must be obtained by those who wish to remain for more than nine days. The island on which this takes place is Saints' Island, a tiny place dominated by a magnificent church which cost almost £100,000 to build, and surrounded by hostels for clergy, and accommodation for men and women. A few whitewashed cottages and a small chapel are the only other buildings on the island. Looking from it one sees only hills and, in the distance, the blue Donegal mountains. During the pilgrimage, from the moment the pilgrims land on the island, each individual feels himself isolated from humanity and in touch with the infinite. The pilgrimage to Lough Derg represents a spiritual 'cure', a cleansing of the soul of acquired impurities, a great mental catharsis for the troubled and the doubtful. Those who wish to read a powerful account of what this pilgrimage was like in the past will find it in Carleton's *The Lough Derg Pilgrim,* though I think that Catholics should be warned that this account has been deemed to be disturbing to those of their faith. But apart altogether from the religious aspect of this great annual event, the visitor, whatever his religion may be, can hardly fail to find in it and in the unique surroundings an impressiveness, a remoteness from this world that is salutary for the over-civilized.

2

Sligo and Mayo

Whether Bundoran or Sligo has been chosen as a Convenient Centre, no visitor should miss the trip by bus or car along the Coast Road which connects the two towns. It is perhaps better to travel southwards, if the scenery is to be enjoyed in stages of increasing interest. On your right is the Atlantic, on your left mountains, and soon you can see Ireland's famous table mountain, Ben Bulben. This is the country of W. B. Yeats, whose mortal remains by his own wish now rest in the shadow of the Ben or peak. A few miles along the road you will pass by Mullaghmore, a most select little resort favoured by those who prefer its quiet and exclusive atmosphere to the hurly-burly of Bundoran. And then Grange, from which you can go by boat to Inishmurray, an island inhabited by fisherfolk and noteworthy for its antiquities. Here is a large *Cashel,* a pre-Christian stone fort which in the sixth century St. Molaise transformed into a monastery: a good example of the way the early Christians in Ireland utilized what remained of the old order to establish the new. Here also you can see a good example of a 'beehive' hut: a pagan or early Christian structure of uncertain date and conjectured to be a domestic building. There are many of these ancient beehive huts on the western islands, and it is curious that in parts of the Dingle Peninsula, where they abound, the people still often build farm outhouses on that old model: a circular or oval stone foundation with stones laid on it in diameters which decrease in length as the rows are erected, until a space remains at the top which can be stopped by a single stone. Such an edifice is called a *clochán* in Gaelic. I cannot look at one of those old beehive huts without trying to imagine what life in them was like. Pagan Ireland was not famous for its stone buildings and, from all that we read and know, even the palaces of the kings and princes were made of wood: which explains why none survived. But if even kings and princes lived in wooden structures, why should some people choose to build with stone? It is somewhat remarkable that, although there is a considerable number of *clocháns* still existing in a good state of preservation, nothing in the way of an ancient household utensil, pot or implement, nor indeed anything of any kind that is identifiable, has ever been found in any beehive 'dwelling'. I write 'dwelling', for so they are usually called. But were they *dwellings*? There is no proof that they were, and I doubt very much whether they were habitations in the ordinary sense of the word. Might they not have been used by pagan anchorites or priests as retreats? Who can tell! But, to return to Inishmurray, this little island is rich in antiquities. There are three mysterious pillar-stones which may date from that very remote period of Iberian influence; there are many old and inscribed gravestones; and two holy wells and rock basins. Much of all this has still to be explained.

From Grange you have a good view of the strange shape of Ben Bulben. Yeats enthusiasts may wish to pause at the little village of Drumcliff, for it is in the Protestant churchyard here that the body of the poet lies. His grandfather was rector here; and this country *is* Yeats. One has only to stand and look at the landscape to appreciate why the poet drew inspiration from it, for he rightly decided when still a young man, perhaps even when still a mere boy, that no source of inspiration is likely to yield better results to a poet than the soil from which he springs.

Drumcliff is within walking distance of Sligo, a centre from which you can visit the adjacent counties of Mayo and Leitrim, and also enjoy a number of very beautiful sights, including Lough Gill and its island, the name of which Yeats has driven into the minds of thousands: Innisfree.

Sligo is the next Convenient Centre on our list, and no town in Ireland is more beautifully situated for either the visitor who wishes to remain in one place and thence to explore surrounding country, or for the plain holiday-maker who likes to have all the amenities of popular seasides mixed with those of a civilized centre. In the town of Sligo itself you have a prosperous community with a vigorous Protestant element, a fine seaport in a closed-in, sheltered bay, the River Garavogue which divides the town and has most streets leading to its bridges. Parts of Sligo town have a quaint old-world atmosphere which I remember once thinking reminded me of parts of Carcassonne: near the gracious Norman Church of St. John, for example, and the Abbey and the Cathedral. Various external influences have contributed to make the Sligo people what they are: a kindly, hospitable folk without many distinguishing qualities that I know of, but with the good points of the Donegal, Fermanagh and Connacht people, a soft accent and an easy way of conversing. Both Catholics and Protestants here have that quality to be found among nearly all the Donegal people which I, personally, find refreshing and in great contrast to some manifestations I have noticed elsewhere and on both sides of The Border. In Donegal and Sligo you will not find mean and narrow bigots: Protestant regards Catholic as a fellow-man to be judged by his behaviour as a human being and not by his religious label; and Catholics regard Protestants in the same way. It seems to me that this sort of humanist attitude should develop naturally when the numerical majority of one side over the other is not great. But this is not so, or not always so, for there are many places in the Six County Area with a minute majority of Protestants or Catholics in which there is none of the calm atmosphere of toleration to be found here in Sligo or Donegal. I attribute the good qualities of Donegal and Sligo people to a divine gift which I should very much like to see extended. The only trouble in Sligo that I have ever read of was closely related to the Corporation. For many years, that body, if accounts are right, lived in a sort of Utopia of its own creation in which a man need not bother much about anybody else. Whoever could carry municipal 'Take-no-heed, let-it-rip!' to the finest shade of quietism was regarded among the élite of Sligo as doing work to qualify for beatification. There were protests, but those good people showed amazing patience and toleration with their sit-tight Corporation. It seems, on looking back, that I was in Sligo when this Utopia was flowering. But such is Sligo that I, a mere visitor, did not know anything about it and never a word was whispered to enlighten me. Sligo is one of those places that, if some local matter were to reach the powder-magazine stage at which a mere spark can cause an upheaval, the stranger would be told: "It's nothing! Just a local argument!" And if that is not consideration and encouragement for the timid stranger, I do not know what is! Incidentally, I heard that the Corporation had improved in recent years, and when I asked *how,* my Sligo correspondent wrote back: "You ask how our people have improved and I'm sorry I can't tell you." I enquired of some men of the present moment, and they all say Sligo's affairs have in recent years greatly improved—for which some of them seem rather sorry as *"there's not the local fun there used to be"*. There I leave it. The main point is that Sligo is a very pleasant, easy-going town which extends its welcome to all comers. If you should be interested in architecture, statuary, memorials, town-buildings, or even in the structure and appearance of the domestic house, this town will provide the most exacting collector of artistic aberrations and of æsthetic scrambled or addled eggs with all he can cope with. The easy-going tolerance of the Sligo people has permitted a succession of town authorities and county notables, among others, to mark their lovely site with some of the strangest works of Victorian vulgarity. But it so happens that, like most of the statues in London, those of Sligo maintain a dignified comicality which expresses the irony that may have existed in the soul of their creators.

Outside Sligo, on the north side of the Bay, is Rosses Point. It can be used instead of Sligo as a Convenient Centre. Rosses Point and Strandhill, which faces it on the other side of the Bay, are popular seaside resorts and, of the two, the first is highly esteemed by golfers because of the course which, my golfing friends assure me, stands on a level of goodness with those of Portrush and St. Andrews. Not far away and dominating Strandhill is Knocknarea, a round-backed elevation on the summit of which is a very big cairn called in Irish *Misgán Maedhbh,* which means Maeve's Monument, Maeve being that famous Queen of Connacht of the Ulster Cycle, she who organized the great Cattle Drive of Cooley. Maeve has been adapted into English folklore as Queen Mab. In Ireland there are many places called after her, and we have to admit that she must have been a very remarkable woman to have not only monuments such as this (circumference about 600 feet) erected in her memory, but to have left what has grown into the considerable Irish and the minor English folklores derived from it.

Those who have read their history are no doubt aware that many of the ships of the Great Spanish Armada—*La Invencible*—were "wrecked on the West Coast of Ireland", and, except in the works of a few English writers interested in Spain and Spaniards, that is about all we ever read or hear of those wrecks. The year in which this great event happened —the decisive naval battle took place in 1588, July 21st–29th —was in one of Ireland's very distressful periods. It was after the failure of another of those periodic rebellions of the Irish, on this occasion one that was followed by a particularly vicious policy on the part of Queen Elizabeth's deputy in Ireland—a policy in those days considered to be a fully justifiable sequel to an English victory that had been bought at a high price. The Irish rebellion was widespread: the Deputy's forces were severely defeated at Glenmallure by the O'Byrnes in County Wicklow. In the Central Plain the O'Mores and O'Connors almost succeeded in undoing Queen Mary's Plantation and liquidating the Planters. The revolt spread to Ulster and, had the Irish co-ordinated and organized their uprising a little better, the whole of Irish, English and Spanish history afterwards would have been different. It was

England's power-struggle with Spain which set the course of Elizabeth's policy in Ireland, because the Catholic Irish looked to Spain and Rome for help to get rid of their English invaders, and Philip II of Spain looked to Ireland as useful geographically and as a possible source of man-power. An Irish rebellion was for Philip the very helpful act of an ally and, because of the international struggle, one which Elizabeth had to deal with severely and bring to a state of satisfactory finality. Thus, when the Irish were defeated in the field and the military victory of the English was as complete as it could be, the next essential step in English policy must be to see that rebellion could not recur until after the 'Spanish Question' was settled.

The policy upon which the English now embarked in Ireland was deliberately to lay waste the country, destroy crops and the seed for next year's crops, drive off cattle, and in general to take all precautions to create famine conditions. To read the English accounts of the devastation thus created is, if it were possible, more harrowing than to read the Irish. Here, to give some idea of what Ireland was then like, I quote these few words of an English eye-witness: ". . . in short space there was none almost left, and a most populous and plentiful country was suddenly made void of man and beast." That was the state of Ireland when the score of Spanish ships surviving from battles with the English Fleet and the elements came to the west coast of Ireland in their attempt to make their way back to Spain. Some of them were wrecked on the Donegal coast and islands, some on the rocks around Killybegs, Ballyshannon and Bundoran; some on the Sligo and Mayo coasts, some in Galway and Clare; and some in Kerry. The stories often heard to the effect that the people in parts of the west of Ireland look very much like Spaniards "because survivors of the Great Armada settled there and intermarried with the natives" can largely be discounted. They do look like Spaniards: that is because many Celts resemble many Spaniards in appearance and also—I think the weightier reason—because of the early and considerable influx of peoples from the Iberian Peninsula which must have taken place.

The visitor still presumably has Sligo as his Convenient

Centre, and so can be reminded that it was on the Sligo coast that a Captain Francisco de Cuellar of the Great Armada was washed ashore when his ship was wrecked. It was an inhospitable shore inhabited by people who were now starving and savage after some years of being hunted and harried by their conquerors. The ordinary Irish people could not always distinguish between Englishmen and Spaniards: to the English the Spaniards were more dangerous enemies than the Irish. Many of the Spaniards had ducats, gold ornaments and precious stones. And so the fate of many wrecked Spaniards was a terrible one. But, when an Irish chief appeared on the scene, things were different. Recognizing their allies and fellow-Catholics, the Irish 'aristocracy' rescued and gave hospitality to the few survivors of the Armada who were lucky enough to fall into their hands. Captain de Cuellar was one of the lucky Spaniards. His is a name to be remembered, for not only did he survive, but he made his way back to Spain and has left an account of his adventure. This is the only account existing that was written by one of those survivors of the Great Armada—the commander of the galleon *San Pedro*—who landed in Ireland; a most interesting and precious document from many points of view. It is in the form of a letter dated 4th October, 1589, and still kept, so far as I know, in the Academy of History in Madrid. James Anthony Froude mentions it and, after the full Spanish text was published in 1885, it became available to the general reader, but now seems to be forgotten. It is of special interest to students of Irish history, for here is a unique source-book, an eyewitness account of that Ireland and also incidentally of the wreck of some of those galleons. I need not here recount Francisco de Cuellar's adventures more than to say that, having been left for dead, he revived and wandered across County Sligo until he fell into the hands of the O'Reillys, whose fortress—a pocket of the Resistance—was at Rossclogher Castle, County Leitrim, near Garrison. It was there than Don Francisco began to write the narrative which (as I translate it for a purpose other than this) I find to be enthralling, in that it throws light into many a dark little corner of our Irish social history. No document that I know gives a more objective statement of an age which, in Ireland especially, was a very terrible one for ordinary people. . . .

We must leave Captain de Cuellar and County Sligo for Mayo, but before so doing I revive again an old chestnut. If you ask an Irishman where he comes from, and Sligo is his homeland, he will say, "From Sligo, thank God!" But if he should come from County Mayo he will say, "From Mayo, God help me!" The reason for this is that whereas Sligo is a comparatively prosperous and fertile county, Mayo is mostly a poor and bleak one. It is so poor and bleak along parts of the coast and on the islands that here there is *Gaeltacht* where the people speak Irish among themselves and in their homes. *Gaeltacht* and poverty are almost synonymous.

Westport is a Convenient Centre for this part of Ireland. From it you can visit Achill Island, connected to the mainland by a bridge, and the largest Irish island. It has become a favourite place for those whose holiday can run to at least a fortnight, but to get the full benefits of Achill, at least a month is required. From Westport you see and can walk to Croagh Patrick, St. Patrick's Mountain, from which he banished snakes from Ireland, and now a place of a great pilgrimage. The coast north of Westport is rugged, picturesque, impressive. At Westport you can play golf, fish, bathe—and from it you can walk in, over and around mountains to your heart's content. You may find that there is something about these mountains in the west of Ireland—here in Mayo as in Connemara to the south—which penetrates the soul, and you begin to realize why it is that the people of the *Gaeltacht*—small farmers, fisherfolk, turf-cutters, sheep-breeders, wool-weavers—with their simple life in these "wilds" are normally so gentle but capable of being roused to strange extremes and excesses, when they can be dangerous. The stranger is not likely to witness such moods. Towards the stranger these people maintain a calm, polite dignity. Big families you will find in that wild west—the average is eight children—living in little stonewalled, thatched and whitewashed cottages from the doors of which, as you pass by, you will get the pleasing aroma of the turf fire. They earn so little in the way of money, those people, that the Englishman or American or, indeed, almost any townsman wonders how they can exist and *"be so happy"*. The chief reason for their happiness and lack of the 'anxiety neurosis' and ultimate insanities of our modern civilization is, as I see it, because in their minds they have a picture of all their problems here and hereafter, and in their simple way of life those problems can be solved—usually by unremitting application to simple and satisfying work. A man sees his ewe give birth to a lamb, the lamb grows into a sheep, and is shorn for wool or sold, the wool is woven into cloth, the woman of the house makes clothes for the family and sells the surplus: a cycle which solves the clothing problem and even does a little more. The way of life of these people is one of little cycles, each of which completes itself, all of them contributing to a healthy, satisfying existence, an absence of being bothered about this and that and the other footling things and major frustrations of our higher culture.

Although the southern part of County Galway is rewarding in many ways, I think most people find the north-western districts—Iarconnacht, Connemara and the Joyce's Country—more exciting in every way. If you should travel south from Sligo, calling at Westport, in Mayo, and are making for Leenane in Galway, you should find a reason, at any cost (and it need not be much), to visit Killary Harbour. This lovely little place is situated on an inlet or fjord which, for sheer beauty, has nothing to fear from Norwegian competition. The country around here and on to Leenane, another beautifully situated town, is not only a sportsman's paradise, but it is dominated by those Twelve Bens or 'Pins', most famous of all the blue mountains of the west. My mind is not now concerned with these facts, which you will find in every guide-book, but with a famous name associated with Killary and Renvyle rather than with them or the big and impressive Kylemore Abbey not far away. The name is Granuaile, short for *Grania ni Mhaile,* anglicized as Grace O'Malley. She is one of those formidable female immortals whose names adorn Irish history from its beginnings. This lady, if you please, was a pirate—a freebooting, buccaneering seawoman who flourished in the reign of Queen Elizabeth. In English history we first read of her in a letter written by Sir Henry Sidney (father of the more famous Sir Philip) to Elizabeth and referring to our pirate as Grany Imallye and as a "most famous feminine sea-captain" who, presumably as a sailor of fortune, "offered her services to him in Ireland or Scotland" with "three galleys and three hundred fighting-men". Sir Henry comments that 'Grany' brought her husband with her when she spoke with him and that "she was as well by sea as by land more than Mrs. Mate with him". Her second husband this was, the first being one of the ferocious O'Flahertys of Ballinahinch, near Leenane. Killary fjord and harbour was her headquarters. She practised the art of piracy and freebooting up and down that coast and among the islands. But she was caught and served a term of imprisonment. Why Grace was not hanged I do not know: unless it be that, while in prison, she made it known to her captors that she would serve Elizabeth. The details are obscure, but Grace decided to go to London and see the Great Queen. It seems that Elizabeth was so ready to meet her that she took lessons in Irish in order to be able to greet the distinguished pirate in her own tongue. There is no doubt that Elizabeth sincerely admired that woman of mettle, for she off-hand pardoned all the piracy and freebooting. Furthermore, the English Queen was polite, generous and kind to Grace O'Malley and so sincere that the Irishwoman was deeply touched and even decided to abandon her freebooting. She returned to her Castle near the entrance to Killary Bay and close to Renvyle and Lough Fee. It is recorded: "Ever bearing cess and paying Her Majesty's composition rent and did utterly give over her former trade of maintenance by sea and land."

And so Grace O'Malley became Granuaile of Irish story, the woman with as much physical courage and daring as any man: *Grania ni Mhaile* becomes Granuaile, which is another way of expressing Cathleen ni Houlihan or Dark Rosaleen or Ireland herself, that brave and beautiful female of the sentimental poets and of worshippers at the female shrine. The lady chose, of all places, Killary Bay for her headquarters, which proves that she was a woman of very good taste.

3
Galway—the Aran Islands

This County of Mayo (the people there pronounce it may-oh, stress on the *oh*) and the neighbouring County of Galway are the country of the O'Malleys, of "the ferocious O'Flahertys", of the Joyces and many others whose names are famous. The City of Galway (said to have been a city two thousand years ago: the Magnata of Ptolemy) is notable for the obscurity of its history before the Anglo-Norman invasion and for its clear and often turbulent history from then onwards. It was the O'Connor stronghold when the Norman Richard de Burgo (or de Burgh, anglicized as Burke), nearly fifty years after the landing of the invaders, captured it (1232) from Irish resisters and colonized it with a number of families, the members of which were to become "more Irish than the Irish". When Cromwell was later putting into practice his terrible edict (1653) which offered the Irish east of the Shannon the choice of going "to hell or Connacht", those families kept themselves aloof from the Irish natives and, for this reason, the Cromwellians sneeringly gave them what was intended to be an opprobrious description—"The Tribes of Galway"—which the Galway people accepted, but later as a term of honour and distinction. When in this city you come upon the names of Blake, Lynch, Skerrett, Bodkin, Brown, D'Arcy, Ffrench, Joyce, Morris, Martin, Kirwan, Athy, Dean and Faunt—all Norman, English or Welsh names, you note—you have the name of a descendant of one of those Tribes.

The Irish owe a debt of gratitude to the Tribes. In spite of all difficulties, those cool-headed Anglo-Normans succeeded in advancing the well-being of Galway from a state of horror and misery to one of comparative affluence. They made it a great port and trading centre from which corn and other local products were exported to England, France, Spain and even to Italy. The city imported from those countries interesting merchandise which was lacking in Ireland. The Galway wine trade, for example, became a very flourishing one. Such was the trade between Galway and Spain that, to this day, you will find down by the quays a Spanish arch and some dilapidated old houses with what seem to me Spanish *patios*. But Galway's trade was ruined with the rest of Irish trade by laws imposed by conquerors acting on behalf of 'interests' which did not wish to have their profits reduced by this active competition. Today you can wander through streets near the port where you will see the melancholy remains of the tall old stone warehouses of that vanished Spanish trade. Galway also had its 'Irishtown', like that of many other cities and towns in Ireland: a part in which the native Irish were segregated in order that they might not contaminate their lords and masters. This part, still called the Claddagh ('beach' or 'sea-shore'), is, as its name indicates, near the harbour. When I first visited it many years ago, the Claddagh was a colourful little quarter mostly inhabited, I think, by fisherfolk, and then one still saw there what one now sees only in some part of the *Gaeltacht*: the red petticoats, kerchiefs and often very beautifully embroidered shawls worn by women. The Claddagh had its 'king' and celebrated its own feasts, among which might almost be counted wakes for the dead, for, considering that these were poor folk, their wakes were often elaborate and costly affairs. The Claddagh is still there. But gone are the lovely-looking old thatched and whitewashed cottages with their brightly painted gates and little patches of gay flowers. Alas, they were insanitary; and had their cattle. Now their place has been taken by commonplace modern cottages not nearly so good as the small villas one sees in 'ribbon development' on the outskirts of industrial towns in England. The modern Claddagh is hygienic—and uninteresting. Why the modern should necessarily be made dull and uninteresting, especially when it has to replace something picturesque and with a tradition, I cannot tell. Galway in this follows the trend of our times. Yet, you can still buy a Claddagh ring—two hands holding a crowned heart—a symbol related to seafaring.

Galway is the most 'foreign' city in these islands. Not only has it this distinction, but it is a Convenient Centre from which Connemara can be visited, as well as a long list of places, antiquities and buildings of great interest, and providing thrills for the most blasé stranger. From Galway you

Connemara Turf Cutter at Work
ITA

Derry City on the Foyle UTDA

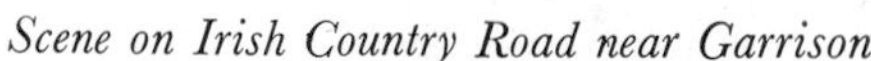

Scene on Irish Country Road near Garrison

UTDA

can go by rail east to Ballinasloe ('the mouth of the ford of the hosts'), and about nine miles farther east of that town you will come to Clonfert Cathedral, which is, architecturally, one of Ireland's most beautiful buildings. A gem. This Cathedral is no bigger than an English country church. The site was chosen, not because of a populous community (for there is none thereabouts), but because it was known to be the place selected by some holy man of a remote period to seclude himself from the world and its wickedness. The doorway is Romanesque of the twelfth century. There is nothing in all Ireland to surpass it in exquisitely extravagant stone decorations. Clonfert is worth a day of any visitor's time for this marvel alone; and for the equally beautiful east window.

On the way back to Galway you pass Aughrim, where there was a famous battle on the 12th July, 1691. You may remember that the Battle of the Boyne was fought in that month the year before. This was the Williamite War. At Aughrim, Orange William's troops were led by the Dutchman Ginkle. The Irish were helped by French troops under St. Ruth, their own leader being Sarsfield, a man of great military skill and boldness. The Irish lost the battle of Aughrim—experts say St. Ruth was to blame—and those two battles were followed by the final struggle farther south, from which came the Treaty of Limerick, on the 3rd October, 1691. It ended those wars but solved nothing. The winners broke it. Following that Treaty was the famous 'Flight of the Wild Geese', the voluntary exile of thousands of Irishmen who went to all parts of Europe and became soldiers of fortune, or settled to become citizens in the new countries of their adoption. Pass on from Aughrim, traveller, but remember that the name of this village is written into Ireland's history with the blood of her sons.

*

There are few real Gipsies in Ireland, though there are some 'duddekais', wanderers with gipsy blood in them. But in the west there are still many 'tinkers', and I think that there must be gipsy blood in some of them. Half a century ago it seemed as if tinkers would present a social problem in Ireland, so numerous and widespread were they, and organized, if the word can be applied, in 'tribes'. One can hardly call those who remain—they are often referred to as 'travellers'—anything but family groups which hang together loosely and move from place to place with the seasons and for such events as fairs and races. In the old days the tinkers did much useful work mending pots and pans, or making small household articles which they sold or exchanged, and living a care-free, colourful existence which brought them into story and song. They had their own system of marriage and moral code, but as they seldom committed any crime worse than an occasional stroke of violence, and generally after they had 'drink taken', they were not regarded as a bad nuisance. The sticklers for law and order and regimentation looked askance at them. They were nearly all poor, those old tinkers; and their life was not easy.

How different are the tinkers today! They are still wanderers, each group with its regular places of call. But now they are considerable dealers in cattle, horses and the bigger things of life, such as cars and lorries. One can meet a rich tinker now; real poverty among them is rare. They turn up at important fairs, do their trading, have a carousal, and move on. When the men get drunk, and sometimes the women also, they become quarrelsome, and often there are fierce fights. The main characteristic of the tinker we now meet is his aptness to 'fly off the handle' into a sudden rage about what ordinary people might regard as a trifle; and then he can be a dangerous and very violent creature. Hence, it is advisable to be cautious with tinkers from noon onwards, for if a tinker has had a few drinks, he may feel inclined to trail his coat, and is better left alone. I saw a tinkers' fight in Galway one Fair Day, or rather after the fair had finished. It was a long-drawn-out business, the principals being two men who, I learnt afterwards, had quarrelled because one told the other that he was a bad man. The man thus accused said he was a good man. And so the row started at the top end of Eyre Square in Galway with an exchange of blows and no great harm done. What interested me most was the way the women entered into it, taking sides and, while each side was ready to fight, they tried to solve the problem by agreement or arbitration among themselves. In the middle of it all their 'king' turned up, a handsome, solid man of muscular physique, with his wand of office in the form of a good ash-plant with a useful knob. I cannot say that the king impressed me with either his intelligence or his personality, and I felt thwarted and disappointed when two Civic Guards came along and, so to speak, cleared the square with a wave of the hand.

The tinkers are no great problem to the authorities now, excepting perhaps to the collectors of taxes! All the same, there should be a film or two in these picturesque wanderers, who deserve to be 'documented' before they disappear. There is nothing quite like them outside of Ireland.

*

In Shop Street, near Eyre Square, is St. Nicholas (Collegiate) Church, founded in 1320, a pre-Reformation edifice built by the Normans and one with many interesting associations. This now Church of Ireland property is notable for a triple nave and a pyramidal belfry, in which there is an old French bell from Cavron in Normandy. The church, though built in different periods, is uniform in general design, and is altogether pleasing and impressive. What I found of most interest in this church were its associations, especially the story that, before he set out on his great voyage which ended with the discovery of America, Columbus heard Mass there. If the story is not true, it is a good one. I cannot discover a reasonable foundation in fact for it. As is well known, Columbus was in Portugal and Spain for some years before Santagel and Abravanel produced the finance for his voyage, and there is no really reliable record of any visit by him to Galway either immediately before his departure or, so far as I can find, at any other time. What we do know is that, in order to persuade possible backers for his project that he was a great 'navigator', Columbus told some very tall stories about his travels, one of them being that he had visited Ireland. This may or may not have been true (confirmation is lacking), but, if he went to Ireland, Galway would have been a likely port of call. That would have been years before the voyage of discovery and the events which immediately led to it. The part of the Galway story to the effect that a Galwayman went with him on his first voyage is undoubtedly more likely, for there is in the authentic crew-list a record of an Irishman whose name is not given, but who is described as *Guillermo Irés*—William the Irishman—having been a member of the crew of one of his ships. On this hangs a tale with a very Irish tang about it, so that one cannot altogether rule out its probability. When the three ships prepared for the expedition of discovery were anchored at the little Spanish port of Palos, near Huelva, it was found at the last moment that some of the men were missing. A visit to the calaboose could provide substitutes, and there is surely a probability that among these was found our famous Irish William! A familiar picture comes to mind: that of a sailors' carousal ending in a brawl with the arrest of William and others for being 'drunk and disorderly'—not a very serious offence, but by no means an uncommon one.

Some years ago in Spain, when I was engaged in research about Columbus, this story and its possibilities fascinated me; yet I was unable to find evidence to substantiate it beyond the bare record that 'Guillermo Irés' was one of Columbus's men on that voyage of discovery—a fact which nobody can dispute. Some writers say that he was a certain Rice de Culvey, but I have not seen evidence which would confirm the truth of this. There is nothing very remarkable in the presence of an Irishman at such an event as Columbus's discovery of the western continent. For we have it in the *Landnamboc* of Ari Marson that, when the Norsemen went to America centuries before Columbus, they found Irish-speaking people on the mainland there. And in the *Eyrbyggja Saga* there is mention of a merchant, Gudleif Gudlangson, "who was blown to a strange land far to the West of Iceland and there found a strange people who spoke Irish". With their usual modesty the Irish have not laboured their claim to priority in the discovery of America, being content to leave it to the Norsemen to establish it for them. That they were well 'in on it' need not be doubted. They merely failed to exploit a good thing, but many of them have since made up for the previous failure.

*

In Market Street, near the Church of St. Nicholas, you

should look for a slab of black marble on which you will see the words *Remember Deathe, Vaniti of Vaniti, and all is but Vaniti.* This slab was placed in 1624 on the mansion of a Galway merchant, James Lynch Fitzstephen, to commemorate a very terrible incident in his life when he was chief magistrate or mayor of the city in the year 1493. When the original mansion (in Shop Street, at the corner of Abbeygate Street) was demolished to make space for widening the street—that would be about a hundred years ago—the slab was removed to its present position. The story of James Lynch Fitzstephen has been told and retold with innumerable embellishments until I feel timid about even mentioning it; but the fact remains that, stripped of the embellishments, it still has in it the elements of great tragedy, and there is background with a sufficiency of incident and of variegated colours to make a novel, an opera or a play. The term 'Lynch Law'—summary execution without legal authority—comes from the incident in question and, by one of those curious perversions, the name Lynch is now attached to the barbarity. But the truth is that the incident on which the term is founded was an act which had behind it the full authority of the law, the extraordinary feature of the incident being that, when the lawgiver could not find an executioner to hang the lawbreaker (his own son, in this instance), rather than see the law thwarted, he came forward and himself filled the office of the hangman. It was a case of fulfilment of the law in the utmost logic, whereas 'Lynch Law' is the opposite! Why the calumny should have attached itself to the name I do not know, but it is about time that the strictly legal aspect of the story should be made clear. It was an act of legal justice which that magistrate felt had to be fulfilled in the interests of authority, of established law and order, of urban discipline—even if he had to do it himself and the criminal was his own son.

James Lynch Fitzstephen was one of those many Galway merchants engaged in the profitable trade with Spain—in those days Galway had a fine commerce with Spanish ports, and her merchants often visited Spain. Fitzstephen was very friendly with a Cadiz merchant named Pedro Gomez and, on one occasion, having had a most pleasant time in the Gomez household, he brought his host's son back to Galway for a holiday. Young Gomez, as a guest of the Fitzstephen family, met Walter Lynch Fitzstephen, the Galway merchant's son, who, the story goes, was engaged to a desirable local girl named Anna Blake. At this point one version of the story presents us with the usual triangle: the course of true love between Walter and Anna did not always run smoothly; the young Spaniard found Anna attractive and, if we are to believe it, took advantage of tiffs between the lady and her suitor to pay court to her. Another and more poetical version has it that the Spaniard grew to think so highly of his friend Walter that he did everything in his power to bring Walter and Anna together after their lovers' quarrels. What does seem to be reasonably authentic is that the Spaniard and Anna saw much of each other, danced together at balls and what not; thereby provoking jealousy in the heart of Walter, as might be expected. Then came a day when Walter, who, apparently, had been visiting a tavern and had warmed up somewhat, returned home to catch young Don Gonzalvc Gomez and Anna Blake seated together in a quiet corner of the Fitzstephen garden and in what he regarded as a compromising situation. Here the story again varies. Walter drew either a sword or a dagger, killed Don Gonzalvo, and took refuge in the house of one Seamus Mac Hugh, a retainer of the Lynch family. The body of Gonzalvo Gomez was soon discovered, and it was not long before the chief magistrate and his men were on the track of the murderer, who confessed to the crime. Then followed the trial, at which James Lynch Fitzstephen presided, found his son guilty, and sentenced him to be publicly hanged. Again the story varies: they could not find a hangman because no hangman was available; hangmen were available, but none would undertake the job of hanging Fitzstephen's son, because of the respect in which the Fitzstephen family was held. Either the young man must remain unhung or his own father must hang him. The father and a priest spent the night before the day of execution in the cell with Walter Lynch Fitzstephen. Embroideries on the story are that the hangman was by this time being fêted in the town because he had abandoned his office; that a widow O'Shaughnessy, whose son Chief Magistrate

Fitzstephen had condemned to be hanged, was now going about boasting of the curse she had put on the Fitzstephen family; and there are innumerable others. What is quite certain is that Fitzstephen and his son Walter duly appeared before the great crowd gathered in front of the Lynch 'Castle' or household. The two figures appeared in the arched window above the main portals and, in full view of the assembled people, Fitzstephen placed a noose around his son's neck, kissed him on the brow and launched him into space. The sequel to the story is that the act wrought such havoc on the magistrate that he was a broken man and never again showed himself in public. To complete the tragedy, James Lynch Fitzstephen fell into a physical and mental decline and died in "great mental distress".

I have given this old story space and retold it in my own way because it is, first, an example of how much story there sometimes is behind a few words on a slab of stone in this country, where almost every stone can tell a story. Secondly, because it exemplifies how far a ruling magistrate in Ireland in those days was prepared to go in order to maintain his idea of justice. Thirdly, because it is the only example I know of a magistrate under British rule having to become executioner, hangman of his own son. Finally, because of the effect which his act of justice had on that magistrate. With that I must leave it to the moralists to work out the natural justice of it all, and to ponder what Anna Blake was left with to turn over in her mind for the rest of her life. There may be something in it to explain why Fitzstephen's act of justice became perverted into the term 'Lynch Law'.

*

From Galway you can go to the Aran Islands, and, if the weather is fine, the one-day trip is very pleasant. The vessel which takes you goes to Kilronan on Aranmore and, weather permitting, to Inishmaan and Inisheer. The journey from Galway to Kilronan lasts about four hours, and, on a good day, you will have a fine view of the Connemara coast and of the little communities at Barna, Spiddal, Inveran on that coast, and, to the south, you will see the uninviting Clare Mountains and Black Head. Even on a 'calm' day you will feel the Atlantic roll. On arrival at Kilronan you will see what you have never in your life seen unless you have been here before: the miraculous expertness with which those islanders handle their *currachs*—canoes or coracles, in English—astonishingly seaworthy craft made of lath and tarred canvas, and so light that a man can carry one on his back. The first time I went out in an Aran Island *currach* one of the men looked at me whimsically and said: "I see that your hair is not parted in the middle. You must be very careful, Mister, or you'll have us all in the water." Aranmen manipulate the canoes with wonderful speed and instinctive adroitness. Those frail craft can carry surprising weights and, what seems almost beyond belief, the men have been known to transport animals from the island to the mainland seven miles away in their eight-foot craft. If you have seen the film *Man of Aran,* you will know that these islanders can weather the huge Atlantic waves in their angriest moods. It is a great sight to see the men load their canoes from the ship, and when one considers that the slightest mistake of judgment means that they are thrown into the sea and the *currach* sinks, one is lost in admiration at the skill of it all.

The Aran Islands are notable for their innumerable antiquities, their cruel surface on which 'fields' are made of seaweed carried up from the beaches, yielding the poorest of livings to those sturdy people. You can get a jaunting-car at Kilronan, and, for a matter of shillings, see the main sights of the island—including *Dun Aengus,* a great prehistoric fort on the edge of cliffs that are perpendicular, which ought not to be missed. Most of the drivers of the jaunting-cars know the history of Aran very well. I found one man who could tell me the story of almost every stone we passed as we drove to Gortnagoppel (the 'Field of the Horse') where Liam O'Flaherty was born. As Peadar O'Donnell is the prose-poet of Donegal, Liam is the prose-poet of Aran and the western *Gaeltacht,* especially in his short stories, many of which good judges agree to be masterpieces of observation and of feeling for Nature and that life. To me the people of the Aran Islands are of more interest than the islands or their antiquities. Galway is said to be the most 'Irish' city in Ireland. If that is so, the mainland city hardly knows Irishness. The proof of this strikes one when an Aranman is seen walking along a Galway street: a tall, muscular man who carries himself proudly and walks with a quick springiness which indicates a great reserve of strength. A day trip to Aran is better than none. To know the islands moderately, a month or six weeks may be required, and no visitor will ever regret his island holiday.

4

Connemara and the Joyce's Country

When a person who is not from Connemara hears the word, he usually takes it to mean a fairly large area in Connacht: say, the part of Mayo and Galway west of a line drawn from Westport to Galway City. The *real* Connemara is a comparatively small district around its capital, Clifden: say, the part of Galway west of an irregular line drawn from near Leenane to Cashel on Bertaghboy Bay. It is in this small area that the visitor should be most interested, at all events on his first visit, after which he may devote some attention to the Joyce's Country which lies west and south of Lough Mask. In that part of Galway south of these two districts and known as Iarconnacht, he will find very little but stones: except along the coast, where there are some pleasant little villages, including Spiddal, a centre for the teaching of Gaelic.

In the British Isles, in Europe and in the world, Connemara is unique. But before attempting to indicate why it is unique, let me assure the reader that he ought not—except in exceptionally busy holiday seasons—to have difficulty about finding suitable accommodation, for the district has long been a favourite one for those who like fishing and shooting. There are hotels and guest-houses which cater for rich, yes and for *poor* also—because he who seeks can find accommodation in Connemara at prices as low as any in these islands. With this preliminary assurance, I shall say briefly why this stark and austere region should interest many visitors.

Connemara has its name from one Conmac, the son of Fergus and Maeve of the royal house of Connacht. It is

Gaelic-speaking, sparsely populated, and its people live by fishing, agriculture and cottage industries, of which spinning and weaving are the principal. Agriculture! As you travel along by bus or go along the smaller roads by car or push-bike, all you can see are those dominating Twelve Bens—conical mountains of which the central peak Benbaun rises to 2,393 feet I am told, the others decreasing in height to Benbrack, 1,922 feet—these, and poor land of peaty quality all cut up and divided by little lakes and innumerable rivers, some of them brawling their way through stones, twisting and turning and mostly teeming with fish. The fish in these rivers must be, I should say, Connemara's only wealth, but I have heard some stories from people there to the effect that the best fishing is reserved for visitors, and that a Connemara man with line and rod, pulling out fish after fish, is a sight not seen often enough. But, after all, one could not live on those fish alone. Something must be done with the land, such as it is. One can cut turf in most places. One can grow potatoes and cabbages. And one can graze a horse, a donkey, and the parts around the Bens are not too bad for sheep. Certainly it is not as bad as the Aran Islands, but some parts of the Aran Islands are about as hopeless for making a living as anywhere on earth. There remains the Ocean—the Atlantic which rolls in on that whole coast, sometimes with a rage which dismays the most intrepid of those fearless men of Connemara; and makes the risk of going out in their remarkably seaworthy hookers—their shape and rig are peculiar to those parts—far too great. When the weather is good and they are not working on the land—two considerations which subtract greatly from time otherwise possibly available—out go the sailors. They come back with good or bad catches of herrings or mackerel and a few other fish. Around Clifden there is good lobster fishing. But lobsters are diet for the far-away select who are not Connemara people!

You can have a wonderful bus-ride from Galway to Clifden through Oughterard, Maam Cross, Recess, Ballinahinch, Roundstone, with the Twelve Bens on your right, the Atlantic horizon to the left, crossing little bridges, and passing through that incredibly irregular land of little lakes, slight undulations and uncountable streams and brooks. The road seldom runs straight for more than a few minutes' travelling. From Galway to Clifden is about fifty miles, and the journey takes two and a half hours. You leave Galway in the morning, have a good day in Clifden, and return the same evening—and in the evening you may see one of those unforgettable Connemara sunsets. This, the loveliest of all the bus-rides in the world, costs only a few shillings return!

I have often amused myself by thinking of the least costly of those pleasures which not only provide us with a feast of visual loveliness, but also feed the soul and spirit; and nearly always end with my mind turning on what I have seen in Connemara. Paul Henry, Charles Lamb and others have painted this scenery, but, with all respect to the artists, I do not think that any man can catch and paint these colours because they so often change from one moment to the next. If you should not be able to visit Connemara and see for yourself what it is, then read Walter Macken's fine novel, *Quench the Moon.* He has caught the spirit of the people and their disturbing and yet strangely satisfying country better than any other writer that I know.

The Joyce's Country cannot be seen quite so easily. If the visitor wishes to see it quickly—and I hope not—he must either hire a car or go there on a push-bike. Better still to walk through it, which need not be an exhausting effort. Either Maam Cross or Leenane would be a good headquarters from which to explore this most interesting countryside on the edges of Loughs Mask and Corrib. It is mountainous and watery—I do not mean soggy, but well rivered. The expert sees a difference between its people and those of Connemara —due to a differing environment which provides a less harsh economy. If anyone should be desirous of a really superb walking-tour, this is the part of Ireland to go to: *first.*

CHAPTER III

SOUTHERN COUNTIES

With deep affection and recollection
I often think of the Shandon bells,
Whose sounds so wild would, in days of childhood,
Fling round my cradle their magic spells:
On this I ponder, where'er I wander,
And thus grow fonder, sweet Cork of thee;
With thy bells of Shandon,
That sound so grand on,
The pleasant waters of the River Lee.
The Bells of Shandon, by "Father Prout."

1

Limerick and the Shannon

As a Convenient Centre for visitors, Limerick insists on being placed high on our list, and for several reasons. It is the third city of Ireland, it is a busy port, it is near the important Shannon Air Port (at Rineanna), and from Limerick you can travel by boat up the great Shannon waterway for miles and miles, seeing sights and enjoying yourself all the way. What country can compete with Ireland in inland waterways? None that I know. And of those Irish waterways, if the Erne comes first, the Shannon has a good claim to rank second. As for Limerick as a Convenient Centre, one might add that, excepting possibly Dublin, no Irish city has within such easy reach and in almost every direction so many places and buildings as the Shannon port. The American who is pressed for time and wishes to 'taste the flavour' of old Ireland can do so most satisfactorily here. He steps off one 'plane to catch the next.

Limerick was founded by the Norsemen as a fort on the great river system up which they could navigate their long, shallow craft, to penetrate almost to the centre of the country on their marauding and pillaging expeditions. For this purpose they found it ideal. Limerick is notable for that; and also because it is 'The City of the Violated Treaty'. When Patrick Sarsfield, one of Ireland's most respected leaders, surrendered to William's Ginkle on the 3rd October, 1691, he did so on honourable terms; and the Treaty was solemnly signed on the now famous stone. One of those terms was to the effect that Roman Catholics in Ireland should enjoy and continue to enjoy the privileges they had under Charles II. Alas, the Treaty was repudiated, and the Irish were again back where they had been before all the blood was spilt. Those Irish have set up the Treaty Stone on a pedestal—made a public monument of it!—on the Clare bank of the Shannon—a permanent reminder of English treachery. Considering that in European and, indeed, in nearly all the history that we know, hardly a treaty that matters has not been broken by some régime which considered it expedient to do so, it seems, therefore, a little hard on the English that they should be singled out for this permanently conspicuous advertisement. But there it is; and there it seems likely to remain.

Limerick strikes the visitor as very much alive. It is a pleasant, prosperous city, with many fine Georgian streets, and Arthur's Quay—this, a very beautiful sight. The eighteenth-century Irish poet Bryan Merryman lived in Limerick, although he was a Clareman, a rationalist and a humanist who must have been a white blackbird in that area of intense and uncompromising Catholics. If you have not read his famous *Midnight Court,* you must do so, and you have a choice of three translations: one by Arland Usher—now unhappily out of print [1]—which I find very pleasing; one by Frank O'Connor—banned by the Irish censor—which I find very lively; and one by Lord Longford—with a printer's cut—which I find close to the original and in other ways illuminating. I hear that a friend is working on a 'literal' prose translation, and that should be fun for censors, if it ever appears. The aspect of Merryman's work which I find most refreshing is that it shows very clearly what an advanced mind a back-of-beyond Protestant *and republican* Irish schoolmaster of that period could have. Those with preconceived ideas of the 'backwardness' of the Irish mind should read Merryman, and rid their heads of nonsense. This extra-

[1] It is included in *1,000 Years of Irish Poetry* (published in New York, 1947).

ordinary man of genius ran his little hedge school at Knocknageeha. He had mastery of four languages: Irish, English, Latin, Greek. And his mind was that of a citizen of Europe, of a 'good European' rather than of a good Irishman. I could not buy the Irish text of his fine poem, though I hunted for it everywhere. Parts are moderately Rabelaisian; and therefore it is not approved by those who would save the souls of those who read Irish. Those people seem to have forgotten just one thing: that in the *Gaeltacht* there remains—vanishing, no doubt, but still existing—the oral tradition. The traditional storyteller and reciter can be found, and I have an acquaintance who, on return to London from a holiday in West Kerry, told me with joy of an evening by the turf fire, when a hearty old man recited in Irish *The Midnight Court* from beginning to end to an enthralled audience of men and women who rollicked and laughed to raise the thatched roof. I do not think that official censorship can ever keep down such stuff as this poem.

From Limerick you can go to the next county, Tipperary, though first you may care to see Kilkee and Lahinch, in County Clare, and, maybe, Lisdoonvarna, which is Ireland's spa. Here are sulphur springs with other elements which those with rheumatism and glandular troubles find beneficial. It is a highly respectable town, mostly frequented by well-to-do people who 'take the waters' solemnly and look solemnly and searchingly at one another. I dislike the whole atmosphere of the place, but then I dislike all spas, and this is by no means the most objectionable of them that I know. You may put my dislike down to mere personal prejudice, but I have marked this place with the beautiful name. Go to it if you think it will do you good. It will do you no harm.

On to Tipperary, 'Fighting Tipp', a great country for huntsmen, a great country for fine people, and a country with a wonderful history in Ireland's 'Troubles' of the 1920s. This is the country of Dan Breen and the Tipperary Brigade; of Solohedbeg, Knocklong and other famous incidents in that ruthless guerrilla warfare . . . Brave Tipperary and the Sweetest Girl I Know! In Tipperary is Cashel, with its Rock dominating the town; and that masterpiece, Cormac's Chapel.

The people of Cashel are lively, but some of them run to the other extreme. Catholics know about Purgatory, but how many of them know of its connection with Cashel? Thereby hangs a tale!

It was a man of Cashel who evolved the idea of Purgatory which was accepted into the canon of the Roman Catholic Church by Pope Gregory the Great, who defined and formulated it. The idea was first stated in a vague form in the first century by an Irish Celt named Fursa, to whom it came as a vision. Then the man of Cashel—Tnúthgal, anglicized as Tundale—a soldier of Cormac Mac Carthaigh (one of the Marcarthys) fell into a trance one Wednesday "while sitting at table, and during this trance beheld the vision which he related to an Irish monk named Marcus". For further details of how the idea of Purgatory arose from those Irish visions, I must refer the reader to the work of a more authoritative writer than myself on this difficult subject: Fray Anselmo Tommasini, O.F.M., who, in *Irish Saints in Italy,* expounds it all learnedly, and informs us that Dante took Tundale's Vision and turned it into the Divine Comedy. "The Italian poet," says Fray Anselmo, "took the poor dross of the Irish visionary's prose and turned it into the pure gold of poetry." Poor dross indeed!—when it was the original idea. I mention this to give some idea of what a Cashelman can do. He can plant a seed from which may grow a great tree. From Cashel has grown Purgatory; and from Purgatory one of the very great poems of the world. Without Tundale—who knows!

2
Killarney and Kerry: Puck Fair

The County of Kerry is called after an ancient king named Ciar (pronounced kerr), whose kingdom was a small piece of country near the present county town of Tralee (the 'Strand of the Lee'), which has so much history that it deserves a book to itself. The town is closely associated with the great Desmond family, but all you can see to remind you of those people is the site of their castle, now mostly concealed by business premises. The old Kingdom of Desmond was divided up by the English King John in 1210, and the western part of it made into a shire or county on the English model. Although I have marked Killarney on my list as a Convenient Centre for the visitor, I do not mind confessing that I myself would prefer the less exacting and more restful atmosphere of the fine town of Tralee as a headquarters from which to make excursions to the famous Lakes and other parts of this wonderful area. However, Killarney has to have its place of honour; for it is everything that is implied in the term 'Tourist Centre'. Tralee is in itself an interesting town; Killarney is not. But Killarney is within walking distance of the Lakes, the nearest of which lies about a mile and a half south of the town, and this, and the fact that the people of the town and neighbourhood have had long experience in dealing with all sorts of visitors and tourists, gives it a fair claim to priority. Whereas Tralee lists five hotels and one guest-house, Killarney lists sixteen hotels and five guest-houses: this, for a town of less than six thousand inhabitants, is good going. One has only to move outside the town of Killarney and walk in any direction for a very short time to be well into some of the most beautiful country which Ireland has to offer.

I do not propose to say much about Killarney, for, in regard to amenities and scenery, any tourist office will supply the prospective visitor with all the basic information likely to be required. There is *no* part of this County of Kerry in which you will not find remarkable scenery, most of which follows a pattern of mountains and lakes, the mountains extending well into the neighbouring County of Cork. The famous Lakes of Killarney are three: the big Lower Lake (Leane), the Middle and Upper Lakes, these two being very much smaller than Leane. One notes that they are called by the English word 'lakes' and not loughs (more correctly lochs), as such stretches of water are usually called in Ireland. It is out of politeness to English and other visitors, whom the considerate local people would not wish to see straining their throats in efforts to pronounce that ugly Irish guttural. This in itself indicates some measure of the care and attention given to visitors, most of whom are well advised to deliver themselves wholeheartedly into the hands of the

Thatched Cottage—Co. Donegal
ITA

kindly and loquacious guides, carmen, boatmen and other willing helpers, who seldom fail to entertain and instruct. I have been surprised to find how many English people there are who believe that the famous Blarney Stone is somewhere in the neighbourhood of Killarney, but of course the *real* Stone is at Blarney Castle, in the County Cork. I am assured that if a visitor who is unaware of this important fact asks some of the self-appointed guides at Killarney where it is, the answer is to the effect that *any* stone in Kerry will be as effective as the one in Cork.

There is everything for the tourist in this well-organized centre: jaunting-cars with old-fashioned drivers who know everything; motor-cars with drivers who are efficient and less talkative (some of them); boats for hire and trips to Innisfallen on the Lower Lake, and to O'Sullivan's Cascade (a lovely waterfall amid greenery and oaks), and to Dinis Island. The last is well worth a visit, for here in this 'soft' and temperate climate you can see vegetation of which much is tropical and in tropical profusion. Kerry is much maligned for its heavy rainfall—I use the word 'maligned' because the fall is not the same in all parts of the county. Some parts *are* wet, very wet; and Killarney is not the driest part of the county. The MacGillycuddy Reeks nearby and dominating the landscape are responsible for catching the water-laden clouds. They are the highest group of mountains in Ireland, a great rugged and very irregular mass running from the Gap of Dunloe to Glencar and from Laune Valley to Cummenduff. From Killarney you can easily go to the coast, and you should make for Glengariff, in Cork, with its lovely Bay and innumerable attractions. Or you can make your way down the coast of Dingle Bay, and to Irish-speaking country with the village of Dunquin: from which you can go to Great Blasket, the only one of the Blasket Islands now inhabited. This is where Tomás Ó Crohan wrote *The Islandman,* beautifully translated from the Irish by Robin Flower, and also the birthplace of that other Gaelic writer Maurice O'Sullivan, who wrote *Twenty Years a-Growing,* also beautifully translated by Moya Llewelyn Davies and George Thomson. If you cannot go to the Blaskets, you can read about their simple way of life in these two books. From Killarney you

Devenish Round Tower and Abbey —Lough Erne
UTDA

can go to Muckross Abbey and to Killorglin. There is the Abbey, Muckross Lake—and Muckross itself, a little village with a fame of its own.

I never see or hear the name of the little village of Muckross but I think of the fame it has acquired because that man of a unique blend of genius, foolishness and rascality, Rudolf Erich Raspe, who wrote *The Adventures of Baron Munchausen,* spent his last days there. Although his death (1794) is recorded in the Parish Register of St. Mary's Church, and he is no doubt buried thereabouts, the actual place where he was interred cannot be traced. His only memorial is his remarkable book and some praiseworthy original work to his credit (sometimes mixed with discredit!) in other fields. The attempts hitherto made to piece together the strange and sometimes criminal activities of Raspe, and to fix the dates on which some of them occurred, usually include a statement to the effect that the first version of Munchausen's *Adventures* was written while he resided in Cornwall (1782–1788), but there is general agreement that in the last years of his life he 'elaborated', as he certainly embroidered, that first version into one now regarded as 'complete'. It is highly significant that the elaborations and embroideries were *added* in those last years when he had the experience of appreciating how Kerrymen can tell a story when once they get going. It is known that there really was a person named Munchausen—Baron Hieronimus Karl Friedrich von Munchausen—who, over after-supper libations, amused his guests by telling them very tall stories allegedly about himself and his wonderful adventures. Raspe's chronicle might be a satire or lampoon, as some say it is. I think it is neither, but merely the result of the author's conviction that he had something amusing to write about, for it is all stated with that solemnity which, when successful, as this is, constitutes a good literary joke. The final version at times reads like extracts from the Irish Mythological Cycle! These parts have a spirit that is not in the least Teutonic, and is in contrast to the somewhat heavy-footed tread of the remainder. I wonder whether this little speculation on my part will find any supporters? Not that it matters greatly, because we all know that the good Baron could not hold a candle to even a second-rate Kerry storyteller when it comes to imaginative elaboration. Almost anybody in Muckross could beat him if set to it.

The people of Kerry are, taking them all round, as good talkers as you will find anywhere—except maybe in the neighbouring County of Cork, which in this respect is unique. There is also something robustly pagan about the people of the countryside and villages of both these counties. The mention of the pagan spirit brings us to Killorglin and its famous Puck Fair, which is, as far as I know, the last surviving pagan festival in these islands. I do not include in them some of those modern manifestations of 'Druidism' we know of, because I do not regard them as having quite the same authenticity or sheer pagan spirit as the Killorglin festivity. This merry event has to be experienced to be believed.

It has never once been my good fortune to witness Puck Fair (an event which takes place in August each year, usually about the 11th), and the more is my sorrow. Whatever may be the immediate or superficial attraction of this annual festival—and it is well worth seeing—there is behind it a long, untraceable history which without doubt goes back to pagan Ireland. I believe that whoever would persist in research would find that, basically, it is similar in symbolism to pre-Christian celebrations and other Nature Festivals held in many parts of continental Europe and among primitive peoples elsewhere. As it now is the only festival of its kind held in these islands, it has unique interest. There used to be at least two other Puck Fairs in Ireland, but the last of them faded out nearly a century ago. Before attempting to explain the Killorglin event, let us see what actually happens there.

Although they happen at the same time, Puck Fair consists of two sets of activities which fit well into each other. The first is the assembly in Killorglin of a large number of farmers and others from the neighbouring countryside and often from farther afield. Their purpose is a simple one: *business.* They go there to sell or buy cattle, horses, pigs, sheep and anything else of interest to them and their way of life. That side of the Fair gives it an important local economic background and justification, because much money changes hands. The Fair lasts three days; most of the serious business is completed by the end of the second. Concomitantly with business is the old ceremony of the goat, the 'puck' as it is called, from the Gaelic word *poc* meaning a buck-goat, and that old ceremony provides the excuse for the less solemn aspect of the Fair which, with it, quickly takes on the full bloom of a high-spirited and very lively social jollification dissimilar only in degree from what we read of as Bacchanalia. And so, business and pleasure go on together and they all enjoy themselves.

The three days of Puck Fair comprise the following programme:

First Day: Gathering Day. From all arts and parts all kinds of people, men, women, children, with their animals and in their vehicles or on foot, make their way into Killorglin. Soon the little town is packed with humanity and animals; and the dealers are busy. For the women and the children this is a great annual outing, in which they are able to relax from the cares of life and obtain a release from the hard, normal monotony of existence. For the men it may be the most important day for business in the year. All this in the packed streets, the crowds dressed up and in festive mood, provides a very happy atmosphere. When evening of the first day comes, say between six and seven o'clock, the band turns out, a parade is organized, and everybody is ready for the remarkable ceremony in which takes part as fine a *pocán* or he-goat as can be found in the Kerry mountains. The band of pipers, drums and other instruments now leads a procession in carnival style in the direction of the market-place, where the ceremony of the Enthronement and Crowning of Puck is to take place. After the band follows a line of ponies with boys riding on them, and one sees little banners, coloured ribbons and paper. Next comes the lorry with the great Puck himself, usually a magnificent animal, standing there in quiet dignity as if he was only getting what is his due from those humans. He stands on a plank platform for all to see, with a maiden colourfully dressed at each corner of the vehicle's floor. If you should meanwhile be in the market-place, you would find that a great platform arrangement in three tiers or floors and about forty feet in height has been made ready. On the bottom floor there is dancing to the music of a melodeon or accordion for the amusement of the multitude already assembled all around it. The floors are about twelve feet by twelve, the top one being reserved for Puck, the bottom one for the dancers and musician or musicians, and the middle one for, apparently, those influential people who can get there, including, maybe, the Press and photographers. Each floor is reached from the one below by a ladder. The whole stand is decorated, and each corner at the top has a pole with a banner flying.

The parade ends beside the platform-arrangement in the market-place, and now begins the elevation of the goat. The top is removed from his stand, the goat is hoisted up with his frame, and both are installed on the top platform. Now comes the Crowning of Puck with a crown made of a piece of thin metal in circular form and of appropriate design. The ceremonial goat is then turned in all directions for everybody to see and to be photographed in all his elevated grandeur. He remains there for the rest of the Fair, thoroughly enjoying the generous supply of foodstuffs and tit-bits fed to him by ever-watchful attendants, and greatly admired by everybody. Need I say that parade, elevation, coronation, exhibition and the photographing all take place in an hilarious atmosphere, in which everybody present enjoys himself, from the innocent child who sees in it only sheer fun to the solemn folklorist who looks on in wonderment searching his memory for parallels and thinking maybe of some festival in the Homeric age in Greece or of some fertility rite in pre-Columban America or in Polynesia? Here is a pagan atmosphere in the twentieth century, symbolizing the tough old paganism that lies not very deep underneath the skin of those Irish!

Second Day: The Fair. Now the real business is done. The dealers argue, bargain, agree. The money changes hands, and the transactions are concluded with a libation. Women and children wander about looking at the shops; the roundabouts reap a rich harvest, the side-shows are packed. Puck stands aloft happily munching a cabbage or perhaps, as a special treat, some ivy leaves or, surreptitiously, a sugar-bag! The day rolls on to its end, and then the night, and so on to the morning of the third day. If anybody sleeps nobody else is aware of the fact.

Third Day: The Scattering. On this day the Fair and business work themselves out and, for the most part, it is a day on which everybody gives himself up to enjoy what remains of the joyful three-day break. Ceremoniously Puck is taken down. Music, dancing, and now there is the concluding parade from the place of coronation. Little by little, slowly and in a well-satisfied manner, the multitude disperses out along the roads and homewards to the four points of the compass. It is well called the Scattering. The great annual event of Puck Fair, to many locals and most visitors a wonderful 'binge', has ended. It is a festival initiated, organized and carried out to the last detail by Kerrymen mostly from Killorglin and close by. Solemn citizens from more imposing centres of civilization such as Tralee or Killarney affect to be rather ashamed of Killorglin's Puck Fair as an exhibition of the primitive, the barbarous and what have you. It was such people and the clergy who were mainly responsible for the disappearance of other festivals of this nature, no doubt because they regarded them as pagan survivals to be discouraged. I have not seen or heard that the Church has condemned the Killorglin Puck Fair. It might be difficult to suppress, if any foolish men should think of such a thing. Not only is it a harmless safety-valve for the people, but it is economically of considerable importance to them. Although it never died out entirely, there was a time when it attracted far less attention than at present. It is good business; and thrives accordingly. As it is now, it is also a very healthy link with an incalculably remote past. I hope that it may long continue to thrive as such and not be spoiled by racketeers from outside.

I cannot here attempt any serious appraisal of the origin and original significance of this curious survival, but of two things there need be no doubt. It is essentially pagan; and no evidence exists of how or when it began or why it survives in Ireland only at Killorglin. Those seem to be the only certainties; otherwise we merely speculate. It is legitimate to speculate that Puck Fair in its early manifestations was (*a*) connected with agriculture, and (*b*) related to the harvest. It *might* be a survival from some old fertility cult, for the buck-goat was sometimes regarded as a fit candidate to be 'king of fertility' and crowned accordingly. One can reasonably keep an open mind on that point and not entirely rule it out of our reckoning. But we must also remember the almost innumerable manifestations here and there over the world of the 'corn spirit' which, in many folklores, was cunningly conceived by those who drew life and sustenance from the soil and represented by them as a god or ruler to be sometimes worshipped, sometimes placated or flattered, and nearly always in the form of an *annual festival* about or just before the reaping of the final harvest. Those who are sufficiently interested can turn to Frazer's *Golden Bough,* in which they will find the case of Dionysus as a goat and, most interesting in relation to Puck Fair, the 'corn spirit' represented as a goat. It seems to me, keeping Ireland in mind, that this might prove a fruitful line of enquiry. For, after all, is not Puck Fair an annual jollification, with its surviving ceremony of Crowning the Goat, the occasion of much business relating to a pastoral existence, and taking place on a date which may have been later in astronomical time, but is now in early August by our calendar, yet is not even by this date very far from the final harvesting? We must leave it at that, though there is one point the reader may wish to have cleared up. What happens to Puck after the Fair? Answer: he just goes home again. They used to auction him, but that indignity has ceased. A new *pocán* is chosen for coronation each year. And so the pagan survival goes on. . . .

3
Cork

Draw a line on the map from Limerick to Cork, and you will notice that the whole of that south-western seaboard is marked with great inlets, as if the Atlantic Ocean had worked roughly cutting away land to make bays that are natural harbours. Compare the whole of the western seaboard with that of Norway, and you will see that, whereas the Norwegian seaboard is cut in a fine filigree pattern, that of Ireland is bold though hardly less irregular. No wonder Britain long used some of those Irish inlets as naval bases, for there are none better in these islands. Lough Swilly in The North and

Bantry Bay in The South can each provide perfect anchorages for the combined fleets of the world. As naval bases for Britain, they no longer exist. The Republic, aware of its vulnerability and military weakness in a world armed to the teeth, tries to maintain a neutrality on the model of Switzerland.

Cork Harbour is one of these magnificent natural havens for ships. The city is named Cork and the port *Cóbh* (pronounced cove), the port being the one where visitors from the United States disembark. For this reason alone Cork is a Convenient Centre. The American visitor can use it to see Killarney, to work his way up or round to Dublin; and, of course, to see the City of Cork itself as well as the surrounding county of the same name. Cork is a delightful city, charmingly situated, populated by about 90,000 meridional people whose nature is in marked contrast to that of the hyperboreans of Derry. It is curious how a southern aspect affects people: in Spain the Andalusians are light-hearted to the point of frivolity in contrast to the Asturians and even more stolid Basques; in France the Marseillais and people of Provence are irrepressibly gay compared with the down-to-earth Normans and serious Pas-de-Calais folk. Similarly, the people of Cork have in them much of that southern levity, and I do not think that the visitor will be far out in regarding them as the Marseillais, the Sevillanos or the Neapolitans of Ireland. Corkmen at times tend to become so exuberant that one feels they may have caught a touch of the southern sun. Pay no attention to this, for it is merely a part of their cheerful nature. And what a gift of the gods it can be!

When in Cork there are two things to do: walk and talk with the natives. First wander aimlessly about this charming city and stop from time to time to enjoy to the full such beauties as the spire of Shandon. In this peregrination you will inevitably walk down Patrick Street, a fine shopping centre above a branch of the Lee, Cork's lovely river. Ask somebody to point out to you the bronze statue of Father Mathew by Foley, and then walk on to Father Mathew Quay, where there is a Memorial Church with a graceful lantern spire to that good man Theobald Mathew (1790–1856), whose name is immortal in Ireland. From Father Mathew's statue you can take a motor-bus to places near and far: to Glengariff, Killarney, Limerick, to many parts of Cork County, and even to Dublin. Steamers run to and from *Cóbh,* and if you are inclined to seafaring and wish to make the journey to England, you will find a shipping service. In your walks you should inspect St. Finnbarr's Cathedral, the most impressive building in the city (seat of the Protestant bishop), in the early French style, designed by William Burges: a modern building on an old church site, consecrated in 1870. Having wandered about, you may have acquired a thirst and, if you are not a follower of the doctrines of Ireland's greatest temperance reformer (and therefore the greatest of all her idealists: none other than Father Mathew), you should visit a Cork pub. I write the word 'pub.' deliberately, for it is an ordinary Cork *pub.* you must first visit, before you go on to hotel bars, saloon bars, smart public-houses and chromium plate, where Cork talkers are more disciplined and usually less interesting. In an ordinary Irish pub. there can be fun, and it need not be a question of consuming great quantities of alcohol or getting drunk, though you may meet tempters who believe that Ireland sober is Ireland stiff. The whole point about visiting an ordinary pub. in Cork is that there, rather than in the more solemn atmospheres of uppish bars, you will meet the Corkman at his best and most congenial. The Irish small pub. is in any case an institution worthy of every visitor's attention, being more than its English counterpart and usually combined with the grocery and maybe several other kinds of commerce.

It is possible that interested parties who read this book may wish to know something about the Irish public-house: the pub., or premises licensed to sell alcoholic liquor. The *shebeen* or unlicensed amenity also exists in most Convenient Centres, but on that interesting subject I cannot expand, it being one for the more enlightened specialist. Visitors from across the Irish Sea will not find in Ireland what is known in England as the 'tied house'—the premises which are owned by brewers, have a manager paid by them, and must accept for stock and sell what the brewers supply. Irish individualism could never be satisfied with such a system. In Ireland we have everywhere houses that are entirely 'free' and can sell what they please in the way of alcoholic beverages. My own rough estimate (based partly on personal observation and partly on the researches of others who are deeply learned in this profound subject) is that in urban communities there are 2·3 public-houses for every 100 of the population. There are not in any part of Ireland many of those isolated or road-side pubs. which one finds so happily placed in England to relieve the thirst of the traveller and to cater for the local yokel. This means that, if one wishes to drink, one must be in a hamlet, village, town or city—a good rule for the illustrious to remember. You will notice that I do not make any distinction between The North and The South in this important question. For practical purposes, the only real difference is in the prices of the drinks, which are approximately the same in The North as they are in Britain; and much less—sometimes almost 50 per cent. less, as I write, in The South—because of the difference in duty. One might add that in The North the modern pubs. come a little closer to the English model, and, although the northern are good friendly establishments, there is not so strong a tendency when they are 'modernized' to aim at the extreme of glossiness, of lavish display of chromium plate now found in progressive pubs. of The South. Also, I have a strong feeling that this is one of the branches of human endeavour in which The South surpasses The North: public-house efficiency, that is. But I am not prejudiced, for I have enjoyed libations in all four provinces, and I cannot say that my experiences in Ulster have been less happy than those I have had elsewhere.

Outside the cities women do not in Ireland drink standing at public-house bars. If a woman goes with a man or men into a pub. and drinks are called for, she and they are politely ushered into a 'snug' or a back room. This is a general custom. Public bars are for 'men only'. The stranger must accept the rule and make the best of it, and is well advised to do so, for, if the great natural courtesy of the average publican should cause him to relax the rule, if there are in the bar local drinkers, they are sure to feel a little uneasy in the presence of strange females whose cool behaviour, however innocent it may be, will nearly always be regarded by them as a form of brazenness unbecoming to the weaker sex.

For the rest, the Irish pub., and especially the small town pub., can be a most interesting establishment, in which the visitor with wits will learn as much about the habits and customs of the natives as anywhere. The Irish publican is usually a man of importance and substance, a man of independence, influence and great local knowledge; a good talker, and often a character. You will find him friendly, helpful, sympathetic. Furthermore, if you like good drinks, you will often get surprises, and discover that he has all kinds of excellent wines and liquors. In discussing this with an English friend, he told me that on one occasion he and a couple of companions were hiking through County Monaghan, and had brought sandwiches with them. After a good morning's walk, one of them said: "I wish we had a bottle of good wine to drink with our lunch." They came to a village pub. and decided that here they would at least find some of the wine of the country—stout. But first they would enquire about other wines. To their complete surprise the publican produced half a dozen bottles of vintage-quality Bordeaux, Burgundy and even Châteauneuf-du-Pape. Stroking a bottle of the last, the good man said: "If you don't mind paying a shilling or two more, this is the wine *I'd* recommend. *Châteauneuf-du-Pape*! Why, the name's enough!" As he wiped the dust from the bottle and wrapped it in a piece of paper he gave a brief lecture on 'wines for walkers'. Burgundy—a little too heavy. Bordeaux—very good. But, after drinking his own choice, the hikers would "feel like Finn MacCool!" It is tempting to linger on this pleasant subject of the Irish pub., but were I to do so, I might forestall the joy which every intrepid traveller should find for himself.

The subject of drink here prompts a digression. Scotch whisk*y* and Irish whisk*ey* come from the Gaelic words *uisce* meaning 'water' and *beathadh* meaning 'of life' (pronounced ishkay-bah): 'water of life', or, as the French have it, *eau de vie*. The origin of this widely appreciated tipple is lost in the mists of a remote antiquity, but it seems possible that a knowledge of the process of distilling was brought to Ireland by Phœnician traders long before the Christian era. Certain it is that, when the Anglo-Normans invaded Ireland in the twelfth century, the native Irish had long been whiskey drinkers. Distilling was established as a *domestic art,* one widely practised without any sort of restrictions or taxations. Whiskey was much favoured for medicinal purposes, and samples of this valuable medicine were carried far outside Ireland by missionaries who disseminated a knowledge of its wonderful qualities among less-enlightened peoples. In the reign of the English King Henry VIII some expert Irish distillers settled in Pembrokeshire. Others are reported to have made their way to the islands off the south-west of Scotland. The making of whiskey in Ireland long continued to be a domestic art, but in Scotland it quickly developed into an *industry*—so that in Tudor days the Scottish products already began to be appreciated by discerning English drinkers. No need to explain further a branch of history of which the ramifications reach to every corner of the earth where Irishmen, Scotsmen and Englishmen have set foot. Let us be content to note that the *domestic art* of making whiskey was first evolved by the Irish; and that it was first developed into an industry by the Scots, later by the Irish. Scotch whisky and Irish whiskey are not the same drink: the processes of making differ; Irish whiskey is usually stronger and has a flavour of its own. The best 'Irish' and the best 'Scotch' are rare and heartening medicines, each having stalwart partisans who are ready at any moment to propound or discuss the respective merits of the two great distillations and make comparisons based on subtle tastes, preferably on practical tests. *De gustibus non est disputandum*: the argument as to which country's product must be awarded the honour of superiority over the other is likely to continue as long as makers conscientiously observe the sacred old rules of the art. Scotland now has the major industry. But the making of whiskey continues as an industry in both The North and The South of Ireland—the domestic art has been almost but not quite killed—and from North and South are exported to most parts of the world valuable cargoes of this greatly appreciated 'water of life'. Export trade brings profits to manufacturers and distributors, useful returns to the two Governments, and to those who finally drink the golden liquid a most pleasant if temporary relief from that tyrannous censorship the intellect normally imposes on our senses and behaviour. The Celts have never been notable for allowing too much power to this censorship. In this matter of distilling, their domestic artists must be counted among those great pioneers who first gave to suffering humanity the formulæ for happy releases. If the releases are not abused, they can enable those who so desire to acquire wings on occasion, or seven-leagued boots, and thus harmlessly to escape from immediate cares and frustrations with no more physical effort than is required to lift glass to lips. . . .

It was in a Cork pub. that I first learnt what was something new to me and proves to be a sidelight on the social revolution of the twentieth century which is affecting the whole world and may lead to the Third World War. As this is likely to be a matter of deep concern to most people, it must be dealt with. We were on our third or fourth drink when a small, ferret-faced man in an Ulster coat, wearing a soft hat at a tilt and not of our party, fixed me with an electric eye and said, pointing straight at my nose: "Do you know, Mister, that it was a Corkman who emitted the spark which struck the tinder that set fire to Russia in the year 1917? No! Well, 'tis a fact, a solemn fact as true as God's in heaven! To be sure he was a Protestant, bad cess to him!—oh, I beg your pardon, no offence to anybody here. William Thompson was his name. Have you ever heard or read of him? I expect not. Well, look him up, Mister, look him up! There's an article in *The Bell* that'll tell you all about him." I did look up William Thompson in *The Bell*, and found that what the man said was near enough to truth to be startling. This is not unusual in Cork talk. Furthermore, it fitted in with something else. Nothing can be more amusing for any people than to hear or read what others think of them, and the Irish are no exception in this respect. Some years ago I cut from *Punch* a passage in a dramatic criticism which amused me. A comparison was made in it of the similarities between the Irish and the Russians, and, although I have always thought that those similarities are many and often striking, what amused me about the *Punch* list was that the most striking were completely missed and the others were based on a misreading of both Irish and Russian character. Mind you, it may well be that *Punch* was being humorous, my own sense of humour failed to rise to this occasion, and I do *Punch* wrong in taking it seriously—in which case the laugh is on me. Never mind, I must mention the similarities between us and the Russians as listed. This is what is written: "I can offer no revolutionary theory of race to support it, but the fact remains that both peoples (Irish and Russians) are great theorists and poor executants; immensely dramatic talkers with a vocabulary of great breadth; mystic, philosophic, and unusually aware of the world of the mind; very witty, very lazy and very melancholy; romantics and yet notably ruthless; and in addition to these common qualities they both distil a spirit of the sheerest flame and they both live on tea. Surely there is a deep significance in all this, if one could only think what." Well, Mr. Punch, as we are in Cork, I may as well let you and the rest of the world into the secret, which may cause astonishment. There is a formidable instance of some Irish theorizings having been effectively put into practice by Russian Executants. For it was a Corkman—as we all now know—who was responsible for the Russian Revolution. I looked it up and this is how it came about. His name was William Thompson, and he was born in 1785 at Clonkeen, Roscarbery, in the County Cork, of a Protestant Anglo-Irish family (*they* are the ones who cause the great troubles). Thompson showed himself early in life to be unconventional almost to the point of being an eccentric: he began to fight for all sorts of advanced and impossible ideas, such as the rights of women, the need for co-operative farming and marketing and, most astonishing for an Irishman of his time (or, it seems, of any other time—James Connolly excepted), he preached Socialism! Thompson the Corkman was in fact the *first* person in Europe to write a treatise in terms of what the Marxists call 'Scientific Socialism'. This work was his famous *Directions,* but it was a mild effort in comparison with that which he published in 1824 under the disturbing title of *An Inquiry into the Principles of Distribution of Wealth most conducive to Human Happiness, &c.* In the *Inquiry* this thinker modified or blended with his own ideas the thought of William Owen, the economics of Ricardo, the libertarianism of William Godwin and Benthamist individualism: "To apply to social science the ascertained truths of Political Economy, making these and all other branches of knowledge subservient to that just *distribution* of wealth which tends most to human happiness." Here was high explosive!

Neither Cork nor Ireland nor Europe paid serious attention to Thompson's ideas when the works appeared. Cork regarded him as a man with a swarm of bees in the bonnet. Yet Thompson had grasped and propounded essentials of tremendous importance to human destiny, but if his contemporaries were blind to them, there was somebody who later grasped their terrific significance: no other than Mr. Karl Marx. So, with acknowledgment in a footnote in *Das Kapital* some forty-three years later, Thompson's ideas were paraphrased, amplified and sharpened—to appear in final Marxist form in the famous *Gotha Programme* of 1875. And was not that one of the most important of the wells from which Lenin drew the ideas which he put into practice in the Russian Revolution? Thompson deserves his monument—in Cork or Moscow or both, but we must leave the decision to those great cities. Few Corkmen have sprung a greater argument in this world, great as they are in the sphere of argument and dialectic. I need not continue the story more than to record one other thing which this remarkable Corkman spotted: that what science has to do must be for the *happiness* of mankind or, if it is not, we are better without it. How right Thompson was! Scientists who work for power-politicians make horrors possible.

4

Waterford—Wexford—Other Centres

It is a matter of 25 miles or so from Cork to Youghal, near the next County of Waterford, and there are several reasons why Youghal (politely pronounced yaw'l: correctly yo*ch*il, with guttural *ch* and meaning 'yew-wood') is worthy of a visit, the first thing being that it is a pleasant and interesting little seaside place. You can have a lovely quiet holiday here. The whole town consists of one charming Main Street, which runs parallel with the shore and harbour, and has quaint lanes going up and down from it. Youghal is famous for its delicate point lace, and it cherishes the memory of an Englishman who brought two things to Ireland which the Irish hold in high esteem: the potato and tobacco. Not far from St. Mary's Church is a fine Elizabethan mansion called Myrtle Grove, in which Sir Walter Raleigh lived at different times between the years 1584 and 1597, he being one of a band of select English gentry who were given excellent estates in Ireland as a reward for their services to Elizabeth in putting down rebellion in that country. Raleigh was given some 42,000 acres of the land confiscated from Desmond estates. Those were the days! But he made rather a mess of his affairs, and sold his holding to the Earl of Cork for the mere song of £1,000. Those estates would now be worth anything from one to two million pounds; but there you are. In the garden of Myrtle Grove you can see a yew-tree under which Sir Walter is reported to have 'drunk tobacco', or in other words, enjoyed a smoke, while he read Spenser's *Faerie Queene* in manuscript. The most important event in that unfortunate man's life from the Irish point of view is that here also he planted the first potato that grew in Ireland. A learned man has recently written a treatise libelling the Irish potatoes, but the Irish continue to enjoy them just the same.

Tramore, farther east along the coast, means 'big strand', and it certainly has a very fine beach. This is a popular resort for fairly well-to-do people, and among the other amenities provided for them are a well-equipped Hydro for physiotherapy, a golf-course, some excellent hotels and guest-houses; and there is also a racecourse. Perhaps the most pleasant features of Tramore are its grand situation between two headlands surmounted by old towers on the beautiful little Bay of Tramore; and its proximity to Waterford, which is one of those places that I have listed as Convenient Centres. You can judge its convenience by merely looking at the map: within day-trip distances are East Cork, Cashel in Tipperary, the lovely town of Kilkenny, the southern part of County Carlow; and almost next door is Wexford, with the cross-channel port of Rosslare for Fishguard. I strongly advise people who live in the south of England to keep their eyes firmly fixed on Wexford and Waterford as Convenient Centres to make for in their Irish visit. They are both easily reached. From Wexford you have within reach Kilkenny, Carlow, East Tipperary and south Wicklow, with its interesting and beautiful Wooden Bridge and Avoca of the famous Vale. I cannot pretend to give even a catalogue of the extremely rewarding places, scenery, interesting roads and landscapes which come within rail and bus radius of those two centres, Wexford and Waterford.

Waterford was one of the early and important Norse settlements, and it was also the bridge-head for the first English invasion of Ireland by Henry II in 1172. And in 1649 the city stood up so well against Cromwell that he was compelled to abandon his siege, though it was taken by Ireton next year. These are incidents in the long and often turbulent history of the city. But it has claims to distinctions on the gentler side: the famous glass manufactured there in the eighteenth and nineteenth centuries, for example, and killed by a ridiculous excise duty imposed in 1825, though it lingered on until about the middle of the century. The greatest of all 'English' actors, Charles Kean, was born here; and also Vincent Wallace, composer of operas; and the family of Lord Roberts. But the visitor will probably find more comfort in the excellent amenities and situation of this city on the bank of the gentle River Suir expanding into the estuary of the fine harbour which rewards with its really beautiful Quays.

The quaint old town of Wexford was also a Norse settlement, but the long-memoried Irish are more likely to think of Cromwell when it is mentioned; for, when he took it in 1649, he razed its churches and massacred the garrison. It was from this and other episodes of his ruthless campaign in Ireland that arose the worst curse an Irish person could put upon another ("The curse o' Cromwell on ye!"). One still sometimes hears it, but I think that its use must be dying out except on the part of old Irish people and some writers of fiction who have Irish characters in their works. It is about five miles from Wexford to Rosslare; and Rosslare, be it noted, is not only the cross-channel port, but it is a popular seaside in its own right, with amenities, golf-course and the possibilities of many interesting excursions, including one as far afield as Glendalough in Wicklow.

*

I hope that by this time I have made it clear that my chief purpose as an adviser on 'Seeing Ireland' is to draw attention to a comparatively small number of Convenient Centres rather than offer detailed guidance and information in the manner of a guide-book or book of travel. There are many important places and interesting sights which I should like to mention at greater length, but to do so is not strictly necessary in this simple and mainly *geographical* aim of telling the prospective visitor *where to make for* in order to be well placed for seeing a particular area. If I have succeeded in this, my aim has been achieved. I have not mentioned Leix (or *Laoighis,* which used to be Queen's County and still is to many) or Offaly (which was King's County and maybe still is to many, as *Dun Laoghaire* is Kingstown and *Portlaoghise* is Maryborough and *Cóbh* is Queenstown). Clonmacnoise ('meadow of the sons of Nos') in Offaly is perhaps the most interesting of all Irish holy places, and notable as the place in which the *Book of the Dun Cow* was compiled in the twelfth century, also for its Seven Churches. But I must mention by themselves two towns that can hardly be considered of interest other than as Convenient Centres: Mullingar and Dundalk, the first in Westmeath about halfway between Dublin and Galway, the second in Louth, just south of The Border. Mullingar is roughly near enough to being the geographical centre of Ireland not to require explanation why I insist on naming it as a Convenient Centre for the visitor. It is the key to three counties and to the Central Plain. As for Dundalk, this is the Convenient Centre from which are easily reached Monaghan, Cavan, the very important pagan burial-place of *Brug na Boinne* and the really wonderful ruins of Monasterboice, each of the last two being worthy of a book to itself. The difference between them which will appeal to the average visitor is that *Brug na Boinne* must be felt to be appreciated, but Monasterboice can provide visual enjoyment to satisfy most people. Both are survivals of a great past, the former of a remote and dim past, the latter very old, but capable of being judged in terms which Christians understand. Monasterboice has a ninth-century Round Tower, two old churches and three Celtic crosses, of which two are superb examples of the sculptor's art and the finest to survive in Ireland. The site of these wonderful ruins and survivals is a very beautiful hillside. In its choice for the holy purpose we see a perfection of harmony with Nature in the senses of those artists and craftsmen who worked this miracle.

CHAPTER IV

BORDERLINE INTERLUDE

"The Dormouse is asleep again," said the Hatter, and he poured a little hot tea upon its nose.

The Dormouse shook its head impatiently and said, without opening its eyes, "Of course, of course; just what I was going to remark myself."

"Have you guessed the riddle yet?" the Hatter said, turning to Alice again.

"No, I give it up," Alice replied; "What's the answer?"

"I haven't the slightest idea," said the Hatter.

"Nor I," said the March Hare.

From LEWIS CARROLL'S *Alice in Wonderland.*

THERE is one thing which I do *not* intend to do in this book, however important it may seem to many possible readers. That is, to attempt to deal technically with the politics of Partition or, as it is usually called in Ireland, 'The Border Question'. The Border *exists.* I think it can be said of it that neither the people of The North nor of The South *like* the idea of this arbitrary, artificial frontier; and that each would be glad to see ended those politico-religio-economic difficulties which brought about its establishment and continue to keep it in existence. I give the wise piece of advice once given by George Bernard Shaw to the effect that, in a controversial matter, the only thing a sane person can do is to read and study both sides of the question and then form his own opinion about it. And to this I will add my own advice to visitors: do not, either in The North or The South, glibly express your opinion about this Border Question. Content yourself with some vague generality.

Ireland, as the map shows, is a natural geographical unit. The Irish used to divide their island into five provinces; later it became the four we now know by the merger of two. The final division into counties or shires—initiated by King John—began in the seventeenth century after the Cromwellian Settlement and the Plantations had been completed. Hence, Irish counties are now shires on the English model. This division has been found so convenient that I have never heard of anybody who wished to see it altered. But we need not forget that the pre-English political headquarters of the province of Ulster was at Tara, well in the Twenty-six County Area; and that the grave of Ireland's patron saint, St. Patrick, is at Downpatrick, in the County Down, well in the Six County Area. Armagh, in The North, has been, since St. Patrick's time, and still is, the Roman Catholic primate's see and the ecclesiastical headquarters of the whole country. Of the forty-three 'High Kings' of old Ireland, no less than twenty-five came from Ulster. At Enniskillen, that fine town —with 56·9 per cent. Nationalist and 43·1 per cent. Unionist vote—which now regards itself as a stronghold of Protestantism and of loyalty to England, began in 1594 the Nine Years' War in defence of the Gaelic way of life. On Cave Hill outside Belfast in 1791 was founded by the Protestant Wolf Tone the Society of United Irishmen—a unity of all religions —pledged to make Ireland an Independent Republic. One could go on listing facts such as these which show that from time immemorial the lives of the Irish people, North and the rest, have been and are interlocked and interdependent. And Border or no Border, in many ways they must willy-nilly continue to be so.

The Border cuts off from the Irish province of Ulster its three counties of Donegal, Cavan and Monaghan. A line beginning at Lough Foyle drawn along the inner edge of Donegal, the south of Fermanagh, Tyrone and Armagh as far as Carlingford Lough, represents the present frontier. Along this frontier are established on each side and at chosen places those 'control' stations with which travellers going from one continental country to another are familiar; but here controls are gentle, officials on both sides polite. Some of those Irish control points correspond with railway stations; most of them are on roads. Those visitors likely to have to cross The Border in either direction by a route other than rail, must be warned that all roads that lead towards and cross The Border are classified into 'approved' or 'unapproved', and *only on approved roads is traffic permissible.* You can be severely punished if caught on an 'unapproved' road. So look out! As Ireland is everywhere a country remarkable for its great number of 'boreens' (little roads, lanes), some of them mere tracks, the number of 'unapproved' roads crossing The Border would at any moment be difficult to compute, especially as new paths tend to appear and old ones to fade out from disuse. Whereas on the Continent and elsewhere it is usual for a Frontier Line to be drawn to divide peoples of different races, religions, ideals, politics, culture or way of life, one of the many problems and not the least in difficulty which faces the authorities on both sides of this Border in Ireland is that the people on each side of it are often men and women of the same family. In some places one part or street of a town is on one side of The Border, another part or street is on the other side. You will even find a house of which one room is in the political North, another in the political South, The Republic!

Next, as you have already been told, Ireland is a country of much water and many waterways: great sea loughs, great inland loughs and rivers. Two great sea inlets—Carlingford Lough, between Counties Down and Louth, and Lough Foyle, between Donegal and Derry—have lines on the map to mark The Border, but nothing on the surface of the water to indicate where it is. Then there is a part of Upper Lough Erne, which runs across a frontier line. And there is, for example, Lough Melville, of which one bank is in Leitrim in The South and the other in Fermanagh in The North, The Border being the north bank! Thus, a row-boat touching The Border may have its stern in The Republic! Rivers run from The North into The South as Nature inclines them, no matter where The Border is. If you take into consideration that the people on each side of this Border of 240 miles have lived for generations beside or intermixed with each other, that they are Protestants or Catholics, Irish-Irish or Irish mixed with English or Scottish settlers and Planters or their descendants, we begin to realize that the word 'Border' in its Irish connotation may represent something unique in the way of frontiers. At times it all reminds us of Alice in Wonderland! When we look closely at it, leaving aside the serious and often very grave implications, many of us can hardly fail to see its comic side. Looking at it objectively I often wonder why somebody does not give us some sort of 'documentary' of The Border: scientific, economic, social, religious, anthropological. Although there are innumerable

Border anecdotes and stories, some of them very amusing, it would be interesting to have some serious documentation, if only for the benefit of posterity. Perhaps the reason for the absence of such a survey is that those capable and otherwise willing to undertake it believe that this embarrassing borderline state of affairs will not endure, and may be regarded as a passing and not very important episode in Irish history.

Here I can attempt a mere bird's-eye view of a few aspects of The Border. Let us begin at Lough Foyle in the north and make our way south and eastwards, ending at Carlingford Lough.

*

I have read somewhere—I cannot trace where, but I think the story is Stephen Gwynne's—of what went on and, for all I know, may still be a cause of entertainment on both sides of Lough Foyle which, the map will show, comes between County Londonderry and County Donegal—the first being in Northern Ireland, the second in The Republic. Lough Foyle is never, at its broadest point, six miles across; and territorial waters end at three miles from shore. Thus, the two jurisdictions overlap, and at times there must be parts of the Lough which are either the business of both sides, or, as more often happens, nobody's business. Most of the time neither side bothers about these problematic and potentially troublesome areas, and in fact nothing very grave happens in them to worry Border officialdoms. But Nature takes little heed of man-made laws and at times She steps in to disturb the peace. Lough Foyle illustrates this. First, at low tide the area of water contracts, and the only navigable passage refuses to keep strictly to midstream. Secondly, salmon on the way from the sea to spawn in either the River Mourne (Northern Ireland) or in the River Finn (The Republic) have to use the Lough and, at low tide, the deep channel which irregularly winds its way down it. To add to these complications, fishing-rights of Lough Foyle are claimed by a commercial company which bought them from the London Irish Society that, in turn, had acquired them in the wonderful days of the Plantation. Those fishing-rights as originally acquired were a monopoly, and a very strict one, meaning that even owners, other than the company, of land on the banks of the Foyle were forbidden to fish. To round off this setting for the comic opera, the High Court in Dublin refused to recognize the monopolistic title. What an opening this provided for salmon poachers! There is probably no human being on this earth who more dearly loves poaching than an Irishman, for he regards all Nature as shared by him and at least partly his by the Divine Bounty which provides such excellent food as salmon and in such convenient places as Lough Foyle—convenient for Irishmen, whether they are ruled from Belfast or from Dublin. In such circumstances local fishermen—Republicans and Orangemen—take advantage of a situation which it would be folly to ignore.

In his solid book *Ulster* (1949), Hugh Shearman writes: "In wartime the frontier produced even more high comedy, for Eire (The Republic) was neutral territory, while Northern Ireland was combatant territory. For long periods goods rationed in Northern Ireland were not rationed in Eire, and you could slip over the frontier and purchase gorgeous but expensive meals on neutral territory. Then, of course, there was a blackout of all lights in Northern Ireland but not in Eire; so, while lights blazed at night in Lifford, you were liable to be pursued by Air Raid Wardens and fined if you showed the faintest chink of light in Strabane, only a few yards away across a stream and inside Northern Ireland. Then the fact that the United Kingdom and Eire began to work their clocks differently produced some further strange drolleries, and the position was further complicated by the fact that people in some country parts of Eire accepted neither Eire time nor British time, but kept on going by sun time. Thus you might leave the city of Derry at ten o'clock by British double summer time and travel for an hour into Donegal and find that it was still ten o'clock, this time by the locally accepted sun time. There is a story that two men were fishing at opposite sides of a frontier stream when it began to threaten rain, and the Eire citizen called across to the British citizen: "Hi, you'd better get your coat. It'll be raining on your side in an hour's time." Mr. Shearman refers, of course, to the period of the Second World War when, by all accounts, the goings-on along that Border were in degrees of fantastic 'lawbreaking' at times not far short of what we read of in *Hajji Baba*.

What appeals to many is that which happens on Sundays along The Border. The *shebeen*—unlicensed drinking-place—having almost disappeared in The North, unless you are a member of a club or a resident in licensed premises, you cannot buy an alcoholic drink in Northern Ireland on the sabbath. Northern Irishmen are of a breed not easily thwarted or daunted, especially when thirsty, though they are on the whole a God-fearing and respectable people little given to lawbreaking unless politics or religion are involved. Hundreds, aye, thousands of fine Northmen at times turn their eyes towards The Border on Sundays and, when the weather is fine, if you should happen to be strolling along one of those 'approved' roads, you would be compelled to acknowledge that they were very highly approved, for you would see an unending procession of vehicles making for that paradise over the frontier where all travellers and well-behaved men of good-will can find their hearts' desire in the matter of liquid refreshment. Special trains have often been run to relieve the roads of this heavy traffic and to provide facilities for those who do not possess or have not access to a road vehicle. In the summer months—the holiday season—the great border-crossing movement of thirsty Northmen is at its height. I cannot but feel that all this is to be highly commended, for it tends to sociability among the people who live on the two sides of the frontier: there is a broad and deep humanity about it not lost on either Northerners or Southerners. The remarkable feature of it all is that there is rarely any 'trouble'. Hence, the traffic indicates, if it does not prove, that if those people were left to themselves untroubled by politicos and some others, they could get on well together.

*

Regular trade between The North and The South goes on over The Border through the official controls and Customs. But certain economic factors are conducive to a considerable irregular trade: smuggling. The direction of the smuggling is governed by market prices, which often vary. Thus, when butter is cheaper in The North than in The South, there is an inclination for it to move from the Six County Area into The Republic. That is the governing economic law of smuggling which, like other commercial occupations of mankind, must show a profit—in this case a good one because of the risks run by those who engage in it. When an article is cheaper in The South than it is in The North—it is the Customs' tariffs on each side which cause most of the differences in market prices—then there is a movement of that article northwards. The Border smuggling reminds us of water, which finds its lowest level as it flows: goods chosen to fetch a profit to the regular smuggler are taken across The Border by the easiest and safest route he can find. As we have some idea of what that 240 miles Border is like and of the often irregular, difficult nature of the land and of the mystifications which a labyrinthine waterway such as the Upper Erne can add, one cannot but feel that the Customs' officers on both sides would have to be supermen to catch all those loyal Ulstermen and pious citizens of The Republic who yield to the temptations of filthy lucre. Besides, there is a sporting element in smuggling which Irishmen enjoy; there is the pleasure which most of them get from outwitting and defeating authority in any form.

There are changes of smugglers' routes from time to time and occasionally overnight as authority brings them under its microscope: what may be a well-beaten track today is abandoned tomorrow; what might never have been thought of as a route becomes one overnight. And so it goes on, the lively and intense battle of wits with, so far as one can estimate, hundreds of smugglers big and small, wholesale and retail, trading in bulk or small quantities, but operating throughout the twenty-four hours of each day, Sundays included, and often even during the favourable hours of divine service. Transport vehicles engaged in this traffic have included almost everything on wheels, from lorries to perambulators; from old tin-lizzies to ass-carts. Living contraband is often walked or swum across The Border: cattle, sheep, pigs, greyhounds. The greyhound has been regarded as a fine animal to smuggle. I have heard of an instance when a smuggler and his greyhound were stopped by officialdom, and the smuggler merely released his dog, pointed whence they had come, and whispered in its ear: "Home, Mick!"—leaving the bewildered officials to deal with a baffling situation. How could one prove that the owner of the dog was involved in an illegality?

Cattle being profitable contraband, much ingenuity is exercised to get the beasts safely over The Border. Jokes are made about it, and the visitor may hear some good tall stories of what is said to happen. For example: that the noses of cattle are anointed with saltpetre to prevent them from lowing as they wind their way through a danger-zone. Pigs, it is said, can be prevented from squealing at the wrong moment by filling them with Guinness's stout. Cattle with white spots have the spots painted out so that they do not show up in the dark. Shoemakers along The Border, it has been whispered, enjoy a profitable side-line in the manufacture of felt footwear for animals scheduled to be walked across. The tallest Border story I have heard is of a Leitrim cow into which a republican vet sewed some valuable watches and jewellery. The cow, of course, was swum across Lough Melvin to the Fermanagh shore, where she was received, escorted into a nearby operating theatre, relieved of her jewellery and turned out to graze in a nice green field. She was a good milker and became known as 'Timekeeper'. I do not vouch for the absolute truth of these stories, and I must say that I cannot swallow the one about the Carlingford Lough sheep. As you know, sheep follow a leader. That particular Carlingford Lough sheep was trained to swim in the dark at the head of great flocks, which dutifully followed it across the unmarked Border in the lake and, the task achieved, it plunged again into the water and swam back home! . . .

The Border has had an effect, not only on social and political relations between The North and The South, but it has affected industries and trading. It is fortunate for The South that its Border counties—Donegal, Monaghan, Cavan—are for the most part agricultural, and hence business has not suffered very much in them. But they and The North have suffered by the cutting off of a free traffic in northern manufactures. Londonderry had a good free trade with Donegal: some of that has been lost. Distributive trades have been affected all along The Border, always for the worse—apart, of course, from such advantages as professional smugglers may take from them by stealth or under deliberately closed eyes. Newry used to be a centre for distributing sugar over a considerable area; The South must now import sugar through Dublin, if its own new sugar industry cannot supply what it wants. The clay for Belleek pottery used to be imported through the republican port of Ballyshannon, a few miles away. Now it must come through Derry.

From Warrenpoint in Down you can cross Carlingford Lough by a row-boat or motor-boat to Omeath in the Republic, or vice versa. There is a considerable traffic across the water every day, especially in good weather: you will see fleets of small craft packed with travellers who, for one reason or another, wish to cross the line of The Border that is marked on the map but not on the water. It is an interesting experience to leave a shore representing one State, get into a small boat, and in no time to land on a shore opposite representing another State. Those who live at these strategic points cater for the traffic. At Omeath, on the Republican side, you will find, near the little pier to which the border-crossing craft are moored, a row of stalls well supplied with all those articles which happen to be in short supply or more expensive in Northern Ireland just over the lough: clothes, tobacco, nylons, canned goods, etc., etc. These stalls are for the special convenience of travellers who may not have had time or opportunity to lay in a stock of what The North regards as subject to control, scrutiny or taxation. On reaching the northern side there may or may not be a Customs' scrutiny, but those Customs' examinations on both sides of the Border tend to be very erratic, incalculable affairs: one day travellers might be put through a very close inspection, and the next you might not see one Customs' officer in that same place. There were places, and they may still exist, where Border officials shut offices and went home at the end of a day, leaving The Border unwatched by night. The reason seems to be that, unless the Governments at Dublin and Belfast maintained the vast legion of officials required for a night and day watch along every inch of the 240 miles, they could not hope to catch more than a fraction of the contraband that passes. If they did catch it all, the fines and taxes would not pay for the officialdom. And they could never catch it all! So, let most of it rip is the unwritten and unspoken working rule. But, just to impress the public that the controls are there, from time to time there is a swoop on some chosen place, and border-crossers are minutely and ruthlessly inspected. It is a good enough system as such systems go; and northerners and southerners make the best of it. They make the best of it in their own sweet ways. Human nature being what it is in those parts, making the best of it means that few people are averse from taking an occasional risk and, if they happen to be caught—well, it is just too bad. But nobody on either side of that Border thinks any the worse of the law's victim.

To the stranger, to the Englishman, American or person of any other country but Ireland, what I have written about The Border may seem to be the final proof that this is the Land of Beautiful Nonsense. Possibly it is. Yet, I can assure them all that, whatever the politics of it may be, the *people* all along both sides of The Border are friendly disposed towards each other. I have not read or heard of violent or otherwise serious incidents arising from plain politics or religion; although minor and often effective gestures are not unknown. In regard to the views of the two sides, there is a relevant story of two young Border Irishmen from one of those towns where one part of the community lives in Northern Ireland and the remainder in The Republic (also known as Eire). One of these Irishmen was from the part in The North, the other from the part in The South. They had both enlisted in Britain's Royal Air Force in the Second World War and found themselves together as mates in the crew of a bomber in a raid over Berlin. Shells were bursting all round them. The Northerner, the story goes, chose that particularly hellish moment to say to his friend: "I suppose *you'll* be a supporter of De Valera?"

"I am not," replied the Southerner, and then after a pause he added: "All the same, I think there's a lot to be said for oul' Dev. He kept *us* out of *this* b—— war, anyway."

"Aye, true enough," said the other, "although I've no time for neutrality meself in this war. I think we all ought to be in it. Don't you?"

"Oh, now, I'm not so sure of that," said the Southerner. "Why, you have no conscription in The North, have you?"

"No fear!" replied the Northerner. "Although our Belfast Government wanted to have it right enough, but the British wouldn't let them." Pause. "And the British were right."

"Right? How do you make that out? If ye think everybody should be in it, why were they right not to have conscription in the Six Counties? That doesn't make sense to me."

"Why not?" the Northerner replied. "Ye see, if they'd had conscription in The North, all the boys there would hate it, and do ye know what they'd do then? Cross the border into Eire, so that they could go from there to England and *volunteer* for the British forces and avoid conscription. Oh no! Conscription wouldn't work with us."

"I see. Well, after all, you must be Irish like the rest of us!"

That is what it amounts to. And the visitor to Ireland will find that neither the politics of The Border nor anything except those 'frontier controls' need detract from the pleasure which both sides offer.

CHAPTER V

NORTHERN IRELAND
OR THE SIX COUNTIES AREA

As I went a-walkin' tae Moneymore Fair
I spied a wee lass sittin' combin' her hair:
She gied me a glance o' her bonny blue eye,
An' says I tae myself: "I'll come back by an' by,
Back by an' by,
Back by an' by,"
An' says I tae myself, "I'll come back by an' by."

From *Ramble Away*, a Ballymena version of an anonymous old song, quoted in *Ulster Songs and Ballads* by Padric Gregory.

1
Belfast and Armagh

For our present purpose we shall assume that Belfast is the landing-place, a Convenient Centre in itself, and also a good starting-point from which to reach any of the other Convenient Centres in the Six Counties.

Enjoyment of the Irish scene begins before landing if you travel by ship to Belfast, and this is one of the advantages of sea over air travel, which otherwise wins marks for speed and some say comfort. If you are one of those travellers who gets out of bed an hour or so earlier than is strictly necessary in order to stand on the deck of your ship and contemplate the approaching landscape, this is an opportunity not to be missed. Belfast Lough is four miles long before the ship reaches the narrows. On a clear day you should get a good view of the hills and fields, of the houses on each side of the shore, as well as of the shipping on the Lough itself—the latter always an interesting feature, as this is an impressive port. The fields, you will notice, are really green!

Belfast (*bel* = entrance, *fearsad* = sandbank or bar: thus perhaps 'the entrance by or over a sandbank'), which the natives pronounce 'Bĕl*fahst'*, with a fierce stress on the last syllable, is situated on the River Lagan. You may not see much of this river in the city itself, because, except where it runs into the Lough, it is inconspicuous and uninteresting here, though not unimportant for shipping. The sight really worth seeing as you approach the city is the fine harbour and great shipbuilding works, the latter being not only the largest but also one of the finest and most efficient in the world. Your ship will pass the shipbuilding yards, and you will not only hear the rattle of riveters at work, but you will have a close enough view of the iron 'scaffolding' and vastly complex structures and cyclopean cranes or gantries which surround and dominate the hulls under construction. With binoculars you may be able to pick out the unfinished liner, battleship or tanker, and few people, even though they may dislike modern industrialism, but are thrilled by the spectacle of so much human energy and ingenuity as those yards unfold. Your ship goes on and you land. What you see is anything but encouraging. A drab quayside. And up and down it are equally dull warehouses, from some of which may be wafted to your nostrils new and unaccustomed aromas by which the expert can decide their contents. There is one thing about this Belfast quayside which may really impress you: the hurry and bustle and energy on all sides. You are seldom kept waiting long for a porter for your luggage or for a taxi to take you to your hotel, or your railway or bus station. A Belfastman will pounce on you before you know where you are, and you will find yourself moving in a way and with a speed that you may not have expected of Ireland.

This city of nearly half a million people is devoted to industries: shipbuilding, linen, tobacco, iron-founding, rope-making, aircraft; and to many of the lesser ones such as whiskey, if this can ever rightly be called a lesser industry. If you intend to make Belfast your headquarters, *see the city first* and get it over before you sample the surrounding country. I shall not conceal my opinion that in Belfast itself you will not see much that you cannot see in almost any industrial centre in Britain. Its noteworthy monuments number about a dozen, among which are the capable-looking City Hall, the Queen's University, the College of Technology, the Courts of Justice, the Museum and Art Gallery, St. Anne's Cathedral and the Albert Memorial. These are functional rather than architectural masterpieces. Six miles outside of

"Giant's Grave" or Cromlech—
Kemp Stone, Dundonald, Co. Down
UTDA

Parliament Buildings—Stormont, Belfast UTDA

Belfast Castle UTDA

Belfast at Stormont are Parliament Buildings, perhaps the most impressive modern edifice in the Six Counties. If you start from Castle Junction in the centre of the city, you can either walk or go by bus to Stormont. On the trip you will have a good view of the Lagan from Queen's Bridge, and at the same time not only get a general idea of the harbour and shipyards, but also a taste of the countryside. Another interesting outing is to the public park and zoo at Bellvue by the Crumlin and Antrim Roads, which are also on the way to Hazlewood, the Floral Hall, Belfast Castle and the Dunmore Racing Track. Crumlin is a name which, you will find, crops up fairly often in Belfast. A Flanders master-spinner named Louis Crommelin was one of the many Huguenots who came to Ulster in the time of William III. This Crommelin was a great craftsman and a man of all-round ability. He made Lisburn his principal centre of activities, and achieved considerable local fame, for he introduced many new ideas, of which the local people took full advantage. They are grateful in Belfast to the memory of Crommelin.

I always think that a big city, and especially a big industrial city like Belfast, is not the right place for holidaymaking, and therefore I want to get the visitor out of it as quickly as possible. This city, there is no need to conceal the fact, cannot compete with Dublin for interest. If you must have an urban holiday, I recommend Dublin, Cork, Limerick, Galway or, in The North, Londonderry or Enniskillen—all of these being of more interest than Belfast, a city which I think is best contemplated from outside. So that, if I do not dwell on Belfast itself, it is because the assumption here is that it is merely being used as a Convenient Centre for Antrim, Down and Armagh, and not as itself the holiday resort. By all means see the sights I have mentioned, and if you are that kind of person, go also and visit Harland and Wolff's great shipyard (if they will permit you, which they might). Go also and see Gallaher's tobacco factory, a linen mill, a rope-works, a distillery—and marvel. But, to my mind, of more interest would be a walk down the Falls Road, which is Roman Catholic, cut across to the parallel Shankill Road, which is Protestant, and see whether you can tell any difference between Protestants and Catholics. You may not notice it, but there is! Very fierce passions lie dormant most of the time in these two streets, but from time to time some little incident acts like a match to a powder magazine. Then the lid is blown off. There have been some very unpleasant incidents around there. They do not often happen, but when they do there is shown a primitive ferocity which I should not like any visitor to witness. It makes me sad to think of what I myself once saw in Belfast. Let me not create the impression that Belfast is anything but a very Convenient Centre from which to visit Counties Down and Antrim, and even Armagh. But, before thinking of those lovely counties, you should first visit Cave Hill, a bus-ride and pleasant walk from the city. This Hill overlooks Belfast, and from it you get the best possible view of the city, and, if the city is like any other industrial city at close quarters, you may be rather surprised to see how beautiful it can look from the top of Cave Hill. This is in many ways a point of vantage. Apart from the view of the city, of Belfast Lough and the surrounding countryside, which are beautiful, there are on the Hill and nearby some interesting historical survivals: MacArt's Fort and the Scottish baronial Belfast Castle, built by a Marquess of Donegall about 1870 and now owned with its grounds by Belfast Corporation. It is a show-piece. Within bus-ride are the site of the residence of Con O'Neill, the last Irish chief thereabouts, who died in 1559; and the Round Tower of Drumbo. Nearby is Shaw's Bridge, a very pleasant outing.

County Down, to the south of Belfast, and with good bus and rail facilities, is a restful county. The people are mostly of English or Anglo-Irish descent, and it is in this pleasant land that the famous Mountains of Mourne 'run down to the sea'. Down is rightly called the 'county of contrasts', for pictorially it has nearly everything: mountains, hills, green fields, sea-loughs, rivers. In it you will find pockets of old Irish-Ireland; and, of course, much of modern Anglo-Ireland. Modern seasides: Holywood on Belfast Lough, and Bangor, Donaghadee (stress on -dee) on the Irish Sea; and Rostrevor and Warrenpoint to the south. And many charming small places along the coast. There is in this county an exceptional geographical feature: the large sea inlet with a narrow entrance which makes Strangford Lough an inland salt-water lake. Newtownards is at its north end; Grey Abbey on the north-east side; Portaferry on the south of the north shore; and Killyleagh on the south bank. Have you ever had the experience of a holiday by an inland salt-water lake? Not in the British Islands—unless you have visited Strangford Lough. The visit is well worth while. There is nothing about the places on this Lough of the hurly-burly and restless vigour which one usually associates with popular resorts situated on the 'outside' sea, for here, inland, you have, as well as the inland sea, the farmlands all round you, and on the other side of Strangford Lough more farms, little cottages and green fields. This may not be the most colourful or the most wonderful landscape in Ireland; it is certainly one of the most restful.

Down is a very fertile county, nearly all capable of being farmed, cultivated or utilized to advantage—in contrast with some of those other stony and almost barren Irish areas of which the most striking feature is often their very bleakness. There is not much 'bog' in Down, not many old woods; though there are many newly planted ones, and so the landscape in many parts is nicely varied. Perhaps the most striking feature of this county is the very long coastline—200 miles in a county of only 50 miles in length—chiefly due to that great Strangford Lough inlet. There is one place which the historically minded visitor *must* see: Downpatrick. Here St. Patrick landed in A.D. 432 on his return to Ireland for his great Mission which christianized the Irish Celts and initiated Ireland's 'Golden Age'. Downpatrick is for other reasons of great historical interest. It was known in early times as 'The Fort of Celchar' (*Rath or Dun Celchar*) and so called after *Celchar,* who was one of the Red Branch knights or heroes. It was also called *Dun Leth Glas* (meaning obscure), from which the county got its name, the word Patrick being added to mark the saint's landing-place. This is also the country of the de Courcys, of whom the first to arrive was the Anglo-Norman, John de Courcy, in 1177. From the moment of his arrival and onwards for centuries Downpatrick was the scene of struggles and battles between the Irish and the invaders, of burnings and pillagings, and of little peace. As might be expected, there are survivals hereabouts of interest to the antiquary and historian. There is what remains of an interesting old cross. But the battles have eliminated what would be of most interest, and today no trace remains of the de Courcys' Castle or of the once famous old Houses of the Franciscans and Cistercians. Almost in the middle of the town you can see the parish church, of which the tower dates from 1177. All around and about this modest little county capital and cathedral town of Downpatrick will be found old ruins, dolmens ('Giants' Graves'), stone circles of druidical origin, pieces of old Christian churches and a great *dun* or fort. Christianity was first preached in Ireland at the place called *Sabhal,* meaning a 'barn', and now called Saul, this barn having been placed at the missionary's disposal by the well-wishing Irish chief Dichu. Here a little church was erected. Here St. Patrick died in A.D. 493. What a history this little place has! Burned by the Norsemen; rebuilt; sacked by an Ulster king; ravaged by Edward Bruce in the fourteenth century. Here also is the very early Church of Raholp. At Struell are the Holy Wells of St. Patrick, once a minor Lourdes for pilgrims and those stricken with disease and disability. Not of least interest are the many prehistoric monuments around Downpatrick, especially the stone circles at Ballyalton and Ballynoe and a grand 'Giant's Grave' at Lough Money. For a quiet, pious or contemplative holiday Downpatrick is your place. For the opposite, choose Bangor, in which the atmosphere is physically more invigorating.

A fine holiday-place in Down is Bangor, a town which spreads itself along the sea front for what may be as many as four miles when this is read. Here you will find good bathing facilities, yachting, public parks, sports' grounds, golf-course, and the long front promenade where the city-worn Belfast people stroll and take the air as they admire one another, gathering strength from the invigorating air for another spell of city turmoil, grind and business. At Bangor over a thousand years ago was a great monastic school which sent its teachers and exported its learning and culture to semi-barbarous England and to the blacker corners of continental Europe. Dance-halls, cinemas, amusement halls and the theatre signalize the modern spirit of the town. Where the monks once chanted their hymns, perhaps to the accompaniment of a gentle harpist, you may now hear jazzed-out 'Rudolph the Red-nosed Reindeer' or whatever happens to be the latest anthem of the crooner.

These extraordinary contrasts—of the ultra-modern alongside an antiquity often dating back to prehistoric times—greatly contribute towards making Ireland unique. You will find the contrasts in most of the big Irish towns: modernism in the form of cinemas and jazz-halls surrounded by very old survivals. County Down has these contrasts, as well as those already noted in its landscape and configuration.

You might with pleasure make an excursion to Newtownards, first calling at the popular seaside resort of Donaghadee, and then go on to the beautiful Ards Peninsula, south of these towns. The number of possible excursions from Belfast to the south, that is, to the County Down, is almost without limit: along Belfast Lough; to Groomsport, where King William and his men under Schomberg landed in 1689 to help in the politics of the day. And there is little Comber, where they make whiskey. Those who like the atmosphere of a little fishing village will find it at Portaferry at the narrow entrance to Strangford Lough, a delightful spot which any artist would enjoy. You must not forget that farther south there are the towns of Warrenpoint and Rostrevor on the sea-inlet of Carlingford Lough through which runs The Border. Tourist offices will provide lists, and I need not continue what might here become a dull catalogue. There is enough in County Down to fill many excursions from the 'Convenient Centre' of Belfast, and I should be surprised if a visitor who has sampled this good, comfortable and friendly county does not find in his outings some place which he deems worthy of a longer holiday, a more prolonged visit, to itself.

You can make of Belfast your Convenient Centre for Armagh. The County of Armagh is noteworthy for several reasons. Apart from its green fields and fine orchards—it is the great fruit-growing area of Ireland and, in spring, one great blossom—this is the Saga Country of Ulster. Navan Fort, near the city of Armagh, was the pre-Christian Emania, the King of Ulster's capital and headquarters of the Red Branch Knights, those Irish heroes who stamped their memory on Irish history and are immortalized in the *Táin Bó Cuailnge* (see Part I, Ch. IV). The capital town and county are called after Macha (*Ard Macha,* 'Hill of Macha'), but, as there were three Machas, it is not certain whether it was called after the queen of that name or after a Macha who, according to legend, might have lived so long ago as 3,000 years. Modern historians and archæologists are little by little getting that misty and legendary past into a perspective which may one day enable us to write dates in old Irish history with fewer doubts than now. But we need not be doubtful of one thing: Armagh is historically one of the oldest places —by this I mean that it has the longest history—in Western Europe. There is a geographical reason which partly accounts for its antiquity. Two great roads leading into the Ulster 'basin' or valley meet just at this Hill. Archæologists speculate to the effect that men of the Iron Age—'Progressives'—invaded Armagh along one of these roads or routes to drive out Bronze Age men—'Conservatives'—into Antrim and Down. The great highway from Tara in The South also passed this point. The other important route came from Monaghan and the Upper Erne country. Hence the Hill of Macha would be an excellent place for a settlement in those days. Next, Armagh is the ecclesiastical capital of Ireland, Protestant and Roman Catholic. The present Protestant Cathedral stands where St. Patrick built his first cathedral, and some of the building you see may date from the 8th century, though we know with greater certainty that it was begun in the 13th and restored in the 18th century. A king of the Northumbrian Saxons was educated at the Armagh School. He was Prince Aldfrid, and in A.D. 684 wrote an account of a trip he made through Ireland. This old town of Armagh reeks of history. What may be of as much interest to the visitor as history is that it is one of the most beautiful towns in all Ireland. Architecturally Kilkenny is, I think, better, and is better planned. The Hill with its two cathedrals, the perfect choice of sites, and the spontaneous, natural and pleasing growth of the town around the hillside give Armagh its unique beauty. For the rest, it is like most Ulster towns: clean, orderly, prosperous and altogether a lively, busy centre for a countryside of farmers and fruit-growers.

Armaghmen are of a good-natured and sturdy race, though I doubt whether many of them appreciate as fully as they might the beauties and great history of their capital town, or of the Saga Country which now yields an income from the cultivation of apples and plums or, as happens, from canned plum-and-apple. It seems a long way from Cúchulainn and the Red Branch heroes to Richhill jam. This is the county of both.

*

Ireland has stamped itself on the United States of America in a way and to an extent that few Irish or American people fully realize. Everybody knows that from the days of the Famine onwards, the Irish emigrated to the United States in great numbers, but it is sometimes forgotten that at the time of the American Revolution there were already some 400,000 Irish Protestants, mostly of Presbyterian stock, and descendants of those who had gone there in the period when Irish Presbyterians were getting as bad a deal from the English as were the Irish Catholics. Those Ulstermen were the stuff of social revolution and republicanism such as showed itself in Wolfe Tone in Ireland. From them Washington got some of his best generals in the War of Independence, and from the Ulstermen came the most fiery of the progressives of that period, the men who signed the Declaration of Independence. In those days Irish Protestants and Catholics worked together, respecting each other's religion and united by common political ideals. Nearly one-half of America's Presidents have come from Ulster stock.

Ireland influenced the United States in another way which is far less widely known. If the Ulstermen contributed the republican ideal, that of American Federalism came from the Celtic Irish who must have been thinking of the loose old Celtic system of communities or 'States', each under its own chief, and grouped together for certain purposes under a king, the five big groups having an *ard-ri* or 'high-king'. American Federalism—separate States with their own governors, and an elected President and a Federal Government over them all—is politically the same idea, with republicanism substituted for monarchism and democracy in the place of hereditary aristocracy. The Celts were the only European people who had this system before it was established in the United States, but the old Celtic form was looser and more elastic than the American. Here is a subject for a hitherto unwritten thesis. From some such system as that of the Celts may yet come World Federation.

To come down closer to earth, the map of the United States is sprinkled with Irish names, many of them multiplied several times. There are in the United States a score of Dublins and Waterfords; and there are Donegals, Westports, Sligos, Limericks, Corks and Lismores. One can find on that same map Galway, Wicklow, Dundalk, Ennis, Cavan, Belfast, and I do not know how many other Irish place-names. The Gaelic language was once well known in some parts of the United States, and I have read somewhere of a political campaign in North Carolina about 150 years ago in which Gaelic was the principal language. There must be few Irish families who have not kinsmen across the Atlantic, and of these Ulster has a considerable proportion. The influence of Ulster speech on American has probably been greater than that of the Irish-English of the rest of Ireland.

2

Larne—Antrim Coast Road and Glens—Portrush

The next on my list of recommended Convenient Centres is Larne, and, although it is a small place, I would myself prefer to use it as my headquarters rather than Belfast. Larne is not only the port for ships from Scotland, but it has bus and rail facilities to enable you to visit many interesting places. You can get a train or bus from Belfast to Larne, passing Carrickfergus, Whitehead and running by the side of Island Magee (not an island, but almost), and from Larne you can go by train or bus to the town of Antrim, which is situated on Lough Neagh, the largest fresh-water lake in these islands. Fishermen, bird lovers, hikers and those who like smooth sailing or rowing find that in Lough Neagh and its surrounding country—it touches County Antrim, a small piece of Down, Armagh, Tyrone and Londonderry—there can be the ideal holiday. By sailing round the Lough you see five of the six counties of Northern Ireland. If you fish in it you might catch a fighting black Boddagh, which you would not easily catch elsewhere; on its shore you might see a yellow wagtail, which you would see elsewhere only on Lough Corrib; and an insect peculiar to the Neagh sand-dunes. This is a naturalist's country *in excelsis,* but because I emphasize that point, it is not to say that you will not also find in this country much of historical and archæological interest.

I dwell on the advantages of Larne as a Convenient Centre if only for the one reason which I place above all others in order of importance. Not only can you explore the whole of Antrim from Larne, but from this town of excellent amenities, resources and popular amusements you can start out on what I regard as one of Ireland's most wonderful road trips: along the famous Antrim Coast Road. This lovely route runs northwards and then westwards, never far from the sea, and sometimes almost *in* it, passing with cinematograph speed a succession of most varied scenes and giving the fortunate traveller close-ups of hills that are almost mountains, cliffs that almost scare one to look at, bays, promontories and, of unique beauty, those Glens of Antrim some of which come down to the road to give a passing glimpse of their caressing quietude. I have often read or heard of this trip round the Antrim Coast Road as being breath-taking; and that is the simplest and most truthful description it can have. It is some years now since I last went round that road, beginning at Belfast, and following it in Antrim to Portrush, there leaving it to go on through Derry to Donegal. The trip impressed me so much that, although many of the details are blurred, I still have the sensations felt as we went along from one striking view or scene to the next. All of this is *close-up,* not panorama; and perhaps this is what makes the experience unique. I quote with approval the official Guide: "Turning and soaring and dipping, like a swallow in flight, with the sea on one hand and the cliffs on the other, white masses of limestone, dark masses of basalt, with glens running into the country and streams tumbling down into the sea, the road for the whole of its course has a beauty which needs no adjectives. Its country, moreover, is haunted with stories, from the dim past of legend till today. This was the land over which struggled the Macdonnells, O'Neills and O'Cahans, whose castles, once the homes of passion and emotion, are now voiceless ruins."

At Glenarm is the entrance to the first of the Glens, a peaceful little place where you might pleasantly step down for a brief contemplation of its restful beauties. You may be one of those people who prefer to rush ahead, which you can do and inevitably will do with eager appetite for what is to come, for the map shows ahead Red Bay and then Cushendall and Cushendun: the Glen country. The Antrim Glens (or 'glynnes') are, in simple words, wooded places. But to describe these Irish hills and valleys as 'wooded places' is about as adequate as to describe the Himalayas as 'a range of mountains'. I do not think it is possible to give in words any idea of the superlative beauty of these Antrim Glens. Many writers of prose and poetry have made the attempt and have not always succeeded, for the Glens must be seen, experienced, *felt*. Elsewhere I have referred to those Gaelic place-names which roll off the tongue. The Glen country of Antrim serves as a perfect example of the joy and poetry which those old Irish wordmakers must have felt when they gave names to the hills, dells, rivers and valleys which inspired Nature created here. Gaelic scholars do not and probably never will agree about the meaning of many of the names, which have the sound of pure music. For two reasons. First, the poet often mints a word of his own, and the inspired poet will find or make a word which satisfies by its sound as well as by its associative, comprehensive or descriptive power. Second, it is sometimes, but not always, possible to find in another language (in this case English) a word which will convey *some* of the meaning but never *all* of the meaning. For meaning, in such words as those relating to the Antrim Glens, can never be complete unless it conjures up the associations, which are spiritual more often than material. The usually accepted approximate English meanings for the (anglicized) names of the Nine Glens are:

Glenarm—*Glen of the Army*.

Glencloy—*Glen of the Sword* (or *Dikes*).

Glenariff—*Arable Glen*.

Glenballyemon—*Edwardstown Glen.*

Glenaan—*Glen of the Proverb* (also, *Hemmed-in Glen*).

Glencorp—*Glen of the Dead Body* (also called Glencorb, *Glen of the Coaches*).

Glendun—*Brown Glen.*

Glenshesk—*Sedgy Glen.*

Glentaise—*Glen of Taise* (Taise Taobhgeal, Daughter of a King of Rathlin).

Glenariff is usually regarded as the 'most beautiful' of the Glens. The Cushendall–Ballymena Road cuts across it. The visitor who is in such haste that he cannot see this Glen and the waterfalls might as well not come here at all, for the names of the waterfalls (*Ess Na Laragh*—Fall of the Battlefield, and *Ess na Cruib*—Horseshoe Fall) are imperiously inviting.

If a holiday is in mind, Cushendall, Cushendun and Carnlough (in order of size and amenities) are quiet places and, for those who like to walk, climb and wander about with an aim only to look at and enjoy the softer poetry of Nature, these key points can be recommended.

The next fair-sized town on this route is Ballycastle, but to get the best of things it is advisable to take a road with a less finished though not a bad surface for motorists, and go round the coast, passing Runabay Head, Torr Head, Murlough Bay and Grey Man's Path leading to the beach. Here the cyclist or pedestrian scores, for the extra distance involved is only about twelve miles; and the journey can be broken. It is worth breaking at Fair Head to see, or better, to visit Rathlin Island. On the summit of Fair Head are Lough Dhu ('Black Lake') and Lough na Crannóg ('Lake of the Island on Piles'). Rathlin Island is worth a visit—possible by boat twice weekly—if only to see how happy and contented a little isolated community can be in one of the many Shangri-Las which Ireland and its islands have available for the interested escapist. If you intend to visit Ballycastle, or to have a holiday there, you must read or re-read James Stephens' *Deirdre.* For Ballycastle, as well as being a very pleasant modern town, is connected with the marvellous, but in essentials authentic, story of Deirdre and the Sons of Usneach, and also with part of that delightfully Celtic fantasy of the Children of Lir. A jealous stepmother, you may remember, turned the children of Lir into swans doomed to live nine hundred years until released by the ringing of a Christian bell. The swans spent three hundred years on the waters opposite to Ballycastle, but one of the four, Fionnghuala, a girl, perished in her efforts to succour her brothers. The Christian bell rang; the old swans resumed their human shape; they were properly baptized; and they died. They rest together in a single grave, Fionnghuala in the centre, with her youngest brother in her arms and a brother on each side. And so it is that in Ireland you still often hear swans referred to as Children of Lir, the old God of the Sea. At Knocklayd near Ballycastle is a Round Tower which, for perfect preservation, challenges the one on Devenish Island in Lough Erne, is easier to visit and inspect, but smaller and with less interesting associations.

After Ballycastle, the next town is Portrush—a popular seaside resort and also a Convenient Centre with every amenity a visitor can require. On the way you will pass the little town of Ballintoy, near which are some interesting ruins—Dunseverick Castle—famous in the Red Branch Cycle as the home of the phenomenal Conal Cearnac, a powerful and skilful Celtic wrestler and fighter with the sword who held his own always, and was often victorious even when matched against the flower of ancient Rome's gladiators. So the story goes; and who are we to challenge it?—for the Celts made great gladiators, and are still useful fighters. On the way to Portrush you pass the Giant's Causeway, six miles east of the town, and reached from it by a tramway specially built for that purpose. The geologist who has never seen the Giant's Causeway will wish to. The ordinary visitor who likes to see the wonders of the world must see it, for this is said to be one of the seven. I quote the official Guide: "It is alone of its kind, unexampled, unique, a miracle in shape, as if gigantic bees had been its builders and their work had been in stone instead of wax." Legend has it that it was made by that much-overworked Irish giant Finn MacCool. It is, I read in a work of authority, a volcanic formation in basalt. But forgive me, dear reader, I found it a bore to look at after five minutes. It did not startle me the first time I set eyes on it. And I do not particularly want to see it again! But I won't say a word against the Giant's Causeway, for it was probably there before man set foot in Ireland, and it may still be there when some other form of life inhabits the Emerald Isle. The Causeway demands respect; and I respect those who respect it. More I cannot say.

Of Portrush as a popular resort there is much I could say. It is situated on a promontory which is almost an island, and thus gets the highly invigorating Atlantic air from all sides; it is a health resort, a favourite holiday resort for Ulster folk and many others. I do not know of any place in these islands which can compete with it in sheer salubrity, for which it has long been famous. But I do not commend it to those who find a relaxing atmosphere better for their health. You should, I think, be one of those people who like a clean, fresh, bracing atmosphere, and be capable of at least constant mild exercise to get the best of Portrush. Its sea breezes are cooling and, except in the heat of a good summer, Portrush is rarely a place for lounging or sitting about in the open air. There is a fine Blue Pool for bathers, and Golf Links which, close followers of the game assure me, challenge those of the great St. Andrews. I learn not without some surprise that Bowling has become very fashionable here and in other parts of Northern Ireland. That is all to the good, for it is a gentle game. And you have facilities for tennis and other games and, above all, everything that the sea can offer. The country around the town provides excellent walks. As you will see by the map, it is on the top edge of County Londonderry, the city of that name being our next Convenient Centre. But we cannot pass Coleraine, for that would be to insult a fine community.

Coleraine is not merely a thriving, busy town. It is one with many historical associations and many general attractions. I see that it is often called a city, but in Ireland the distinction between city and town is not laboured. The name is poetic, meaning 'corner of the ferns', and it holds on firmly to the right to be called city because St. Patrick himself gave it its name in the fifth century, and St. Bernard of Clairvaux elevated it to the status of city in the twelfth. To me Coleraine is of special interest, because it was the Pictish capital before the Celtic invasion of Ireland. And those Picts—the same race as the ancient *Cruithne* (?)—were a formidable people who fought to the last ditch against overwhelming numbers, held out for years, may not have been completely conquered, and in some places may have thoroughly absorbed their enemies. It is not for nothing that Coleraine people are tough: because, for all we know, many of them may have in them the blood of the first human inhabitants of Ireland! Whoever so desires can start a lifetime of research and study here at Coleraine. Outside of it, at Mountsandel, he can usefully begin on a rath representing remains of the Pictish Royal Palace at *Dun na bheann,* without doubt one of the most interesting of the innumerable forts and fort-sites indicated by the words *Dun, Cashel, Lis* and *Rath* which you will find marked all over the Ordnance Survey Maps of Ireland: Dun Laoghaire, Lisburn, for example, and Rathmines—all once forts—and Cashel in Tipperary, this word usually meaning a round, stone fort. Coleraine is a river-port situated at the end of the navigable part of the River Bann. And the Bann is a good river for fish, especially salmon and trout. For eels there must be few waterways to compare with it. You could do worse than make of Coleraine a headquarters for a holiday, for by so doing you would avoid the crowding and accommodation difficulties of the summer months at Portrush which is easily accessible by bus and rail and even on foot, being only about five miles away. A King of Ulster named Fintan used Mountsandel as a fort. Four miles out, on the hilly way to Limavady, and on the top of a hill, is *Dun Ceithern,* legendary headquarters of the Knights of the Red Branch. Thus, you can enjoy yourself physically at Coleraine, and if you wish to delve into archæology, ancient history, mythology and legend, here is a pleasant and useful seat from which to begin.

3

Derry and Tyrone: Orange Day

Now we come to the excellent Convenient Centre of Derry. The official name of the county and its capital is Londonderry, but no Irishman outside officialdom or law-courts would ever dream of calling it anything but Derry. In Ireland it is snobbery or 'English' to talk of 'Londonderry'; and has been as long as I can remember. The old name of the city was *Daire Calgaigh,* the 'Oak-grove of Calgagh', the latter a Celtic leader who so distinguished himself in England as to be mentioned by Tacitus. When Ulster was 'planted', many places were given English names, or the original Gaelic names were given an English pronunciation from which we have their present anglicized forms. Something rather different happened to *Daire Calgaigh.* The name of the man was dropped, the word *Daire* was retained, and the new masters put the name of London before this and so made 'Londonderry'. But why London, you may ask? Soon you shall know how London came to be so deeply interested in that part of Ireland, but meanwhile note that, although the compound word Londonderry may seem an incongruity, it so happens that, by what I think is a philological fluke, this need not be so. For the word London also happens to be of Celtic origin: *Linn*—pool, *Dun*—fort, and so "the pool by the fort." Londoners need not be told what the Pool of London is. The compound word Londonderry might at a stretch be translated "the pool by the fort of the oak-grove": that is, if your imagination will allow you to regard Lough Foyle—which can provide good anchorage for the combined fleets of the world—as a pool! We had better leave it at that, and explain why and how London came to be closely associated with our Convenient Centre.

It would be interesting to look into the negotiations which took place between the Government of the English king James I and the Companies of shrewd London merchants who had their minds well concentrated on the commercial possibilities which were being thrown open to them by the Plantation of Ulster. We cannot do that here, but must be content to accept as a fact that those Londoners regarded the possibilities as highly promising. In which they made no mistake. James's Government needed money; the London Companies needed new openings for business. The Companies were for practical purposes the Corporation of London. We can simplify a complicated story by stating that Derry and many other 'interests' in that part of Ulster were *sold and conveyed* by the Plantation Government to the Corporation of London. For the purpose of the more efficient exploitation of these new interests acquired by conquest, there was formed in London *The Irish Society*—with no Irishman on its roll. The aims of the Society were to promote *religion, education* and *industry* in the part of the Plantation they had bought. The settlers, under their masters in London, took over the various local 'interests', including the newly named Londonderry, and it was about this time that the division of Ireland into 'shires' on the English model was completed. The Planters set about their work with energy and efficiency, and before long The Plantation began to show excellent financial returns to the City of London. That was the beginning of the long-standing and deep affection which London has for Londonderry. The Governor of *The Irish Society* is an Alderman of London City; the Recorder of London is an ex-officio Member of the Society; and the twenty-four 'Assistants' are Aldermen or Councillors of the English capital. Yet, Derry city's population is 60·1 per cent. Nationalist (pro-Republic) and 39·9 per cent. Unionist or Conservative.

Agricultural land in Ulster was divided out among twelve of those great London Companies whose names are household words: the Goldsmiths, the Tailors, the Vintners, the Drapers and so forth, who in turn usefully sold some of their shares to smaller ones. Some forty London companies in this way became involved in the Plantation of Londonderry county, *The Irish Society* retaining the cream of the interests for itself, this cream being represented to this day by 'lands' in Derry City and Coleraine; and the excellent Foyle and Bann fisheries. The Society is ground landlord of Derry and Coleraine. It maintains a great friendship with those in power in Northern Ireland and in Derry and Coleraine, and not a year passes without exchanges of courtesies and the inspection of its Irish properties by representatives of the great London institution. The Irish Society perfectly exemplifies the working of a fruitful marriage between commerce and politics. There are many people, especially among the survivors of the original inhabitants of those parts and their friends elsewhere in Ireland, who do not regard with too

The Strange Figures on White Island, Lough Erne
UTDA

Ruins of Inch Abbey—Co. Down UTDA

Grey Abbey—Co. Down UTDA

favourable eyes what has happened. But this is not the place to discuss such things, if we are to give politics and religion a discreet miss.

Yet it is not easy to give politics and religion a miss in Derry City, whose turbulent history for three hundred years is little else but war and tension between the Catholics who were dispossessed and the Planters who took over. He who wishes to read of strife and battle, of besieged and besiegers, will find more than enough to thrill him in the history of Derry. And whatever his religion or politics may be, no man can read of the heroic siege of Derry in 1689 without admiration for the strength of will and the marvellous courage of its defenders. As this has become an item in the Protestant part of Ulster's history and pride, which no stranger can appreciate unless he knows something of its background, we dare not ignore it here.

What in Irish history is called the Williamite War (1685–1691) was for England an aside in a bigger struggle than its Irish manifestation. It was all a part of a vast and long-drawn-out struggle between the Reformation and the Counter-Reformation, and involved nearly the whole of Europe. When the English Catholic king James II became sovereign of England in 1685, the Irish Catholics saw in him their champion, and James believed that he could use those Irish Catholics against not only Irish but against English Protestants, whom he desired to see converted to his own faith. James had control of power in England, but the English Protestants, who were in a majority and bitterly anti-Catholic, rather than see themselves brought to their knees, made an alliance with the Dutch King, William of Orange. 'Dutch William' landed in the South of England in November 1688. The weak and vacillating James fled, and in England nobody was now found to fight for his cause, though the Irish Catholics continued to remain loyal to him, hoping thereby to win legal rights for their faith and, at the same time, to 'undo' the Cromwellian Settlement and the work of the Plantation of Ulster, and to free the Irish Parliament from dependence on and subservience to English government. James succeeded in winning supporters, and, with the Irish Catholics on his side and the support of the French

King Louis, turned his attention to this promising territory. By the spring of 1689 it seemed as if he might win there, for only in the north—in Enniskillen and Derry—was there stubborn resistance by Protestants. The real war began in December 1688, rapidly developing into the historic siege of Derry in April 1689, a terrible episode which lasted for 105 days. Every Ulster Protestant's breast swells with pride when he reads, hears or even thinks of the heroic resistance and achievement of the men of Derry before the relief ships arrived, burst the great boom on the Foyle and ended the brave city's agony on the 12th August. Derry had only one man, the execrated Lundy, who even thought of surrender. To this day his effigy is burned by the Orangemen every year in Derry and in many places in Northern Ireland. William of Orange arrived in Ireland in June 1690, and with his forces met those of James on the River Boyne on the 1st July the same year. He won that famous Battle of the Boyne decisively on the 12th July, a date celebrated as Orange Day in The North.

With that brief and inadequate sketch to explain the pride of Derry's Protestant community and also something of its political atmosphere, we may look at the city itself. Derry is one of the loveliest of Irish cities, not only because of its beautiful situation on the River Foyle at the head of the Lough of that name, but because of its picturesque fortifications, its configuration, its atmosphere of dignity, its historical associations and even its antiquity, which can be felt. Belfast is best seen from outside. I should not like to go as far as that about Derry, but I recommend the visitor to take a series of walks out to surrounding points of vantage from which he can see the city, and look well at it. If the day is a good one, you will be able to appreciate the strikingly beautiful setting of this place, especially from above the cemetery and the old Strabane Road. I shall not attempt to catalogue the antiquities to be found in the city itself or in its neighbourhood. But I must record that not six miles away is 'the stone house of the sun'—known as the Grianan of Aileach—which many geographers accept as being one of the five places which the Greek philosopher and pioneer of geographical science, Ptolemy, marked on his Map of Ireland (A.D. 55)—thus indicating that the fame of the place had reached the other end of Europe even by that date.

You cannot fail to appreciate Derry City as a Convenient Centre. With this as headquarters you can visit, not only the whole of Derry County—and you should not miss the Derry side of Lough Foyle, or a trip to the Sperrin Mountains—but also Strabane in County Tyrone, not far away. From Derry you can see a good part of North Tyrone. But, to my mind, one of the most attractive features of this Convenient Centre is that next door, so to speak, you have a part of northern Donegal which I can only describe as a paradise for those who prefer wilder scenery and more varied landscape. Derry is a good centre for fishermen. Ptolemy called the Bann the *Argita,* the 'Silver River'. The River Foyle is a notable waterway. Both are beloved of fishermen. Britons need not take offence when I tell them that fishing in Irish rivers, especially such rivers as the Foyle and the Bann, is a much more satisfying sport than it is in the greater part of Britain —except a few parts of Scotland and Wales. In those Irish rivers you can almost always be *sure* of catching fish!—unless you are a very bad fisherman indeed. But to do so you must study the local art and science of the subject, and follow the advice of local experts until you know the physical appetites and moral weaknesses of those cunning Irish fishes. I would even go so far as to say that fishing-tackle for use in Ireland should be bought there, because all the keen native fishermen I have known have usually been inclined to laugh at the elaborate outfits, the wonderful rods and tackle which sportsmen from across the Irish Sea usually bring with them, and of which much is either completely useless or quite unnecessary. I have myself caught good fish in Ireland with a home-made rod and tackle costing next to nothing; and what *I* can achieve as a fisherman can be surpassed, I am convinced, by the veriest novice who gives the matter as little thought as I have done. I mention fishing only for the benefit of those who are not real 'fishermen'; these do not need to be told anything about their sport by such as I. Those who have never tried fishing could do worse than start where they have excellent chances of catching fish, fine fish, succulent fish such as trout and salmon. Great enjoyment, I used to find, can be had in a little quiet poa——; but I must stop in the interests of law and order.

In County Londonderry, to the south, are the Sperrin Mountains. The Carntochers run like a spine from a few miles below Magilligan Point down east of Dungiven and join the Sperrins to form a natural protection for those who live west of the range. This part of Ireland provides a wonderful walk *along hilltops* from Downhill, almost on the Atlantic, to Omagh, the county town of Tyrone, well inland: fifty miles' walk, in which you will hardly see a human being, but will enjoy the inspiring company of gentle sheep and merry birds, including—so I am told—perhaps an eagle. You will pass through a succession of 'slacks' or mountain passes and gulleys. Only hardy walkers—they need not be climbers in the technical sense—should set out on this thrilling pilgrimage. They will not find its equal anywhere. For a 'walking holiday' it is ideal.

Back to Derry as our Centre, and now we can try the neighbouring County Tyrone and then the very beautiful County of Donegal, which is within walking distance of headquarters.

Tyrone (*Tir*—Land, *Eoghain*—of Owen), once the country of the founder of the great O'Neill family, can be reached easily from either of the two Convenient Centres of Derry and Enniskillen. It is not of great interest historically, this county, excepting the town of Dungannon, which was once its capital and the fortress of the fighting O'Neills. It would not be fair to County Tyrone to omit mention of the fine history of the O'Neill resistance to the invaders. Those who find interest in prehistory should note that Tyrone can provide them with evidence of an Alpine 'Beaker People' who irrupted into Ireland, possibly from the neighbouring island, and perhaps over three thousand years ago. At Beaghmore, in the townland of Dunamore, between Cookstown and Gortin, can be seen what remains of a very important burial-place of those 'Beaker People'. It is in bogland, and was discovered by turf-diggers who little by little unearthed what experts say is a tribal concentration of monuments, probably of a ritualistic nature. The stones are in circles. All around here can be found in the Tyrone hills evidence of the Ice Age of eight thousand years ago or more—that age which fashioned the face of Ireland. Near Coagh, on the border of County Derry, is a massive dolmen with a twenty-ton top stone placed on four great supports. And at Ardboe, south of Quay on Lough Neagh, you can see one of the finest high crosses in the whole of Ireland. In other respects you will find Tyrone a pleasant county for a country holiday. It is like England in its clean towns and villages. But when I think of Tyrone, there comes to my mind Orange Day, for it was in Tyrone that I first experienced a very big and unforgettable celebration of that event.

Orange Day, the 12th of July, usually spoken of as 'The Twelfth', is the great day of the year for the Protestants of The North. It is the Orangemen's Day Out. The celebration everywhere follows more or less the same pattern. Strangers who miss a 'Twelfth' are unlucky, for it is an occasion on which the Protestant Ulsterman shows a side of his nature which surprises those who do not know him well. Perhaps I should say *Orangeman,* for it is the good Orangemen, the Members of the Orange Lodges originally established with the formation of the Orange Society in 1795—a secret society on the Masonic model, founded and organized to 'defend Protestantism and Law and Order'—who are the real enthusiasts, the backbone of the great occasion. Orangeism was the form taken by organized reaction against the Society of United Irishmen which had been founded by the Protestant Wolfe Tone and his Catholic friends to "obtain a complete Reform in the Legislature, founded on the Principles of civil, political and religious liberty" (1791). The spirit and ideals of the United Irishmen are not dead. The Orange Society is still almost as lively as it ever was, and openly displays its heart to the world each year on Orange Day.

I shall attempt to describe briefly the pattern usually followed in the celebration of this Great Day. A centre is chosen as a rallying-point for Members of Orange Lodges with their bands and banners. The men wear orange and blue sashes and rosettes, and they and their followers all sport orange lilies. Each band and its followers usually starts out from its Lodge to march to the rallying-point, but when there is a big rally at some distance away—as there often is—then recourse is had to almost any form of transport which will serve to carry all who wish to go to it. But a March there must be, one covering either the whole route to the rallying-point—usually a big field near a chosen town—or the last mile or so before it is reached. So it is that, from daybreak on the 12th of July, the Ulster countryside is alive and the roads are processioned with men marching to the music of their bands and carrying the symbols of their fanaticism.

Those bands and that music! There is nothing on this earth comparable. Here and there are to be seen bands such as those to which people in Britain or the United States are accustomed, usually fife-and-drum and seldom of brass. But I think that about 90 per cent. of those Orange bands are of a kind specially conceived for this special purpose. In their simplest form they consist of a fife (or two) and a couple (or more) of big drums, though I saw a flute band at Pettigo many years ago—half a dozen or more fluters with one kettle-drum leading and playing a very light tap-tap and roll accompaniment so as not to drown the sweet music of the flutes. And I have seen bands consisting *only* of big drums beating out a rhythm. You may find many variations, but it is always the small bands of a fife or two and a couple of big drums which play the greatest part in those Orange marches. The big drums are, I should say, half as big again as those normally used in military bands, though I do not know their exact measurements. They are usually beaten, not with the usual round and soft-topped drum-sticks, but with canes. The little place called Lambeg, near Lisburn, has long been famous for its great drums, for its drummers and for the drumming-parties at which the Orangemen practised for hours on end their astonishing tattoos and rhythms. Hence the terms 'Lambeg drums' and 'to beat a Lambeg'.

On 'The Twelfth' you may see, as I have seen, *miles* of those primitive bands: big drummers with coats off, sleeves rolled up and beating out a jungle rhythm to the tune of the fifers—a tune inaudible except maybe to the drummers immediately behind the fife. It is not possible to describe in words the effect on the mind of an observer of a series of non-stop processions of such bands converging by different routes on a central rallying-point. If you should happen to be near the point where the drummers finish work and lay down their instruments, you will hear nothing but the roar of the outsized drums. At moments of greatest intensity, perhaps I should say greatest *ferocity* in the drumming, shirts are often discarded, hands bleed from hitting the drums, the perspiration rolls, bodies gleam and are twisted in frenzy, and there is a mad glint in the men's eyes. The rhythms coalesce into a continuous roar, as if a thousand trained lions had formed an angry chorus and, using every bit of power Nature had given them, roared their defiance at the universe. Neither the great rallies of Hitler nor the biggest drumming event of Africa can be compared for volume of sound and evocative power with what the true Orangeman regards as a 'good Twelfth'! On such an occasion one might well hear the old Orange comment: *"They'll be saying their prayers in the Vatican the night!"*

When the multitude assembles in the rallying-field, in the centre of which a platform has been erected, the speeches begin. Now prominent politicians, Orange notables, Unionist clergy and others from the Union-with-Britain camp, deliver their impassioned orations. The Northern Government must stand! The Border must remain where it is! Long live the memory of William of Orange! God Save the King! The crowd responds: To Hell with the Pope! Keep the papishes (papists) in their places! Play up the *Boyne Water*! And *Derry Walls*!

When the speeches are finished, there is a break for refreshment, solid and liquid. Most people will have brought a packet of eatables, or bottles of drinkables. The solemnity and deep earnestness observed up to now vanish. Men and women sit about on the grass, or the men adjourn to pubs. There are sing-songs, and you will hear the traditional songs of the Orangemen, the folklore of the Order:

Nor wily tongue shall move us
Nor tyrant arm affright,
We'll Look to One above us,
Who ne'er forsook the right,
Who will may crouch and tender
The birthright of the free,

But, brothers, NO SURRENDER!
No compromise for me!
We want no barrier stone, boys;
No gates to guard the hill:
Yet the maiden on her throne, boys,
Shall be a Maiden *still.*

—the maiden being the Maiden City—Derry.

Then, towards evening, the bands form up again, and slowly beat their way homewards. Boys-a-dear what a gran' Twelfth! It has hardly passed before those fifers and drummers are practising for next year's Orange Day. So it goes on, that fierce uncompromising old spirt, nurtured on the political and religious hate of centuries, instrument of the most obstinate of irreconcilables. Orangeism must be one of the toughest manifestations of human nature. That is why I insist that Orange Day is so interesting, for on that day we can see and hear something of very deep human emotions which are normally covered. It removes the lid from the pot.

*

From Derry or Tyrone to Enniskillen in Fermanagh is no great journey, nor is the journey from Belfast to Enniskillen, an ideally Convenient Centre for the Erne Country, which all my life I have thought equal to Killarney in what it can show to the stranger. Now, after weighing my feelings, I believe that for an interesting holiday the Erne Country can be regarded as *primus inter pares*. Killarney is better known, but——

4

Enniskillen and the Erne Country

Balor of the Evil Eye, the fabulous one-eyed giant and King of the Fomorians (whom we should remember from the Battles of Moytura), had a wife named Ceithle, pronounced killy. In the far-off mists of prehistoric times Ceithle came to Enniskillen, which is our modern, anglicized form of *Inis Ceithleann* (pronounced innishkillen), meaning 'Island of Ceithle'. That is the origin of the name, from which we may venture to assume that the island on which the original town was built must have been a famous resort even in prehistoric times, or the wife of so powerful a creature as Balor would not have chosen it for her residence when she might have gone almost anywhere. At any rate Enniskillen—county town of Fermanagh—is so called because the central and main part of the town now there is built on an island that lies most conveniently for tourists between Upper and Lower Lough Erne. Fermanagh, you may care to know, is called after *Fir Manach,* the Men of Manach, a tribe of Leinster people who settled there in pagan times. Its capital Enniskillen is a Convenient Centre, not only for the whole Erne Country, but also for road and rail services to the adjoining counties of Cavan, Monaghan, Tyrone, Leitrim and Donegal. For this and many other reasons—some of which will soon become apparent—the visitor could hardly desire a better place than Enniskillen as his headquarters for a short or a long period. Because of its position between the two lovely lakes, this town has been called the Irish Interlaken, but I regard this as unjustifiable and bad advertising, because Interlaken is a dull place in comparison. When you have looked once at its surrounding country, you have had the best it can offer. Not so Enniskillen, for you can spend a long time there and you will not have exhausted either the interest or loveliness of the Erne valley and that great waterway. The Swiss know how to 'put their country across', and do it so well that the modest Enniskilleners think it a compliment for their historic town, situated between two lakes, in comparison with which Switzerland's most attractive lake scenery is uninspiring, to be called the Irish Interlaken! It is to be hoped that Enniskilleners will lose some of their reticence, their innate modesty and their shyness in making known the fairyland around and about their island town, so that the position becomes reversed, and the Swiss will one day be glad to call Interlaken 'The Enniskillen of Switzerland'. That is how it should be. Arise, Enniskillen, and make your voice heard!

The town of Enniskillen has about 6,000 inhabitants; and when I say that this is a town in which religion and politics mean something, what I wish to convey is that the less a stranger mentions either the less chance there is of the feathers flying. Whatever the statistics[1] may show—and they can be left to tell their own story—this town regards itself as a stronghold of loyalty to the King of England and Protestantism. It is proud of its two famous regiments, the Inniskilling Dragoons and Inniskilling Fusiliers, each of which has a long history of excellent fighting, the Fusiliers, known as 'th'oul' skins', having had the honour in World War II of being chosen as spear-head troops in the first allied landing in Italy. Until the beginning of the seventeenth century the town was a stronghold of a famous old Irish family, the Maguires of Fermanagh, lords of that land, who were dispossessed after the rising of Hugh O'Neill, Lord of Tyrone. It was then awarded to a Sir William Cole, who died in 1653, having settled it with a score of English families and held it against Tyrconnel in 1690.

From East to West the town consists of one long undulating street which cuts across the island part from an East to a West Bridge, and from that main street others on the island run down to the Erne, which narrows here. It is a very clean and tidy town, a busy and efficient town, in which the people are sturdy, independent and forthright. And it is prosperous, being an agricultural centre and one for fairs, markets, shopping and all those things material and social which concern the farmers and others of the surrounding country. At the highest point on the island is the Church of Ireland Cathedral, with a steeple dating from 1637, and a nave, chancel and aisles built in 1842 on the site of the old church. In the steeple are two bells known as William and Mary, because they were made from cannon used at the Battle of the Boyne, an event in the struggle in which men of Enniskillen took a brave part, of which every generation is reminded in powerful words on every 12th of July, Orange Day. Overlooking the town is a very pleasant park known as the Fort Hill, on the highest point of which there is a monument to a Peninsular War commander, General Sir Galbraith Lowry Cole, son of the first Earl of Enniskillen. That monument is a plain piece of work architecturally, its chief interest to the visitor being its remarkably fine position. You can climb a spiral

[1] In County Fermanagh there is 53·3 per cent. of Nationalists (Catholics) and 44·7 per cent. of Unionists (Protestants).

stairway to the top, and from there, on a clear day, there is a view of the Erne Country to delight the gods. The great waterway, the islands in the Lower Lough, the blue Leitrim mountains in the distance, the Abbey and Round Tower of Devenish—all are to be seen; and even the great houses, castles and ruins can often be picked out. Beg, borrow or steal a pair of binoculars or a telescope, boldly ascend the Cole Monument on the Fort Hill—and look around on all sides. You will get a bird's-eye view of a considerable part of the Erne waterway and Country. If it is a good day, and conditions are favourable, the memory of this experience is likely to remain as long as you have a mind with which to remember.

In 1618 was founded under Royal Charter the Royal School of Enniskillen, to provide educational facilities for the sons of select members of the Plantation, the new Ascendancy. School activities began at Lisnaskea, but they were later transferred to Enniskillen, and now, at Portora, on the top of a hill just outside the west end of the town, is Portora Royal School, often referred to by those who will make use of egregious comparisons as "the Eton of Ireland". Portora Royal School is not so large, not so populous as Eton, but Eton has no superiority over Portora when it comes to the matters of natural beauty, of situation and surroundings. Some of the playing fields of Portora are on a plateau overlooking the Erne, with a view of impressive mountains and of that wonderful Lower Lough with its green and sylvan islands and its beautiful stretch of water in a great valley one side of which is the greenest of green and the other that Irish mountain blue which cannot be matched anywhere. The playing fields of Eton forsooth!

There have been few periods in the history of Portora when the school did not send out men who made their mark in the important walks of life, as old Portorans still do. It is usual to record that Oscar Wilde was a pupil at Portora. When he became famous his name was inscribed on the school's distinction board. When the great frame-up changed the deserved fame into undeserved infamy, the name was removed to satisfy an iron morality. Time has wrought its own less-prejudiced justice. The name of Wilde has been restored, so all is well again. Incidentally, Portora Royal School has the honour of being the last stronghold of the school or collegiate top-hat. On a famous Twelfth of July, when Lambeg Drums were beaten as never before to give out their primordial rhythms, it is recorded, an Orangeman commented, "They'll be saying their prayers in the Vatican the night!" One cannot help thinking that, when Eton realizes that Portora continues to wear the top-hat while their own toppers have become museum pieces, a proud Portoran may say, "How sad they must now be at Eton!"

Guide-books all insist that Enniskillen is 'beautifully situated', and in this they do not mislead the reader. It is the situation of the town rather than the town itself which most concerns the visitor, as will be seen. The town lies between Ireland's two loveliest waterways, Upper and Lower Lough Erne, which form part of one great waterway having its source far away in the republican County Longford, in a river which flows through County Cavan, joining two other rivers to flow through the southern border of County Fermanagh, and there form the beginning of the irregular and complex waterway called Upper Lough Erne. This Upper Lough is about fifteen miles long and four broad at its broadest part, most of it being more like a big winding river than a lake. It is a fine run in a motor-boat from Enniskillen to, say, Knockninny, about ten miles south of Enniskillen. Or you can go there by car, the objective in either event being The Rock of Knockninny ('Hill of St. Ninnidh') near the little village of Derrylin. The view of the Upper Lough from The Rock is probably the best that can be found. It is rewarding. Nearby is a cave used as a burial-place by the prehistoric Irish, and three of what archæologists call 'dolmens' and the Irish call 'Giants' Graves'. Bellisle, at the north-eastern end of the Upper Lough, is also worth a visit. Here, in a monastery, Cahal Maguire (*d.* 1498) wrote the *Annals of Ulster*, an important source-book for historians. With Enniskillen as headquarters, one can go out and round about on innumerable interesting and rewarding excursions, but before mentioning any more, we must deal a little more fully with the Erne, itself a major attraction.

The Lower Lough provides most interest for the visitor.

This part of the great waterway stretches from Enniskillen to Belleek, from which point it narrows into a swiftly moving river. Lower Lough Erne is about twenty miles in length; at the widest point it is nearly seven miles in breadth. These are *Irish* miles, of which eleven are equal to fourteen English miles, the reason for this seemingly unreasonable difference being simple. Those fortunate gentlemen who were awarded gifts of confiscated Irish lands invented those generous 'Irish' miles; so that a measure referred to in an official grant as so many 'miles' could be stretched a bit when it came to taking possession of the land itself! There were also invented Irish acres, perches and so forth. In this way 'Irish' measures became established on the generous basis which so often infuriates the visitor to Ireland who may not be aware that when, for example, he is told by a native that some place is 'about a mile down the road', it is certain to be more than an English mile even in actuarial terms. When the visitor becomes seasoned, he will know that 'about a mile' may mean a very long walk, for such is the desire to please in the heart of the average Irishman that rather than dismay his questioner, he will minimize the latter's difficulties. I have had the experience of finding that 'about a mile' meant half a day's walk. So beware! From Belleek to Ballyshannon the River Erne is not navigable; there are rapids, a waterfall, and at Ballyshannon a thrilling salmon leap. At certain times this river is stiff with salmon and trout.

Lough Erne, *Loch Eirne* in Gaelic, the 'Lake of the Ernai', derives its name from a tribe of Firbolgs who (in the legend) inhabited those parts. The main waterway has a navigable course of more than fifty miles. From its source to the sea at Ballyshannon in County Donegal the Erne runs about seventy miles, and from source to sea this Erne Country is beautiful, not only from the point of view of the artist looking for scenery to paint, but there is an exquisitely restful, placid atmosphere everywhere. The country of the Upper and Lower Loughs is one long valley which, in the course of incalculable time, the great flow of water making its way to the sea has worn out from the limestone and fashioned in Nature's designs. The soil of the land around the waterway is nearly everywhere excellent for agriculture and grazing, and those vandals who, in so many parts of Ireland, cut down the beautiful trees and exploited the forests, have here left enough to break the monotony of what would otherwise be a landscape of startling and unrelieved green. From the Fort Hill in Enniskillen I have watched sunsets which showed the Upper Lough and the countrysides in their greatest glory. It would be as foolish to attempt to describe them in words as it would be to try to describe the music of a heavenly harpist.

Men of Fermanagh helped the Americans in their War of Independence. One of them was an Enniskillener named William Irvine. He formed and equipped the 6th Pennsylvania Regiment; and was a member of Congress for many years. Another was Colonel Francis Nichols, who also fought in that war and became a member of Congress. The roll of honour is too long for here, but I think the little town of Ballinamallard, a name which scholars interpret variously,[1] has a special reason for local pride. It was from near this little Ulster Auburn that came the MacDonalds, one of whom, the Rev. George Brown MacDonald, fathered a galaxy of most successful girls. One of these fine women mothered Rudyard Kipling, and another gave Stanley Baldwin to England. A daughter of this MacDonald married Sir Edward Burne-Jones (or he may have married her); another married Sir Edward Poynter; another, Edith MacDonald, was a writer; and her brother Frederick became President of the Methodist Church. Where is there another townland in that prolific county—or in any other—that has produced such a galaxy of talents?

I call Ballinamallard a little Ulster Auburn, and I have reason, because I retain some very happy memories of the delightful little town and its people, having lived near to them for two lively years of boyhood. In a radio broadcast recently the postmistress of this village told a story of a blind man who came into the Post Office, presumably to draw his pension. The postmistress mislaid his pension book and could not find it. Whereupon the blind man *pointed* to it and said to her, "There it is, over yonder." And sure enough it was his book! About fifty years ago in my time there was a little

[1] P. W. Joyce gives it to mean 'The ford of the horse loads', from *Bel-Atha na Marlach*.

school beside the bridge which crosses the stream dividing the town. Roll was not always called in that liberal school; the master and his wife had the sort of vision which was immediately aware of an absentee. "Where is so-and-so?" he would say, and somebody would reply, "Outside, fishing." And the good master would then say to somebody, "Go out and tell him that when he's caught one fish—*one* only, mind—he's to come at once to his lessons." Where, oh where, shall we find such good sense today? That school sent into the world better men and women than come from the more scientifically controlled modern educational establishments of today.

Just outside of Enniskillen is Castle Coole, the seat of the Earl of Belmore, surrounded by one of the best-maintained demesnes to be found anywhere in Ireland. The mansion of white Portland stone cost a fortune to erect nearly 150 years ago. It is a fine residence. Fermanagh in general is well decorated with stately residences of descendants of important personalities of the Plantation period. But besides such places, there are many Celtic and even pre-Celtic antiquities which some visitors may find of greater interest. There are, for example, near the village of Derrygonnelly (8–9 miles outside Enniskillen), the Knockmere ('big hill') Caves, on the walls of which are carvings and scribblings which archæologists take to be the work of primitive man and anything up to perhaps 10,000 years old. You may not make much of those markings, and I doubt whether you will make even as much of the strange carved stone figures to be found on White Island, which is not far from Castle Archdale, residence of the descendants of one John Archdale, a grantee of land during the Plantation. On White Island is what remains of a little old church with Hiberno-Romanesque archway—an interesting ruin for Ulster which, I understand, has only one other example of this Irish architecture and, generally speaking, has no ecclesiastical ruins to compare in impressiveness with those to be found in the other provinces—Ulster had no builders with the vision, means and resources of those others. The Hiberno-Romanesque arch is an Irish artistic conception and one of great beauty. Nobody knows the history of this little church on White Island, which is chiefly noteworthy for its seven most curious and puzzling figures. The photograph facing page 256 shows these grotesqueries. Nobody acquainted with Irish carving in stone or, in fact, with any manifestation of Irish plastic art, can look at the White Island statues and feel entirely convinced that they can possibly be Irish as we understand that fairly elastic term. Yet there is to me one thing about them which contradicts that feeling. Some of the *faces* are very Irish! That is, their contours and the expression on them are no longer remote from us from the moment we begin to think of them as 'expression' of human nature. I seem to know somebody among my fellow-countrymen who looks like the second figure from the left! The central figure has a face which strongly reminds me of that of an old Fermanaghman, now long dead, who made a livelihood by carting dung. I knew him well. He looked just like that central figure whenever somebody mentioned in his presence King William and the Boyne.

Who created these figures? When were they created? Why were they created? The flat top of the heads suggests that they had a purpose: perhaps to support something. But what? I do not find any explanations that I have read to be entirely convincing, and to me one of the least convincing is that which interprets them as representing the Seven Deadly Sins: lust, sloth, gluttony, covetousness, pride, anger, envy. If the man of genius who conceived and made those figures did so on instructions to make them represent the Seven Deadly Sins, then he was a born satirist who, in the expressions he has given them—sardonic, derisive, indifferent, contemptuous, peaceful—shows that an Irish imp was at his elbow. This White Island group of figures, rescued from nearby, has now been set up in a row for the visitor to see. It is unique in Ireland and in Europe. The latest date given to the figures is the seventh century A.D., but I think I shall have sympathizers with me when I hold to the opinion that these figures are not Christian in spirit whatever they may be in time. What they really are neither I nor anybody else can yet satisfactorily explain. But do take a morning or an afternoon, and visit White Island to see the little church for yourself and contemplate the enigma of these astonishing statues.

On the way back to Enniskillen from White Island you will see on your right an island with some ruins on the summit of its hill and below them a very fine Round Tower. This is Devenish Island. The ruins are interesting, but that Round Tower is famous for being one of the most perfect, probably the most perfect of all Irish round towers. Devenish Island deserves a visit and, if time and weather permit, you can have a delightful outing and picnic to fill a whole day. You can go to Devenish by row-boat, which you hire in Enniskillen, and it should not take you more than an hour or so of easy rowing to get there. When you land on the island, which is close in towards the north bank of a little lake just off the main Lower Lough, first make for the Round Tower. When you have seen it, you can then visit the other ruins and sit down to your picnic among those on the top of the hill—the best place from which to see the whole island, the Lough and the surrounding country.

Much nonsense has been written about Irish Round Towers, but in recent years archæologists and others have cleared away most of the fantastic stories which became attached to them. It is now held that they are Irish versions of the detached belfry which became fairly common on the European continent in parts of Charlemagne's and his successors' sphere of influence: say, from A.D. 750 to 1000. You will still hear people say and you may perhaps read that these towers are peculiar to Ireland; that they were used as watch-towers by monastic communities in the days of the murdering and plundering Norsemen, and also as places of refuge, and so forth. An entertaining book has been written on the subject by an industrious pre-Freudian investigator named Henry O'Brien, a man of considerable scholarship, but of little judgment or sense of the value of evidence and with a fair number of bats fluttering in his own belfry. The book is called *The Round Towers of Ireland* (1898), and you will get an indication of its evidential value from the alternative title which reads *Or The History of the Tuatha-Dé-Danaans*! The chief value of the book is that it lists and describes every Round Tower or scrap of Round Tower in the whole of Ireland, with much entertaining information about phallic worship—not always relevant. O'Brien quotes an earlier work by a Mr. Keane who states: "Lists of Irish Round Towers have been made to the number of one hundred and twenty; of these, the remains of about sixty-six are traceable." As these Round Towers, or what remains of them, are found in all the four provinces, and the Devenish Island specimen is one which experts agree to be in an almost perfect state of preservation, it is well worth close inspection. First let us be clear about one point: these Round Towers were primarily *belfries.* They are almost invariably to be found near the remains or site of some Christian establishment (church or monastery) or where a Christian community had its headquarters. They are also usually near a good water supply. The larger towers have an entrance well up from the ground and an interior which could have been used for many purposes, for these larger ones usually have openings at various points of the compass to allow daylight into the interior, for ventilation and, of course, to provide look-outs. In time of danger the treasures of the Christian establishment or community could be transferred to such a tower, which in those days must have been a safe, almost impregnable place of refuge. The purpose and possible use of some of the smaller towers are not so clear; these were probably symbolical.

Now for the very fine Round Tower on Devenish Island, usually known as Devenish Round Tower. The Devenish (*Dáimh inis,* 'the island of oxen') Tower is variously stated to be from 79 to 85 feet in height and it has a circumference of 48 feet. It had floors or stories originally, five of them, variously shaped; all excepting that at the top had one window. The top floor—the bell loft—had four windows looking North, South, East and West: useful for look-out points. The masonry of the stately tower is perfect: the stones were cut curved for this special purpose, the placing is well done, and the cement is still as hard as the stones, or harder. The tower structure is plain, that is, without ornamentation, but there is a richly sculptured and quite unusual cornice under the conical cap. Here, directly over the four top windows, are four elaborately carved heads which tradition gives to St. Patrick, St. Columba, St. Brigid—and to St. Molaise, who here founded a monastery in the year 541. Nearby is what is left of the old Abbey of the Culdees; and a mausoleum of the Maguires. Near the east shore stands a little oratory or church built in the early or cyclopean style and sometimes called St. Molaise's 'Kitchen', but more correctly his 'House', for he lived here.

When we look at this little House on Devenish we are looking at something which has survived from the early part of Ireland's Golden Age—from a millennium and a half ago. What a pity the history of Devenish is all so vague, for there should be material in it for a great story. We must leave it in its oblivion and turn uphill towards the ruins on the summit.

Here was St. Mary's Abbey, founded on a date unknown by the Augustines who came to Ireland in the twelfth century. Now it is ruins, but ruins which can tell us eloquently of the beauty of the original building and its four-sided bell-tower. These ruins require expert description which I cannot give. Cloister and main buildings of the monastic community are north of the church; and south of it is an ornamental cross said to be unique. The visitor will note the burial-grounds; two of them are comparatively modern; one may be for men, the other for women. In the Island of Saints and Scholars it was quite a general and, in the case of monasteries, almost an invariable custom to bury men and women separately: to keep the sexes apart in death, as it was deemed desirable to keep them apart while they were alive. In a decreasing number of places, women and men still separate in church while they hear Mass, the women to the left, the men to the right. This does not now apply in the bigger communities and churches, nor is it to be found among the Protestants, though it once was. Throughout Ireland respect for and fear of the temptations of sex are not limited to members of any one religion, for it seems to be an Irish characteristic to have a dread of being what Robert Burns calls, "fash't wi' fleshy lust". A strong all-round social discipline, of which the people themselves approve, applies itself; but, when the Irish leave Ireland and this discipline is relaxed, they suffer accordingly.

The visitor who wishes to see as much as possible of the Erne Country in one day should treat himself to a ride in a car or go on a push-bike on the well-known route which covers a complete circuit of the Lower Lough. One can start from Enniskillen by making for the road along either the north or the south bank. I think it better to 'do' the south bank first, leaving Enniskillen by the west end and going out by the road which passes Portora Royal School. The complete circuit of the Lower Lough is about sixty miles. From Portora you go on to the Castle of the Marquess of Ely, with the remains of the Plantation Castle Hume, then on to Tully and Monea, also Plantation survivals, that of Monea being well preserved. From Monea can be seen the island of Inishmacsaint ('the island of the plain of sorrel'), which has a ruined church of no great interest that I can recall. From Tully onwards you have the mountains on your left: the great big range of Leitrim mountains in the distance, which fall to become hills or plain near the water's edge. The road along here is not in itself very interesting, but the scenery away to the west is impressive and, from certain points of the highway, you will get a magnificent long-distance view of the brilliant green and well-wooded north side of the Erne—as fine a stretch of countryside as is to be seen in Ireland. Next you come to Belleek ('the ford of flagstone'), a bright little town which has the honour of being on The Border. But you can avoid the troubles of crossing The Border and continue your trip within the political territory of Northern Ireland by turning into the road which will lead you to Enniskillen. You might do worse than spend an hour or two at Belleek, to have a meal and look at the pottery. Here they used to make, from a clay found nearby at Castle Caldwell, a beautiful lustreware, and the manufacture still continues, but from materials that come from far afield. Feldspar with china clay and flint added, all ground to a fine powder and mixed with water, make the paste on which the craftsmen and women work. They are artists at Belleek, and if you are that way inclined, you can watch the evolution on or in a piece of Belleekware of an involved and intricate Celtic design. But it is not only this delicate and rather costly stuff that is made. They also make ordinary earthenware goods; and you could not take away with you a nicer souvenir than a Belleek mug made in that pottery. After the Next World War it may be worth a small fortune! You should also see nearby the vast sluice-gates built to control the level of the water of Lough Erne, which you will do well to remember is the greatest waterway in these islands, although neither the Upper nor the Lower Lough is as big as Lough Neagh.

Belleek is a grand centre for fishermen. If you are a fisherman, you can have a good sport there or from the little town of Garrison, a few miles south of Belleek and on the edge of Lough Melvin, a stretch of water about eight miles long by about four in breadth, most of it republican. This charming lake is called after an Irish king, but its chief fame comes from its abundant fish—salmon, trout and perch—particularly the trout. In addition to ordinary brown trout, Lough Melvin has the sonaghan and the gilaroo, which you will never have caught or even seen if you have not already been to Lough Melvin. Or so you will hear. I need hardly warn the fisherman against fishing stories, but I can assure him that the gilaroo ('red boy') is a grand fish to eat, better than the sonaghan, I think, and both of them superior eating to most European trout except possibly some that are found in Hungary.

From Belleek you proceed on the north bank of the Erne to Pettigo, a town half in Fermanagh, half in Donegal, with The Border running right through it: a very busy place at times because it is from there that pilgrims proceed on the final stage of their pilgrimage to Lough Derg in the summer months. I almost forgot to mention Castle Caldwell, which you have passed and may not have noticed; because, although there is a name, there is little else there. No village, nothing —except the fiddle stone. Whereby hangs a tale. Nothing? Just a moment. There is a railway station at Castle Caldwell. From it you can wander through woodland to the ruin of the old Castle, which lies not more than a quarter of a mile away, and is in a very lovely situation near the water's edge. At the entrance to the demesne you will see a stone carved in the shape of a big fiddle, with an inscription on it which you can hardly read. A 'Planter' named Francis Blennerhasset built the original Castle in 1612, but some fifty years later it was bought by a rich Enniskillen businessman named James Caldwell. This James Caldwell and his family have left a fragrant memory behind them in those parts, for they made themselves famous by their lavish hospitality, and James showed originality in the organisation of diversions and entertainments for guests. The tradition was carried on by his heirs. There was something 'flahoolach', as the Irish say (meaning 'princely' in English) about most things those Caldwells did. For example, one of them had his own orchestra at the Castle. Not only that, but he had a great six-oared barge in which he would take his guests and orchestra for outings on the lake, never failing to have with him a liberal supply of fine-quality liquor. What I like about that particular Caldwell is that his custom was to encourage his musicians to participate in the refreshments he took with him in the barge for himself and his merry guests who, by all accounts, must have had some great times. On one occasion an elated fiddler fell overboard and was drowned in the Lough. The decent Caldwells had a memorial stone in the shape of a fiddle erected to the unfortunate man, and it appears that the incident put an end to those musical outings, and from then on the orchestra played only on shore. A poet wrote for them the rule to be observed henceforth:

On firm land only exercise your skill,
There you may play and safely drink your fill.

It is gone, gone—all that sort of thing! Gone are the flahoolach entertainments of the Caldwells, and all that remains are the old ruins and the fiddle stone to mark the sweet memory. This may seem of very little importance to the visitor. But Irish memories are usually sad, and it can do little harm to mark the exception. Besides, it explains the fiddle stone of Castle Caldwell.

From Pettigo onwards for some miles past the village of Kesh you have an experience similar to that which you had at one stage of the trip on the other side of the lake. When you look immediately around you, the landscape is pleasant with fine fields and nice woods, but at close quarters it is not exciting. On the other hand, the view you will have from here of the other side of the lake is exquisite. Cross Boa Island and continue on the route towards Enniskillen, passing another Blennerhasset edifice, Crevenish Castle, built in 1617, and then the old Castle Archdale, built in 1615 by

John Archdale, a man from Norfolk. This was the great period in which the favoured grantees of this magnificent land built their fine residences and founded what were to become the 'county families'—in Fermanagh and elsewhere in The North, and often well across the present political Border. White Island, already mentioned, is about two miles from Kesh in the bay of Castle Archdale. In the Second World War this part of the northern bank of Lower Lough Erne was used as an Air Force and flying-boat base: a very important one it was in the Battle of the Atlantic.

Before you come to Enniskillen you will pass Florencecourt, about seven miles out from the town, said to be the finest mid-Georgian house in Northern Ireland. This is the seat of the Earl of Enniskillen. The grounds and some interesting caves can be visited, but you must first obtain a permit from the Estate Office in Enniskillen, which also issues permits to visit the Marble Arch, two miles from Florencecourt. This Arch is at the exit of an underground river—there are innumerable underground rivers running in the limestone hereabouts. A beginning has been made to explore this subterranean world of Fermanagh. It was first visited in 1897 by the intrepid Edouard-Alfred Martel, pioneer of speleology, and famous for his underground explorations in many parts of Europe. But much work remains to be done before the Fermanagh underworld is opened to visitors.

And so you continue to Enniskillen, passing through the second town of the county, Irvinestown; a clean, bright little place with a nice market square. On your return to Enniskillen you may want to rest your head after seeing all those beautiful and interesting places encountered in the trip round the Lower Lough. It is a pity that the Upper Lough cannot be dealt with in the same way: I mean, by proceeding along a route which keeps fairly close to both the lake and the interesting places. The great irregularity of all that Upper Lough, amounting in parts to veritable labyrinths of little inlets, bays, islands and peninsulas, makes it a region of which it is not easy to see the best without the aid of a local guide. There are two ways of 'doing' it: the first is on land—by car, cycle, bus and/or train (parts only); the second is by keeping to the waterway. My advice is to hire a motor-boat and go by water for a day's outing, taking food and drink with you. You will not see more interesting places than those noted in the circuit of the Lower Lough, or so many. But you will have a wonderful outing. My further advice is that on this trip you should relax and quietly contemplate what you see as the boat makes its way from Enniskillen, turning south where the Erne divides to surround the island town. The current runs against you as you go along and pass the Weirs Bridge. The lake narrows, and from then on the Erne will bewilder you with its complexities.

If you should decide to keep to land, you can see on Lough Eyes near Lisbellaw some lake dwellings or *crannógs* (*cran*—tree, *óg*—little), which survive from prehistoric times. Ireland seems to have been in that remote period a country of lake dwellers, for these *crannógs* are to be found in twenty-four of the thirty-two counties. Macallister gives the number already discovered as 221. Here is work for investigators! A whole story remains to be unfolded, but generations may pass before we can have it. At Lisnaskea, the next town, was once a whitethorn tree under which the Maguires, princes of Fermanagh, were 'crowned' or inaugurated, and so the name, which means 'the fort of the whitethorn tree'. A Sir James Balfour built Castle Balfour here, and two miles away is Aghalurcher where, in early Christian times, St. Ronan founded a church of which the ruins can be seen. A few miles farther, going southwards, is Crom Castle, the Earl of Erne's demesne and place of residence—a delightfully placed modern castle. Around here are what remains of several old Plantation residences associated with the names of Balfour, Butler and Crichton. In the grounds of Crom Castle is a yew tree of gigantic dimensions and maybe a thousand years of age. Tradition has it that one of the O'Neill family who was outlawed in Elizabeth's reign said farewell to his lady under this tree before leaving for a safer neighbourhood. Next comes Newtownbutler, where there is a Northern (British) Customs Station, and south of the town is a 'Druids' Temple' or tumulus, part of which has been removed, but leaving some enormous stones. And then Maguiresbridge, near which is Brookeborough, named after the Brooke family whose residence is at Colebrooke, a mile or so outside the village. Here lives Sir Basil Brooke, Premier of Northern Ireland. Lord Alanbrooke is of the same family, of which the members have distinguished themselves in many walks of life.

You would have to cross The Border to make your way back to Enniskillen by the south side of the Upper Lough. If you are one of those people who enjoy walking or cycling or motoring through pleasant surroundings, the trip is worth while. You might, of course, get somebody to row you across the Lough, and so avoid Border formalities. Or you might not! But you will probably have seen as much as you can take in, and be glad to return again to your Convenient Centre from which, you must not forget, you can easily visit the adjacent counties in both The North and The Republic.

So it is with each of the other Convenient Centres mentioned in the Second Part of this book. You can choose one as you please and work from it to other places. But, although a visit to Ireland can be enjoyed without knowing much about this old country and its long and interesting story, no person who goes there can hope to understand it, even superficially, unless he or she has some knowledge and appreciation of the *Background,* of that which I have treated, as lightly as possible, in the First Part.

THE END

APPENDIX

Some Hints for Prospective Visitors to Ireland

PASSPORTS.—In our times everybody must be in possession of a document of identity. He cannot travel to or from Ireland, North or South, without one. The best document of all is the *valid* Passport, and note that word 'valid'. The Passport must be, not only an authentic one to establish beyond doubt the holder's *present* nationality, but it must be *up to date* and, in the case of certain nationals (but not Irish, British or American), have the right *visa* to permit landing in Northern Ireland or The Republic.

TRAVEL IDENTITY CARD.—Persons travelling between Great Britain and Ireland, North or South, who do not possess a valid Passport must equip themselves with a Travel Identity Card, a much less elaborate document, and issued free of charge by the Passport Offices in London, Liverpool and Glasgow, or, like the British Passport, is obtainable on application at any office of the Ministry of Labour and National Service. (My own view is that, although the Travel Identity Card costs nothing and can usually be obtained more quickly, the valid Passport is worth its cost and the extra trouble. But do not forget, whichever of these documents you decide to have, to obtain it and have it in your possession well before the date on which you propose to travel.)

SAILING TICKETS FROM AND TO BRITAIN.—At certain times of the year and on specific dates during the holiday season, ALL intending travellers to Ireland by land and sea routes must be in possession of a Sailing Ticket. These Sailing Tickets are merely intended to assist those concerned (railway and shipping companies) in keeping a control over the number of passengers to be carried by each ship. Application for a Sailing Ticket should be made well in advance, and to the transport company concerned. (I have found these tickets to be a far more troublesome and nerve-racking business to obtain than either a Passport or Travel Identity Card.) Be warned, and apply well in time for a Sailing Ticket. AND DON'T FORGET THAT YOU HAVE TO GET ONE IN IRELAND FOR THE RETURN JOURNEY TO BRITAIN. Without it, you may be stranded on a foreign shore! Best to apply for the return ticket on your arrival in Ireland, if that is possible. (There are,

I have heard, gentlemen available who will, in return for a reasonable honorarium, assist you to obtain a Sailing Ticket. One of them was pointed out to me in Dublin, and I was told: "That boyo will get you a ticket in a jiffy—in return for ten bob." *Verb. sap.* and for what it is worth!) Note well that in applying for a Sailing Ticket you must be able to give the number of your Passport or Travel Identity Card. You must *first* possess one or the other.

MONEY.—Until the time this is written, there has been no 'financial control' for travellers from Britain to Ireland. This is because the Irish banking systems, North and South, are allied to or a part of the Big Banks of Britain. Ireland, all of it, is in the Sterling Area, the currency is the same as in Britain. So, take with you whatever you wish or can in the way of money. And let Ireland do the rest. It seems unlikely that there will ever be money restrictions between these countries, but if in doubt, you can ask at a Travel Agency.

GUIDE-BOOKS.—The *Blue Guide to Ireland,* edited by Russell Muirhead (published by Ernest Benn), will be found useful by those who contemplate a long visit and much travelling in North or South. Murray's *Guide* I have myself used for many years, and always found it excellent and very reliable. These two are 'general' or 'standard' works, and because of their comprehensiveness and detail, must be overhauled and brought up to date from time to time. This involves the possibility that at a given moment information provided may not take account of a change or changes that have taken place.

Official Guides to Northern Ireland: The Ulster Tourist Development Association issues *The Ulster Guide, Golfing in Ulster, Angling in Ulster Waters* and many other items of free literature to assist the visitor—all available at the addresses noted below.

Official Guides to The Republic ('The South'): The Irish Tourist Association issues a series of Guides, one to Dublin, and one for each of the counties and areas of interest to prospective visitors. It also issues much literature of special interest to different categories of visitors: golfers, anglers and so forth. Available from addresses noted below.

DUBLIN: An official guide is published by the Irish Tourist Association. There is also a bright and useful little *Dublin by Day and by Night,* quite unofficial, but providing information about where to drink, eat, amuse yourself, etc. I have not tested it, but on perusal it seems just what the light-hearted visitor requires.

HOTELS, GUEST HOUSES, HOLIDAY CAMPS, HOLIDAY HOSTELS, YOUTH HOSTELS.—Each year the Irish Tourist Board issues free a most helpful and detailed list covering the Twenty-six Counties. In this part of Ireland the scale of charges decided by the Board may not be exceeded, and the list, which embraces not only the cities and big towns, but nearly every place to which a tourist is likely to go, has all these prices—for board and lodging, per week or longer period, and also for separate meals, bed and breakfast and so forth. A visitor knows beforehand how much these items will cost him in the Twenty-six Counties. There is not much difference between the prices and those for similar accommodation and services in Northern Ireland, though here the prices are not 'controlled'.

MAPS.—Very important. For touring North and South, Bartholomew's maps (one-quarter of an inch to the mile), with contours and in five sections, can be recommended. For the visitor who settles in a 'Convenient Centre' in The South, I recommend the more detailed maps of the *Ordnance Survey* (obtainable from Eason & Sons, O'Connell Street, Dublin). Be sure to obtain the right section! Similar Ordnance Maps are available for Northern Ireland from: *The Ordnance Survey of Northern Ireland,* Armagh House, Ormeau Avenue, Belfast.

TRANSPORT IN IRELAND.—The Ulster Transport Authority (21, Linnenhall Street, Belfast) issues Rail and Road Time-tables, obtainable also at railway and bus stations. Information about travel by bus or railway in the Twenty-six Counties is available from Córas Iompair Eireann, Public Relations Department, 59, Upper O'Connell Street, Dublin.

GENERAL INFORMATION FOR VISITORS.—The two Associations will either provide you with most of the information you may require, or tell you where to obtain it. Write, or, if possible, call:

I. (*a*) Northern Ireland Tourist Board, c/o Office of The Ulster Agent, 13, Lower Regent Street, London, S.W.1.

(*b*) Ulster Tourist Development Association, 6, Royal Avenue, Belfast.

(*c*) British Travel Centre, 336, Madison Avenue, New York.

II. (*a*) Irish Tourist Association, 14, Upper O'Connell Street, Dublin.

(*b*) Irish Tourist Association, 19, Lower Regent Street, London, S.W.1.

(*c*) Irish Tourist Association, Island House, 33, East 50th Street, New York.

INDEX

DUN LAOGHAIRE
BRAY
LIMERICK
CASHEL
TRALEE
WEXFORD
WATERFORD
ROSSLARE
KILLARNEY
CORK
BLASKET IS.
W
E
S
IRISH-SPEAKING AREAS SHADED
S. HORNE SHEPHERD